The Young Woman in Business

Expanded, Second Edition

The Young Woman in Business

Beth Bailey McLean

Oregon State University

Jeanne Paris

Director,
Martha Logan Service

Illustrated by HARRY E. WALSH

 THE IOWA STATE UNIVERSITY PRESS, *Ames,* IOWA

About the Authors

Mrs. BETH BAILEY McLEAN, former director of home economics at Swift and Company, returned to educational fields as Associate Professor, Foods and Nutrition, Oregon State University, Corvallis, Oregon.

She has visited twenty-two countries around the world, noting women at work and Americans abroad. She is author of "Planning Meals for the Family," in the USDA Yearbook *FOODS* (1959), and co-author of the *Meat and Poultry Cookbook.*

Miss JEANNE PARIS is nationally known as one of the most active authorities in her field, now a past national chairman of the Home Economists in Business section of the American Home Economics Association. She is constantly on call for career conferences throughout the United States and has traveled abroad extensively. Professionally, she is director of home economics, Swift and Company, where she heads the Martha Logan Test Kitchens.

Mrs. McLean and Miss Paris have worked with girls in every possible mood and circumstance. Their sympathetic concern for their well-being is reflected throughout this book. Because of their philosophy and training, they are well able to guide newcomers to the business field.

© 1962 by the
Iowa State University Press.
All rights reserved.

Composed and printed by
The Iowa State University Press,
Ames, Iowa, U. S. A.

FIRST EDITION, 1953
Second printing, 1954
Third printing, 1957

SECOND EDITION, 1962
Second printing, 1963

Library of Congress Catalog Card Number: 61-14203

Preface

YOU are a fortunate young woman! Today, in our country, you are accepted as an essential worker in our free enterprise system. You will find that many kinds of businesses need and want young women for many kinds of positions. You are fortunate if you have been trained to do well in a special kind of work and if you have an ambition to succeed and move up to better positions.

What makes a woman successful in business? How do women get positions with prestige, good salaries, and an opportunity to be of real service?

Most women in top positions are there because they have been able to bring special talents to the job and because they realize that women have different viewpoints and different innate abilities from men. They are not feminists; rather they develop an objective viewpoint and consider the interests and welfare of people in general, not just women.

The successful woman is proud she is a woman and therefore accepts the responsibilities of being womanly with all the best traditional meaning of the word. She does not militantly compete with men. Rather, this woman understands that working *with* men adds a challenge and an inspiration which can sharpen her understanding of current problems, develop her ability to weigh facts objectively, and establish her reputation as a real co-worker.

[v]

The impact of the business world may be a bit startling to you, and your first reaction may be to resist the vibrant drive for ideas, action, and results. This resentment or rebellion against accepting the challenge to succeed may be one of the reasons why some business concerns hesitate to entrust responsible jobs to women. But if you have met competition in high school and college life, and have learned to work with groups of people outside your personal friends and family, you should welcome the opportunity of a challenge. This attitude will go far to hasten your adjustments in the business world. And the business world is, after all, a regrouping of people, basically not so different from other groups. The interest in the welfare of one company is the uniting force of this group, instead of the college, the club, or the home neighborhood.

The career-minded woman has an important role to play in today's business. How can *you* start? What are the rules of the game? What are the sociological and cultural obligations you must accept? How can you gauge your progress? What are your chances of success?

Whether you think in terms of one year or twenty, *you,* a young woman who has chosen a business career, can take pride in your choice and resolve to learn the rules and succeed.

The Young Woman in Business is written to help you make a good start and to guide you through some of the experiences you are rather sure to have.

Here are some of the answers we have given to young women like you who have asked about careers in business.

This advice is based on our experiences as well as the suggestions of successful women in many lines of work. These career women are enthusiastic about their work and the opportunities for women in business. They join us in wishing you well in the work of your choosing.

BETH BAILEY MCLEAN
JEANNE PARIS

Table of Contents

CHAPTER 1

Choose a Good Place To Work

YOU are about to choose the place of business where you will spend thirty to forty hours each week. Perhaps you are not planning on a long-term career, but today, more than ever before, women continue working after marriage. This means that for you, a young woman, this new position is very important.

Possibly you have had a part-time or temporary job before. You may not have given much thought to choosing it. You wanted money and were willing to do almost any kind of work to earn money for a specific purpose. If this work was in a field you wished to pursue in later life you were fortunate. But, whatever the type of work, you probably did get valuable experience in working with people of different ages and different interests. You learned that an employer sets rules and regulations for his employees. And you learned that although the pay check looked big, the money did not begin to pay for items you needed —

such as rent, food, and clothing — with enough money left over for a vacation, gifts, and that important savings account for future needs.

These first "little" jobs usually make young women realize the "spending" value of money and the importance of doing the kind of work they like in a place where they can be happy. These

jobs serve to underscore the fact that *a good place to work should be chosen carefully.*

How can you judge a good place to work? Well, think back to your first experience in a business transaction. Perhaps you took a list to the supermarket for your mother. Or you may have stopped at the neighborhood variety store with money for candy. Were the clerks pleasant and interested in helping? If they were, you probably went back often. As you grew older, you began to judge a store by the people who operated it and by the quality of the products sold.

With more experience you began to evaluate offices, banks, and other business operations as well as stores. And, in each case, the people and products or services were the basic factors that influenced you to give them your business.

If your father was in business, you learned to associate another idea with business — namely, that the business had to make money to pay wages to the employees and to make a profit for the owner.

Therefore, from your own experience you have learned three good tests of a business concern:

What kind of people make up the business?
What quality of products or services is produced?
Does the company pay its employees well and make a profit for the owners?

In other words, you can agree with the statement, "A business must be economically sound and socially desirable."

Whether you begin your career in an educational institution, in governmental work, in a trade association, or in a social service agency, these same standards of worth or usefulness may be applied, to a certain degree. A business is based on transactions where goods or services are exchanged or sold for the purpose of making a profit. This means that a monetary profit for the owner becomes the number one objective. From an employee's viewpoint, only a successful company can give you security and opportunity.

Therefore, if you decide on a career in business, you should accept the fact that a business must make a profit to exist. And you must be willing to accept your responsibility to contribute to the financial success of the business. You must be a paying investment and produce a fair return on what the company invests in you in the way of salary, training time, and equipment. It is said that American industry as a whole has an investment of $6,000 to $25,000 per worker.

Everyone likes to be on a winning team. So, in joining the business world, you will find it both more pleasant and more profitable to work for a company that is *financially sound* and that recognizes the importance of having employees feel *financially secure*.

If you are graduating from high school or college, or if you have been working in a field other than business, some advisors will say that *any* experience in business is helpful. They may suggest that your main objective should be to get a toe-hold and then make the most of the opportunity to learn and advance in some line of work.

It is true that few of us are able to pick and choose the job we want. But there is no reason for stumbling blindly into a position without using the information that is available to try to fit yourself for and into the *right job*.

You are fortunate if you have chosen your education and experience to fit yourself for a field of work. You have made a good start on a career if, at the time of graduation, you have a clear vision of what you want to do and where you want to go in your profession.

Unfortunately, many young people have no specific goal. They have not troubled to find out about the great diversity of work in business. They have not thought about the possible application of their school training in terms of useful work. As you know, businesses are not labeled *History 342, Sociology 26,* or *Mathematics 400.*

Let's say that your education has given you a broad, liberal background, with special emphasis on one specific field such as Secretarial Work, Advertising, or Home Economics. Then you will be wise to make a study of the business concerns that offer *different* applications and specializations in your field. Such a position may give you more opportunity to learn and test your ability than a specialized position.

Some women now at the top in their profession have begun at the bottom and worked up step by step in the same field. Many more top-ranking women have begun in one line of work and, through observation, initiative, and an expanding vision of opportunities, have found a new field of work more challenging and more compatible with their abilities.

There is no one road to success in the business field. And very few women who are in executive positions arrived there by luck, through family connections, or by waiting for a break. They got to a top position by *working* for it, not by *wishing* for it.

So, let's say you have the education, the ability, and the will to work in a field of business. Let us consider, then, what is a good place for you to work toward a successful career.

1. Does the business sell products or a form of service such as publicity or consultations? Have you the training, ability, and desire to be useful in such a business and to give your best efforts to promoting these goods or services?
2. Do you like the people with whom you will work?
3. What is the reputation of the company concerning service to the community, relations with employees, and contacts with the public?
4. Are the wages adequate to meet your financial responsibilities?
5. What are the opportunities for training, learning, and advancement?

What Does the Business Have To Sell?

Whether you have lived in a small or large city, you probably have only a vague idea of the many kinds of businesses represented in your community. In a large city, the number of businesses is totally bewildering, even to a native. As one girl said, on coming to Chicago, "There must be thousands of kinds of jobs I've never heard about. How do I know I wouldn't like one of them?" The answer is that no one person can know of all the types of specialized work that go into making our American way of life so successful.

There are classifications of kinds of industries and of kinds of work common to many industries. In the classified section of the telephone directory, businesses are listed by types of industry, as: *Advertising, Insurance, Millinery.* Under each general heading are divisions of each type, as: *Advertising Agencies and Counselors, Advertising — direct mail, Advertising — displays.*

In the classified want ads in a newspaper, jobs are often classified according to the kinds of work requiring special skills and abilities, as: *Research worker in food company, Commercial artist, Insurance saleswoman, Buyer for department store.*

Thus you will see that one type of industry needs workers with many kinds of skills. Again, a person with one skill can look for work in a number of different types of industry.

In a small business, one person may do several kinds of work requiring quite different skills. This may prove to be an oppor-

. . . one person may do several kinds of work requiring quite different skills.

tunity to develop initiative and to test your wings without too much supervision.

In a large company, there is great specialization. Departments are established for related kinds of work, and many people are employed to do the same type of work. In such a department, further specialization is often required, so that a job may be very specific and limited in scope. Thus, in a large company, you may find your training will fit you for work in several different departments. When you apply at such a company, the employment counselor determines where you will be most useful and successful.

Of course, the classified telephone directory, the want-ad section of a newspaper, or any other published list of employment places, is very cold and impersonal. If you are joining the business world, you will lessen your confusion and indirection if you talk with people in your field of work and read all you can about companies in which you are interested.

Some companies employ many persons and have an active recruitment program. To do an effective and systematic job of informing interested, would-be employees, they have booklets describing job opportunities, training, and education required. Some companies may have movies suitable for showing before classes or clubs. A letter or a phone call to the personnel director of the company will bring printed booklets and descriptions of the movies available.

Many companies publish booklets describing the products sold and the services offered to the public. These booklets are offered through professional magazines, talks given by members of the organization, and through professional and civic organizations. A study of these materials will help you learn about the purpose of a company. It may give you some idea of how you might fit into the organization.

When you see an advertisement of a product of a company, read a news item about some activity of the company, or collect other information about the company, ask yourself if you would like to work for that company. Would you feel proud to help in the production and sale of those products? Would you feel proud to say "That's my company." Pride in your work and loyalty to your company are *musts*. The pay check is not a ticket to success.

Do You Like the People With Whom You Will Work?

Did you ever walk into a bank, department store, or office that made you feel welcome and *at home*, whereas a similar place of business made you feel insignificant and uncomfortable?

Every business concern has a *personality* quite as distinct as that of an individual. The people with whom you work play a very important role in determining how well you will succeed in your work. Human relations are so important that unless you *fit in* with an organization, so much of your mental capacity will be spent in irritation and resentment that you will not be free to do constructive thinking.

Of course, much of the responsibility for getting along with the people in any business will depend on your own attitude. Are you too young mentally to appreciate and understand the adults who are in business? When you have reached the age to start on your career you should be socially adjusted so that your interests are broader than *the school* or *the home town*. The real test of a well-adjusted woman is the ability to get along with people of different ages, social positions, educational backgrounds, and viewpoints.

When you see the people who work in a business, try to think of yourself as one of them. Would you like to work with them? Or would you feel superior? depressed? irritated? afraid? distrustful?

A woman who had had many years of business experience was invited to take an executive position with a different organization. The opportunity seemed to be an excellent one. The company was well known and respected. The products produced by the company were of top quality. The executives seemed to be the kind who inspired confidence and for whom it would be a pleasure to work. The one question that remained for her was, "What about the people with whom I would associate in my daily contacts?"

This woman decided that the real test of the rightness of the job depended on the spirit that prevailed among the people employed by the company. Were they happy? Did they think this was a good place to work?

With these questions in mind, this businesswoman paused to consider the people with whom she would work. She sat in the lobby of the company office and watched the young office girls, the gray-haired women, the youthful messenger boys, and the older businessmen. In that large organizations some 2,000 people were employed. Through the lobby, as in review, passed the living spirit of the company, the people with whom she would work! They were intelligent, sincere, businesslike, and friendly. They seemed like a big family working together for a common purpose. They looked happy.

That was the final test. *Then*, this professional woman knew it was a good place to work.

What Is the Reputation of the Company?

Every business concern, whether small or large, has a code of ethics or set of policies which gives the company a *character* or *spirit*. This spirit, which permeates an organization or business, is determined by the owner or by the top executives who manage the business. The employees in the business are selected and trained to carry out this code of ethics in their work with fellow employees and in their contacts with the public.

As soon as an employer hires a worker to help run his business, a new set of relations is established. The greater the number of

The spirit of a business concern is determined by the owner or top executives.

employees, the more complex is the problem of employer-employee relations, because each person has individual wants, hopes, and fears. The multiple-helper situation builds up an increasing need for a *human relations* or Industrial Relations Department. Such a department, made up of a group of trained persons or a single trained person, considers and analyzes problems that arise in the interrelation of the human beings in a company. This work is separate from the departments concerned mainly with the problems of producing and selling goods or services.

The responsibilities of a human relations department may vary from company to company. The usual purpose of this department is to weld all the employees into a family group that works together for the good of all.

Just as the members of a family do not agree, so, too, in a large business you will find differences of viewpoint. However, in modern business, management has set up a system whereby these differences can be discussed and settled with consideration for the rights of the individual as well as the rights of management.

When you consider employment in a business concern, it is important to learn as much as possible about the family spirit, the *working rapport* that exists. Much of your inner contentment on the job will depend on the attitude of the company toward the workers.

This is not the place to discuss the goals of organized labor and the attitude of modern business in regard to labor unions. As a businesswoman you may or may not be required to join a union upon entering employment in a company. But surely you will be interested in reading authentic articles and books on modern labor-management relations. You will want to know the facts about the objectives of organized labor to gain economic security, the opportunity of advancement, equality of treatment, and preservation of personal dignity. You will want to read, too, about management's aims to secure the economic welfare of the company, good industrial relations, freedom to manage, and businesslike relations with employees.

Whether or not your type of work is included in the unionized labor, it no doubt will be affected by the unions operating in the company and by the relations that exist between the unions and company management.

If you are entering a business for the first time, you may have little knowledge of the responsibility assumed by modern business for good industrial relations. Mr. Clarence Francis, former Chairman of the Board of General Foods Corporation, has analyzed this responsibility. "Today," says Mr. Francis, "most managements . . . operate as trustees in recognition of the claims of employees, investors, consumers, and government. The task is to see that each gets a fair share of industry's reward."

This modern viewpoint of *service* must play a vitalizing role in establishing a background for your thoughts and actions when you enter business. When you look for a place to work, try to find out whether or not the company has this concept of service.

Many company booklets and publications contain statements of company policies, ideals, and ethics. But the best evidence of the workability and effectiveness of a code of ethics is the attitude of the employees at work and away from work.

Here is an example of a company statement of principles for enduring, successful business:

Deal honorably with all people.
Operate efficiently.
Research constantly to improve products and services.
Pay equitable wages, provide opportunity for advancement, and maintain a sincere concern for the well-being of employees.
Sell not only products but good behavior as well.
Earn a profit sufficient for the company to fulfill these responsibilities and to provide shareholders with a fair return on their invested savings.

The reputation of a company is not determined by writing a code of ethics, for the written statement indicates the *intent* of management. The reputation is dependent on the *fulfillment* of the code.

Here are some statements of company policies. Would you like to work for such a company?

Our policy has always been to consider our employees as individual men and women, not just workers, and we have tried for many years to merit the confidence and trust of all members of our organization.

The welfare of the company and that of its employees are closely tied together. In the long run, what the company can do for its employees depends on how efficiently we all do our job, and how productive we are in contributing to the over-all success of the company.

In a report to shareholders, John Holmes, President of Swift & Company in 1954, called the personnel *the organization's greatest asset*:

It is axiomatic that the shareholders' investment in land, buildings, and machinery is of the greatest value when the facilities are operated by an efficient, smooth-working group of employees. Our products and our services are well and favorably known to the consuming public through the efforts of our employees, who are loyal to the idea that we make the best products and provide superior service for our customers. The personnel is the shareholders' greatest asset. All through its history, Swift & Company has always been a good company to work for — perhaps not always so good as it is today and certainly not so good as I hope it will be in the years ahead. . . .

I should like to emphasize the fact that industrial relations to be sound must be a two-way proposition. We have a right and a duty to insist upon employees giving the company the same fair treatment that they want and expect to receive.

In conclusion, we should like you, the shareholders, to realize that it is not the efforts of management alone that make a profit possible on your investment, but it is the combined effort of all of us, as employees working together, that assures success. In short, good industrial relations is sound investment.

You will notice that the phrase *human relations* keynotes these statements of policies. Everyone in an administrative position is charged with the responsibility of maintaining good human relations with the employees. The Industrial Relations Department of a company is known largely because of its work on wage-and-hour questions. But the real concept or purpose of such a department covers many services that aid the financial, social, and health standards of the employees. These services help to make the company a good place to work.

Are the Wages Adequate?

The reason most of us work is to earn money to buy the things we need and want for ourselves and our dependents. Very few women work in business just for the luxuries of life. Most of them have one or more dependents, so that the financial obligations of women are often as great as those of their men co-workers.

There are still some inequalities in women's salaries as compared with men's in the same kind of work. But more and more the tendency is to pay a salary commensurate with work done, irrespective of sex. The beginning salary paid a girl graduate may be higher in many occupations concerned primarily with women's traditional interests than that paid in fields formerly considered suitable for men only, such as banking, investments, real estate, law, or insurance.

Salaries are fairly uniform from company to company for the same kind of work. When you start that climb up the ladder or move on toward a top position, you should consider not only the pay check but other benefits that add up to the total remuneration received for the position.

A good place to work is in a company that offers you a salary plus other considerations which must be evaluated in terms of your needs. Listed briefly here are some of the services, or *plus values,* which you should know about in judging whether the salary is adequate:

1. Pension plan, bonus, share of profits, and paid-up insurance are methods used by different companies as extra dividends for good work.

   A *pension* paid to employees at a certain age, usually 60 or 65, after a certain number of years of work may be paid by the company with no contribution from the employees.

   A *bonus* to employees at the end of the fiscal year is another type of "thank you."

   A *profit-sharing plan* is used by some companies to pay employees a percentage of the year's profits either in cash, stock in the company, or paid-up insurance.

   A *cooperative insurance* plan is sometimes used to foster savings by employees and to increase the amount of money paid into the insurance fund by the employer.

2. *Vacations with pay* are usual in positions on a yearly basis. The length of the vacation varies from one to four weeks depending on the company, the length of employment and, sometimes, the rank of the employee.

3. *Payment of dues* in professional societies and reimbursement for certain expenses incurred in the work are allowed for certain positions in some companies.

4. An *Employees' Benefit Association* may be in operation in a company. This is a low-cost insurance supported by contributions

of employees who join this service. It carries benefits to the employees in time of sickness, accident, and death.

5. *Group life insurance* at low rates may be available to employees.

6. A *Savings and Loan Association (Credit Union)* operated by employees for the benefit of employees may prove to be a great help to the beginner.

7. *Sickness and accident payments* may be allowed according to the length of employment by some companies.

8. A *medical department* for consultation and treatment of accidents and illness incurred at work is maintained by larger companies.

9. *Group hospitalization* is available in most companies. Such a plan for hospital care is operated on a nonprofit basis by the hospital corporation. Different classifications are available to employees to allow a choice of benefits and payments. This is an optional service offered under the guidance of the company. Dues or fees are deducted from the pay check.

10. A *cooperative plan for medical care benefits* may also be offered by the company. It is a voluntary service which the employees may elect to join.

11. *Hospital, surgical, and medical insurance,* which is paid for by the company, may be offered to the employees.

12. *Cafeterias and restaurants* operated by the company usually afford savings in the cost of lunches and other meals during working hours.

The cost of living in a location reasonably accessible to work may take a considerable portion of a pay check . . .

13. *Other benefits of a monetary value* may be available in a company. These are usually discussed with an applicant at the time of an interview.

14. *Social security benefits* now cover almost every type of work. According to the Social Security Laws, the federal government collects from the employer a percentage on all salaries up to a certain amount per year. Of this, the company pays a certain percentage and the employee pays an equal amount which is deducted from the pay check. At the end of the year, the employer furnishes to the employee a withholding statement. A booklet explaining this act is available from the Social Security Board or the company. In it are listed payroll deductions and the corresponding benefits.

Other Considerations Which Influence Value of Salary

1. The cost of transportation to and from work may take much or nothing from a pay check.

2. The cost of living in a location reasonably accessible to work may take a considerable portion of a pay check.

3. Specific expenses for the job in the way of uniforms, type of dress, and special attention to appearance, a car for business use, membership in professional organizations, contributions to special funds may reduce a pay check considerably.

4. Occupational hazards which may affect health should be weighed against the salary offered.

What Are the Opportunities for Advancement?

A good place to work means not only congenial co-workers, a company of good reputation and wages, and benefits in proportion to your ability, but also an opportunity to advance in your chosen work.

Some women may be willing to mark time in a job, with no thought of advancement. But today, more and more women have hitched their wagons to a star of leadership. The opportunity for advancement is very important to these career women.

A company's policy for promotions is important to you the beginner, too.

Are promotions made from the ranks?

Are there training classes and other opportunities to learn new skills?

Are employees encouraged to continue to study and learn so as to fit themselves for better positions in the company?

Is there a great turnover of personnel in the company or do service records of employees show that they think this is a good place to work?

Is there a counseling service where an employee may discuss her problems in human relations and receive an evaluation of her ability for the job or for a better job?

Does the head of the department in which you will work recognize the ability of women to do executive work?

Are there women in executive positions and does the company encourage leadership in women?

Is the company sound financially so that you have the right to expect a continuation of the job and reasonable expansion of your kind of work?

These are questions that you must consider if you have some experience and maturity and have determined to succeed in your chosen work. As a beginner, you can have fewer positions to choose from but you will be wise to know the importance of working where opportunities for advancement exist.

How do you find the answers to these questions? Not by sending a questionnaire to every company you know! Employers do not have the time to answer letters full of questions about job opportunities. But you can write to the Industrial Relations Department or Personnel Service of a company. State that you are interested in work with the company and ask for a booklet giving information about the organization.

If you are fortunate enough to have an interview, you may ask if there are training classes and opportunities to advance. No doubt during the interview special benefits and regulations will be discussed.

The Right Job

A good place for you to work is a financially sound company of good reputation where you will associate with people you like and have the opportunity to increase your skills in a line of work that is profitable to you and the company.

CHAPTER 2

Look at the Real You

THERE *is* a position for you. Hold fast to that idea and have faith in yourself. Use your ingenuity to search out opportunities, and keep everlastingly at your objective to find the job that is best for you.

Of course, employers aren't beating a path to your door to beg your services unless you are a most unusual person who has achieved noteworthy success in a noncompetitive field. Very few successful women in this country found opportunity ready-made for them when they looked for their first position. In fact, every beginner is apt to feel that she is ready to begin work at the wrong time, that she has chosen an overstocked line of work, that all her friends are getting fabulous jobs, and that nobody wants an inexperienced worker!

Let's dispel that last worry first. *There are more jobs for beginners than for executives.* Each business is like a pyramid

There **is** a position for you . . .

with a broad base of less-skilled workers and a towering point of those with years of experience and great skill.

It is true that some women make the fortunate choice of a field of work that is in need of help at the time they are ready to work. But if you haven't chosen that training, what's the use of wasting your time and energy feeling sorry for yourself and bemoaning your hard luck? It's a bad habit to develop self-pity. The *hard luck* attitude is a sure way to lose friends and bore people. You may have to work harder to find your job, it may pay less at first, but who can say you won't climb to the top faster? *Kites rise high against the wind.*

Begin to build your plan of attack with an optimistic viewpoint. Never give way to the foolish thought that the world is against you. Remember the story of the little engine that pulled its load to the top of an impossible hill by saying, "I think I can."

You want to get into business. Therefore, start with a business-like, systematic analysis of the problem. You may get help from friends, family, and faculty members who know you. But, since you are the one who is looking for the right position, you are the one to tackle the problem.

Why do you want to work? Is it to earn some money for a few months between graduation and marriage? If that is your motive, then you should think in terms of the smaller positions in a department store, office, or similar location where you can begin at once to earn your salary without a training period. In these positions the employer doesn't expect too much or pay very much because the work is routine and does not require much skill. It isn't fair to accept a position which gives you several weeks of training if you plan to work just a year.

Even though you are a college graduate with specialization in a skill, you will need more training, supervision, and guidance in most positions you take in business. This is an expense to the company. You cannot honorably accept such a position if you do not plan to stay long enough to repay this expense plus a profit in terms of continuous, conscientious service.

If you want a career, before and after marriage, then you should choose your position with the thought of learning and growing. You should be willing to work where you have an opportunity to continue your education and training. The salary should be less important than the benefits you receive from working in the right company under the right supervision.

You can waste a lot of time and effort by looking for a position before you take a good look at yourself. You'll be wise to analyze yourself first, then call on all past experiences and present facilities to find the position where you will succeed.

Here is an assignment that is more important than any one you have ever had. You'll find the best vocational guidance help you can get is to take pencil and paper and answer the following questions:

1. *What do you have to sell an employer?* Rate your personality and your training (education and experience).

2. *What kind of work are you able to do?* State the general field of work and list as many variations or subdivisions as possible.

3. *Where will you be more apt to find your kind of work?* Will a local community or a large business center give you the best chance?

What Do You Have To Sell an Employer?

Your personality is your most important asset. What kind of a woman are you? If you have gone away to school, you've made a break from the family circle and have learned through some rather trying experiences that you as a person are accepted on different terms than you as "Doctor Bell's daughter who attended Riverside Church." But even at school you may have been protected by some of the family, home-town influence. Now, in going into business, you, the woman, must be ready and able to succeed without artificial props. Family influence may help you get a start — but pampering and parental protection seldom help anyone grow!

Personality is an intangible word, yet you have a rather definite idea in mind when you speak of a friend's personality. You refer to the sum of her personal characteristics as these affect you. In the same way, your personality or distinctive personal and social traits may be given different values by the people you meet under different conditions.

Your home, your schools, and your church have taught moral, ethical, and social standards. Perhaps you have thought many of these were a bit old-fashioned. No doubt you've had many a *gab session,* discussing the true worth of honesty, fairness, self-control, tact, tolerance, sincerity, dependability, initiative, cooperativeness, and other traits of character. It's easy in a school atmosphere to decide that good manners are overrated and rather out of style. It's natural that each generation should feel a bit sorry for older folk who seem conservative and intolerant of youth's *self-expression.*

This is no place for a lecture on morals or manners. But this fact is indisputable: *The most essential ingredient in business is the ability to get along with people.* Since the people with whom you will work will have an adult viewpoint of good manners and social adjustment, it is wise to pause and give yourself an honest rating on your personality traits.

It is part of growing up to think of yourself not in terms of "Marybelle of XYZ Club" but "Miss Clay of LMN Company." There is a difference! The transition from school life to the business world will be easy for you, if you are one of the many modern young women who are socially adjusted and have adult standards of behavior.

SOCIAL ADJUSTMENT is a combination of many factors. Of these a sense of humor acts as *a foam-rubber cushion for the hard road of life* and a springboard to acceptance by your co-workers. This does not mean you should be a practical joker, a teller of funny stories, or a comedian. Far from it! But a healthy sense of humor is the best safety valve for the stress and strain resulting from the daily impact of personalities and events in business. Don't take yourself too seriously. Enjoy a good laugh! If you find you haven't a sense of humor, mark this as a handicap and make a conscientious effort to correct it.

PERSONAL APPEARANCE plays a part in determining your personality. Most young women today have learned to appreciate the

The transition from school life
to the business world will be easy, if . . .

importance of good health, good posture, and good grooming. You should realize before you apply for your first position that modern businesswomen must look the part. Outward appearance is an indication of the person inside. Only a genius can afford to be careless of her personal appearance. And even the genius is a more useful member of society if she looks as smart as she really is!

Now that you have had a heart-to-heart talk with yourself and can see yourself as others see you, here is your next personality test.

You as a person have definite likes for certain people and certain activities. You are more successful if your work suits your likes and your temperament. These questions will help you know more about yourself:

1. Do you like to meet and be with people, or are you happier alone?

2. Do you like to be with both men and women, or do you feel more at ease with children?

3. Are you clever with your hands, or are you more successful at mental work without manual demonstration?

4. Do you like to organize and assume responsibility, or do you prefer to carry out plans made by others?

5. Are you creative and imaginative?

6. Do you enjoy finding the reasons for things, and searching for background facts?

7. Do you like selling, competition, and working under pressure?

8. What other likes influence your ability to express your real self?

If you really give thought to your answers and write them down in a list, you'll get a clearer picture of *you the person.* You then can be selective in looking for a position. You'll be better prepared when interviewed and asked, "What do you *like* to do?" That question doesn't call for your autobiography, but your answer will tell the employer that you have given thought to your ability. It will be to your credit to give a positive statement as,

"I like to work with people and I enjoy selling," or, "I like to research and find the reason for things, so I work better with figures and facts than in contacts with people." If you answer, "I don't know, I guess I like to do most everything," the employer is apt to interpret that to mean, "I'm not too interested in anything."

So far, you have looked at your personality and listed your interests. *Have you any prejudices, opinions, physical conditions, or family ties that might affect your success in a certain business?* If so, you should face the facts and decide in what kind of work these will be an advantage instead of a handicap. Religion, nationality, marital status, intense political beliefs, and physical defects may weigh the scales in your choice of a position and in the employer's choice, too.

Have you any definite dislike for a type of work, class of people, or location? This may be due to immature judgment which you can correct. If not, you'll never be very successful in work that emphasizes these dislikes.

Your personality is the result of many influences. But if you want to succeed in business, you must recognize and acknowledge your real self. If you don't like some of the things you find out about yourself, now is the time to begin a personality improvement campaign. It may be comforting to know that most successful people have had to take corrective measures, too!

This self-analysis isn't easy, but it should be an eye-opener. In school, no doubt you have had intelligence tests, temperament tests, and interest tests to guide you in your selection of work. You may have found you can do several kinds of work. Most folk can. You don't have to be a genius to succeed, but you'll be far happier if you can find out now about the *Real You.*

In a talk given to a group of business and professional women, Dr. Lillian M. Gilbreth, widely-recognized industrial psychologist, said that, today, business puts less emphasis on your I.Q. (Intelligence Quotient) and more emphasis on your P.Q. (Personality Quotient). So, if you have good average intelligence, a will to succeed, good health, an interest in people, and a willingness to work and learn, you are off to a good start. If you also rate a high I.Q. you are in the winning class.

When you total your assets to make a good sales story you will include *your personality plus your training.* Training includes your education in high school, specialized schools, college or university. Training also includes those experiences which build up your fund of knowledge.

A study of the women who have reached executive stature in business reveals that some have reached their goals by beginning with general training while others began with vocational training in a special skill. Knowledge gained in both general and specialized training has played an important role in their careers. There is no royal road to success. Many women do not find the right road until they have been in business two or more years. The specialists must study and learn more *general knowledge.* Those with a liberal education must study and learn *specialized skills.*

How do you rate your storehouse of knowledge and your training in a special skill? Are you prepared to enter a field which requires a college degree in a specialization, such as Home Economics, Law, Economics, Medicine, or Engineering? If not, you should look for a position which requires general knowledge and which offers an opportunity to acquire specialized training through experience and vocational study.

The women listed in *Who's Who in America* illustrate the importance of a balance between general knowledge and special skills. Dr. Gilbreth, Wallace Clark Award winner in 1951 in the field of scientific management and the mother of 12 children, is an outstanding example of a woman with specialized training who is loved and respected because of her womanliness and her breadth of knowledge and human understanding.

You will find the list of other women who have won public recognition for stellar performances includes:

publishers and editors of newspapers and magazines;
presidents or directors of manufacturing companies, banks, and department stores;
executives in insurance and real estate companies;
vice-presidents in advertising agencies, photography concerns, and public relations organizations;

heads of research and production departments for cosmetics, clothing, and other products;

buyers;   designers;

creators of clothing, textiles, equipment, foods, and the many other products which contribute to our daily welfare.

Women also have reached executive positions in many fields of personnel work in office management and in supervision or in teaching greater efficiency in the mechanics of business procedures. Then, of course, there are women who have reached professional heights in many specialized fields of the arts and sciences.

It is helpful to look at the stars in the business world. Remember, however, that top-flight women were once beginners like yourself. Take encouragement from their success because they have made it easier for you to enter the business world and to succeed. Some day a beginner may be reading about your career and wondering what kind of a person you are and what you did to win success.

Your ability to do a certain kind of work depends on your personality, your storehouse of knowledge, and your special training, plus experience in your chosen field.

Confidence in your own ability will help you make a wholehearted effort to get the right job. Overconfidence or an overestimate of your ability may result in disappointment when you meet with the realities of business. But most employers prefer to hire a woman who knows what she can do and what she wants to do rather than a timid soul who doesn't think much of herself or her ability.

For the beginner, the most baffling line on that application blank will be *experience*. While you are making the preliminary survey of your assets, take time to jot down all the experiences you have had, both in and out of school, which contributed to your ability to work intelligently and effectively. Did you hold

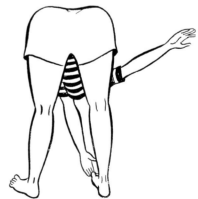

If you don't like some of the things you find out about yourself. . .

any class offices or belong to any organized groups like the Girl Scouts, Campfire Girls, or YWCA? Did you work at home, work during summer vacations, work after school? The experiences need not be limited to those for which you were paid, but paying jobs do give you an edge. Travel, working with people, meeting new situations, participation in sports, training in music or art, outstanding ability in any field of endeavor are experiences which will indicate what kind of a person you are.

As you progress in your career, your experience in your work will become more important. In succeeding analyses of experiences, that first listing will lose significance. But when you are a beginner, you can't afford to overlook any activity that indicates you have been tested and have shown ability in some field of endeavor.

What Kind of Work Are You Able To Do?

It's a happy thought that you probably can do several kinds of work. Most women who make a career for themselves shift their work within their field or dare to work in very different fields. For example, one woman taught clothing construction, became a successful clothes designer, restaurant manager, tearoom owner, and finally organized a real estate company. Do not narrow your sights when you look for your first position. There are thousands of kinds of work of which you may never have heard, but new horizons will open for you if you are alert and make a good start.

Vocational guidance courses in school, books about positions open to women, current magazines and newspaper articles, and, best of all, lectures by and talks with women in business help you select the work you are able to do.

Aptitude and intelligence tests are guides to your ability. *But the very best help will come from your own analysis of yourself and your acquaintance with as many fields of work as possible.*

For example, suppose you have found you are a sociable, observing person who likes to work with people. You like to solve a problem and sell the idea to others. You have training in journalism and have acquired a habit of reading about current events and interesting people. You enjoy writing and have imagination and ability to harness your thoughts into a working, orderly plan. Then you could profit by talking with someone in the advertising field, either in an advertising agency or in the advertising department of a company producing or selling consumer goods.

Suppose, however, your analysis shows you prefer to work with *things* rather than *people* and you are creative and efficient in hand skills. Then check your extra ability to determine whether you would succeed in designing or construction of clothes, fabrics, or equipment. Perhaps your ability fits you for work with statistics. charts, diagrams, and the research needed in banking, finance, insurance, and office procedures.

Home economics training prepares a girl for many and varied positions which are specifically women's work. If you have this training, you have but to analyze your personality and your special likes and abilities to decide whether you are fitted for work in clothing and textiles, foods, equipment, home management, or child development. Do you want public contact work in your specialization, or do you like best to use journalism, research work, or production to express yourself?

If you haven't vocational training, you still have a wide choice of work. Your skill doesn't have to be one of great specialization. Some very successful women have started in business with a skill in typing, plus the desire to learn and the ability to make the most of every opportunity. Women in advertising, insurance, banking, radio, television, journalism, and many other kinds of work have begun by being a good secretary to a good boss. Many women have begun their climb by selling in a department store.

Any selling is good experience. Where could you have a greater opportunity to learn to get along with people, to study human psychology, to become a judge of qualities that make for consumer acceptance of a product, and to get firsthand experience in many of the phases of business operation?

No book or standardized tests can open all the doors to the best work for you. You'll find books, tests, personal contacts, and success stories helpful only as you use these to analyze yourself and to guide you in the general direction of the right work for you.

Any selling is good experience.

CHAPTER 3

Use Employment Help Wisely

WHERE will you find your kind of work? Of course, there are more positions in large cities than in small towns, but that doesn't mean that the best place for you is in a large city. Competition is great and expenses are greater in a large city than in a small town. You may find the best place for you to start is in your home town.

If you have lived in a rural community, you may be wise to look over possible positions in a medium-sized city rather than to get into the confusion of Chicago, New York, Philadelphia, or one of the other really large cities. A big city can be a very discouraging and lonely place for a small-town girl.

On the other hand, if you have ability to do specialized work, you may have to go to the city or locality that is the center for that kind of work. The textile, clothing, and related industries are centered in New York, Chicago, and California. Yet you may start to learn about textiles, consumer preferences, and sales problems by selling textiles in a store anywhere.

The best attitude or approach is to be willing to go wherever you can get a good starting position. It doesn't hurt to hope for a certain location and try to find work there, but you may have to sacrifice important advantages of training and advancement if you limit the choice of location. Two college graduates once wrote a joint letter of application to a company. The letter read:

We will graduate from ————— college in June. Have you any positions in a foreign country? We would like to travel.

The recipient of that letter liked to travel, too. However, she hadn't reached her executive position without hard work on the job at the place where she could learn the most. It took considerable effort to marshal her sense of humor and her charitable understanding of naive youth to answer these two girls who so selfishly limited a job location. Whose expressed qualifications for positions were a desire to have a company finance their travels!

A beau, a favorite aunt, a sunny climate, or a commuting distance from home may be a deciding factor. But it won't impress a prospective employer with your sincerity to make a career of your work.

How Can You Contact Employers?

We might first raise the question, *when should you begin to contact employers?*

There is no one season when business positions are available. This is different from the teaching field where most positions begin at the first of a school term.

Some employers resent having an applicant come in for an interview too far ahead of the time when she is ready to begin work.

Begin planning as early as you wish for your campaign to get a position. The more background information you collect, the better. Generally, it is not wise to write application letters or ask for appointments earlier than *one month* before you graduate. If a position is available, few employers are willing to wait for you.

What about a vacation before you begin to work? In most positions, you will not be eligible for a vacation until you have been employed a year. Therefore, you may be wise to take a vacation and get yourself and your clothes ready before you start work. While you are in school, you should take care of your records, references, and counseling. If you are recommended for a position, you should follow this lead, but make it clear to the employer just when you will be available.

Now to consider the many ways open for you to contact employers.

Counselors in High Schools and Specialized Schools

Many high schools and most business colleges and other specialized schools have counselors to help graduates find the right positions. Often these schools have close contacts with business concerns that need the graduates. Schools are proud of their graduates and want them to be successful. You will find it pays to know and use the vocational counseling service in any school you attend.

College Counsel and Placement Help

1. If you are in college, you will find some faculty members are especially helpful in guiding you into the best place to work. You will profit by getting to know these teachers well enough to visit with them about your future. Ask them how to start looking for your first position.

2. College and university placement offices at the school are the first consideration for the graduate from these institutions. Most business concerns look to colleges and universities for help in filling certain positions. As a graduate, you should take advantage of this service and be sure to fulfill every requirement in the placement office. Too often a girl expects to marry or to have financial security without work. But history is full of cases where fate steps in and this girl wants to, or must, work. Your college records at the placement office are pieces of security and an insurance against the future. Never fail to complete the records and keep them up-to-date.

3. Some universities have central placement offices in some of the large cities. You can get this information from the placement office on the campus.

Employment Agencies

Business placement or employment agencies play an important role in bringing together the employee and the employer. Some employment agencies deal with positions in one field of work only, whereas others are general in scope. The purpose of these agencies is to save both time and money in job hunting and to increase the chance of good job placement by efficient direction.

The selection of an employment agency is very important. Good employment agencies are used by business to get good employees and by experienced as well as inexperienced women to obtain good positions.

A good employment agency evaluates the applicant's education, experience, interests, and attitudes, and then matches these with the expressed needs of employers. Such an agency should give counsel on current employment possibilities, arrange interviews selected because of applicant's background, and follow through until the applicant's employment problem is solved.

Such help in bringing together the girl and the job calls for counselors with specialized training in individual fields. If you can register at an agency through a personal call rather than by letter, you can judge whether or not the counseling service is adequate to meet your needs. If you find the counselor does not understand your special field, you will be wise to try another agency. In some states, employment agencies must be licensed by the state. Regulations and requirements vary so much that a license may not always mean a satisfactory service for you.

Before you register with an agency, try to find out something about the service. For example:

Talk with friends or acquaintances who have used an employment service to find satisfactory positions.

Ask your school counselor or advisor in the placement office about the rating of various employment agencies.

If you are a newcomer in a city, inquire at the Chamber of Commerce, Better Business Bureau, or YWCA. These organizations can advise you about the ethical practices and efficiency of the employment agencies.

Consult with men and women in executive positions who have had experience with employment agencies. They should be able to recommend agencies of good standing which are qualified to be of most help to you.

No standard fee is charged for placement service, but an employment agency of good reputation will discuss the fee

Get your clothes ready before you start work.

Never enroll in an agency unless you read
the contract and understand the terms.

with you. You should read the contract carefully to be certain of
the terms. There is usually a registration fee of about two dollars.
If you obtain a position through the efforts of the employment
agency, the charge for this service may be from 40 to 60% or
more of your first month's salary. This depends on the amount
of your salary and use of the installment plan for paying the
charge. Never enroll in an agency unless you read the contract
and understand the terms. And never enroll if the fee charged
is excessive, or if you have no knowledge of the ethics of the
organization.

Other Placement Help for You

1. A PLACEMENT AND COUNSELING SERVICE is maintained by
some professional organizations, such as the American Dietetic
Association, the Restaurant Association, Home Economists in
Business, the Bar Association. These services are available to
qualified college students. There may be a charge for such a
service.

2. THE YMCA AND YWCA usually have some form of placement service or are able to direct you to such a service. Other
organizations for social service and aid to working women often
give similar placement help. The Better Business Bureau in a
city will have lists of reputable organizations of this type.

3. GOVERNMENT AGENCIES have employment services. These include the United States Employment Agencies, the State Employment Service, and the Civil Service Commission. You may be surprised at the variety of work listed in these offices.

Newspaper Placement Help

1. THE HELP WANTED COLUMNS in a city paper can be helpful to you, but you must be a critical reader. Some listings will be by employment agencies, some will give a box number only, some will list the name of the employer, and some advertisements will be for schools offering classes in a special skill.

You will save yourself time and disappointment if you analyze these advertisements carefully. Usually an advertisement that gives the name of the employer is a better guide to the worth of the notice. However, many times a company does not include the company name if it would cause dissatisfaction among present employees or give information to competitors. Often a list number with the newspaper is your only method of contact with the employer. Here are some typical clippings from a "Help Wanted — Women" column in a city paper:

Best Personnel Service . . . Dress buyer. Large volume department, quality merchandise. Knowledge of all markets essential; Middle West location. High salary.

(If you are a beginner, you'd waste your time to try for this one.)

College Women! Career assignments, claims or underwriting; large all line insurance branch office. Address R.O. 211 — News.

(This might be a lead, if you think you'd like to try insurance work.)

Personnel trainee . . . College graduate with good personality and ability to train for management branch office. No experience necessary. Office knowledge helps. Write P.O. Box 1376.

(This sounds interesting and may be worth a letter of inquiry.)

High School Graduates . . . Good opportunities for bright girls with ability to type and take dictation. Telephone Norwood 6-423.

(Sounds like a business college.)

Office Secretary . . . Receptionists . . . Personnel Workers! I work at James and Company so I ought to know! Working at James' has advantages you won't find in many offices. You have all kinds of little extras in benefits and a liberal merchandise discount that means more clothes and other things for you. So come in and meet us in James' office — you'll be glad you came!

P.S. The pay is good at James and Company. Apply employment office, 3rd floor. Week days 10 to 3.

(Don't you wish you had written this friendly advertisement? Even if you don't want to apply, you feel friendlier toward the store.)

2. THE WORK WANTED COLUMNS in newspapers may serve as a guide for you. If you have a definite skill and special experience, you may want to place an *ad* in a newspaper. Be specific in stating your qualifications. Use the newspaper code rather than your name and address. For example:

College woman wants position export business. Speaks German and French. B.S. Degree in Textiles and Clothing. Training in Journalism. No preference for location.

(A manufacturer, buyer, or seller of textiles, clothing, or interior decoration might be interested in such a notice. Other companies you'd never think of might also be interested.)

The Help Wanted columns can be helpful to you, but you must be a critical reader.

Professional Guides

1. PROFESSIONAL MAGAZINES sometimes carry HELP WANTED and WORK WANTED notices. A trip to the library may help you locate this service. The list of officers and the authors of the articles may be a hint for you to follow.

2. DIRECTORIES of members in special lines of work are issued by some professions. The *Directory of the Home Economists in Business Section* of The American Home Economics Association is an example of such a listing. If several names are listed for one company, you may assume there is a better chance for a beginner than when only one member is listed. Be sure to look for the name of the Director or Supervisor if you plan to write to the company about employment.

All These Are Helps for You

1. LECTURES by women who are doing worthwhile work are sponsored by professional and businesswomen's clubs and other civic groups. If you are in a city, the club notices in the newspapers will give you an idea of what meetings you may attend. Inspiration and a good hunch may be found at some of these meetings. You may get a chance, too, to talk to some of the club members and gain encouragement and advice.

2. COMPANY PUBLICATIONS often give a description of the kinds of work carried on by the company, as mentioned in Chapter 1.

3. REPRESENTATIVES from many companies go to high schools and colleges to talk with seniors or to participate in organized career and vocational guidance programs. Take advantage of these guidance talks and personal interviews to learn more about opportunities for work.

4. PUBLICITY STORIES in newspapers and magazines may give a good lead. Read the business page editorials on *who's who* in the business and professional field.

5. VOCATIONAL GUIDANCE MOVIES and slide films are provided by many companies, trade associations, and professional organizations for showing at colleges and club groups. These will give you a pictorial survey of what a company or field of work has to offer and how to contact an employer.

6. ADVERTISEMENTS of products and services may give you a new idea of a kind of work and a company to contact.

7. FRIENDS AND RELATIVES are listed last, but are by no means least in importance in bringing you and an employer together. It is wrong to refuse to take advantage of this help, just as it is foolish to sit back and wait for family and friends to get you a position.

With this large list of helpful services you should feel encouraged about finding the right position. You've decided what you have to sell, you've mapped your plan of attack, and you've sighted your objective.

CHAPTER 4

Present Your Case Effectively

A LETTER of application or a personal call at an employment office of a company are the two usual methods of presenting
your case. A telephone call is seldom satisfactory but may be
helpful, especially if you have been recommended to the company
and wish to ask permission for an interview with a specific person.
Unfortunately, however, it is easier to state over the telephone
than directly to a person that there are no positions and that an
interview cannot be arranged at this time!

Letter of Application

A letter of application is a thumbnail sketch of you, your
personality, training, and abilities to fill a specific position. Present your case truthfully, interestingly, effectively, and completely
enough to give the essential facts, but not your life history.

The form of the letter. Use white business paper, 8½ x 11,
bond — not note-size or decorative personal stationery. The letter
should be typewritten. If you can't do professional typing, it may
be worthwhile to pay to have your letter typed. A handwritten
letter is preferable, however, to poor typing, erasures, and mistakes.

Single-space and center the message with even margins. Consult a book on letter writing if you are in doubt about forms of

salutation, closing, and spacing. Put your address at the upper right-hand corner with the date underneath.

Try to find out the name of the employer and give her full name and title. If the person's name is not available use the appropriate title for the person in charge, i.e., manager, supervisor, or director. Or, address the letter to the employment office of the company and request it be sent to the proper person. Be sure the name of the company is correct. You would be surprised to know how often applicants confuse names, products, and people of competitive companies. You can imagine how the recipient of such a confused letter would estimate your qualifications for a position.

The content. Your opening sentence should state your reason for writing. Employers receive many letters in a day and have to read quickly. A glance is enough to encourage further reading or to prompt a note to the secretary to "give form reply." Think what you have to say. Plan how you will say it. Try several ways to express your thoughts, then decide which one gives the best picture of yourself. The simplest way to say something is often the best way. Use the personal *I* form. Do not undersell, yet avoid boastfulness such as, "I am sure I can bring many ideas to your department" or "I feel sure I am thoroughly qualified for the position."

Avoid a dramatic, flamboyant style or tricky sentences, yet

You'd be surprised to know how often applicants confuse names . . .

make your letter sound as if you were interested in the company and the position. It is better to enclose a data sheet of your qualifications than to make the letter of application lengthy and involved. Avoid abbreviations of high school or college subjects and also avoid references to them by number rather than name.

State when you will be available for work and give any unusual qualification that you think would make your application noticeable among the many the employer receives.

Your letter of application should state your case so effectively that the employer recognizes your ability to succeed in the particular position for which you have applied.

If you have been recommended for a position, you may enclose a self-addressed stamped envelope and a business picture. But be sure the picture is a recent one taken especially for the purpose of securing a position. You, photographed in a beach costume, in a party dress, or with a group will not help your cause. A good picture may be the deciding factor in your selection or in the request for an interview.

Be sure to give your permanent as well as your temporary address. It's wise to include your telephone number, too. Your application may be kept on file for a year for future consideration by a placement agency, head of a department, or someone else in the organization.

If you have been referred to the company, begin your letter by announcing this fact:

The placement service at ———— college has advised me of a vacancy in your ———— department. I wish to make application for this position. . . .

If you are sending an exploratory letter, you may begin your letter with a question about a vacancy, but it is better to state your case first.

In June, I shall be graduated from ———— with a major in ————. I should like to work for your company. . . .

(*State your experience and specific interests. Keep the letter brief.*)

Enclosed is a data sheet of my qualifications and references. I shall appreciate an opportunity for a personal interview at your convenience. Yours truly,

The close. In closing, type your full name. Omit *Miss* unless there is danger of confusing your first name with a man's name. Put *Mrs.* in parentheses before your name if you are married. Write your name above the typed signature.

One word of advice. Never ask an employer to write you about the kinds of positions available, the salaries, the hours of work. If you wish information of this kind, it is wiser to write to the employment office of a company and request company booklets.

Here are copies of applications received by one employer. Which letters would interest you if you were an employer?

DEAR SIR:

I am interested in the positions ———— Company has to offer college graduates in its Research Laboratories.

Please send this information with a mention of the yearly remuneration that each position offers.

* * *

DEAR MADAM:

I am a senior science major and am interested in work in your company. I would like to know the type of work done, the experience required, the hours, salary, provisions for maintenance, if any, and other information that can be given.

Any information would be greatly appreciated. Thank you.

* * *

(*How could a busy employer find time to write a complete answer to these two unknown persons of unknown ability?*)

DEAR MRS. ————:

Yesterday, Dr. ———— suggested that I write you concerning a position in your department. I have heard so much about the work your staff does and have had the privilege of hearing Miss ———— give a talk about her work. I would like to work toward such a position.

In June, I will be graduated from ———— University with a degree in Home Economics. My major has been Technical Journalism with a minor in Experimental Foods.

Last summer I was fortunate in securing an apprentice position in the Home Service Department of ———— Company in Kansas City. I enjoyed the work very much.

Enclosed is a data sheet of my qualifications and references. If you are interested in my application, I shall be glad to have my college records sent to you and to come for an interview at your convenience.

*   *   *

DEAR MISS ————:

Your talk given before the Business and Professional Women's Club last Thursday was so interesting and stimulating that I should like very much to work under your direction.

I have graduated from ———— and have taken evening courses in advertising at ———— for the past three years. During my school days I was a reporter for our school paper and won an honor for securing the greatest lineage of advertising for the paper.

In high school, I took an active part in the debating society and was captain of the girl's softball team.

"... I took an active part in the debating society. . ."

I have traveled extensively with my family throughout the United States and have kept a scrapbook of interesting experiences on these travels.

I should be grateful if you could find time to talk with me even if you do not have a vacancy in your department.

Enclosed is my data sheet and a self-addressed stamped envelope.

*   *   *

(Both of these letters give a clear picture of a promising young woman. An employer finds time to answer such letters.)

Application Blanks

Many companies have application blanks which will be sent on request. These vary in form from a single sheet of basic questions to a detailed form requesting personal, physical, social, and family history. Fill out these application blanks carefully and completely. Don't forget to mention all the extracurricular activities that indicate leadership, special capabilities, and characteristics.

Data Sheet

The data sheet is a tabulated list of facts, which are easy to read. On this sheet give a complete, truthful account of your personality, education, and experience. Type these — and do a professional job. The accompanying sample is typical.

Letter of Introduction or Recommendation

A letter of introduction or recommendation from a friend should be mailed directly to an employer. It should be written for a specific position. General or open letters of recommendation are of little value. Only in unusual cases should you present a letter of introduction at the time you go for an interview.

Application Photograph

A good application photograph is an important part of getting your records in order before you start to look for a position.

Styles of photographs change, as you will know when you look at your family album. The picture you liked three years ago looks old fashioned now. And besides, you've changed, too!

This application photograph should show you as a well-groomed, alert young woman. You don't have to be a glamour queen. In fact, many employers hesitate to hire the young woman who looks like a movie aspirant. They fear she will be too conscious of her appeal to be attentive to her work, or she will be married before the training period is over. But every young woman has something distinctive about her.

Play up your best features, and minimize the unphotogenic features. Tell the photographer if you know your jaw looks square, your eyes are apt to squint, your mouth is too small, or

DATA SHEET

Name: Age:

Weight: Height:

Birthplace:

Health:

Married or single:

Nationality: Religious
                                               Denomination:

Education:

    High School:

    University: Degree: Date:

      Major:

      Minor:

      Special courses:

Experience:

    Positions — kind, where, employers, dates.

    Summer work:

    Organization activities:

Personal characteristics and qualifications
    applicable to work:

Reference by permission:*

    Credentials may be secured at ————.

    Character references:

    Business references:

    * Always ask permission to use a person's name as reference, just as
you would ask permission for any other favor.

your nose and chin form similar angles. A good photographer will pose you and arrange the lights to avoid accentuating these bad features. Look your best.

Do wear your hair in a soft flattering style. Don't try an extreme (too short, too long, too straight, or too curled) style. Your hair must look well-groomed and neat. It is best to avoid going from hairdresser to photographer because your hair will look too set.

Wear light lipstick rather than dark shades which photograph dark. Keep the line soft and natural. Use eye shadow sparingly. Accentuate a natural eyebrow line. Some photographers suggest no rouge and very little powder. Some professional photographers have an assistant who advises on make-up.

Now for the clothes. Wear no hat, of course. Choose a semitailored suit or dress. Avoid prints and designs which detract from the face. Usually a V-shaped neckline or a soft collar photographs well. Pearls may be worn, but avoid extreme costume jewelry, (especially dangling earrings). Strive to look businesslike rather than collegiate.

When you pose, look at the camera, think of a funny story, and relax. One suggestion is to think how funny it is that you are all dressed up and sitting for a picture. Don't be afraid to smile. A good way to relax the face in a natural smile is to say "cheese." Try it before a mirror and see if you have a pleasing smile. Of course, a grinning or laughing pose isn't apt to bring you a request for an interview!

Do not use a Hollywood pose, a severe expression or any little-girl effect.

Do give the impression of a successful young businesswoman, well groomed, intelligent, and friendly.

Have about twelve small prints made. A photographer accustomed to making application photographs will advise you on the current size preferred. Write your name on the back, and do practice that signature. Even those who don't pretend to read character by handwriting will judge your neatness and straight thinking by the way you sign your name.

You are ready now to send a good photograph with an application letter, to leave one as a reminder of you when you apply,

. . . look at the camera, think of a funny story, and relax.

or to supply a photograph for any need that arises.

Personal Interview

A personal interview to apply for a position can be a very pleasant experience *if* you have laid your plans, rehearsed your lines, and dressed for the part.

You want to get the right position, while the employer is just as anxious to get the right employee. You are trying to sell your qualifications. The interviewer is trying to obtain facts about your personality, training, experience, and general ability to do the work required by the company.

In many companies all applicants are referred to a personnel office where trained workers make every effort to help the applicant feel welcome and at ease. Think of your interview as a visit, not an ordeal.

In smaller companies and for some specialized positions, the head of the department where the vacancy occurs will interview the applicant. This person may not be skilled in interviewing but she usually is interested in people and friendly in manner.

If you are applying for specialized work, write to ask for an interview at a time that is convenient for the employer. Then you will be more apt to see the head of the department. You can imagine that such a person is very busy with department work. Therefore, an interview with an applicant is extra work, especially if there is no vacancy. Even though this employer wants to help you, her schedule may be filled at the time you drop in at her office.

If you receive an appointment for a specific time — *be there on time!* In cities where distances and transportation facilities may cause delays, allow plenty of time to get to the appointment. If someone must wait, it should be you and not the employer who has scheduled her time to see you.

If you have something to read while you wait, you will be less nervous and impatient at the delay. Even the best-run office schedules get snarled at times. *Never bring a member of your family or a friend with you to an interview.* Show that you are mature enough for the job. Do not smoke, chew gum, apply make-up, or prowl around the office while waiting.

Your personal appearance is your first introduction. If you are well groomed and suitably clothed, you can forget your appearance and give your full attention to the interview.

Magazines for women and for the career girl have taught the modern young woman how important personal appearance is in any business position. Department stores have trained saleswomen to help in the selection of clothes for business wear. In fact, there is little excuse for any young woman to appear at an interview unsuitably dressed. Here's a quick review on personal appearance:

HAIR: clean, neat, not extremely styled. A conservative, easily-cared-for style is preferred for business.

MAKE-UP: carefully applied, not extreme.

NAILS: well manicured, with or without colored polish. If polish is used, it should be carefully applied.

PERFUME: very little, if any.

Never bring family or friends
to an interview.

CLEANLINESS: use of a deodorant very desirable. Excitement may make this essential.

DRESS: a suit or tailored dress in a becoming color always a safe choice. Full skirts with petticoats should never be worn. A coat should be tailored, not dressy. Clothes need not be in the latest fashion but should be clean, pressed, and neat. White accessories must be spotless.

HAT: a small, tailored hat desirable, especially in a large city. It should go with your suit and become you. A felt hat is a good year-round choice.

GLOVES: plain, tailored gloves, especially if a hat is worn. If they are light, carry an extra pair to exchange for the soiled ones just before you arrive for the interview. In a large city, gloves are a *must*. Businesswomen wear them to protect their hands against wind, rain, and especially the grime of subways and buses.

PURSE: tailored and neat. Some employers, especially men, may judge your orderliness by the appearance of your purse when you open it to get a pencil or handkerchief.

SHOES: street-wear type (not play or party shoes) to go with tailored clothes. Be sure they are well cared for.

HOSE: selected to complement street-wear shoes. No bare legs or bobby socks! Carry an extra matching stocking in your purse as insurance against a runner.

Perhaps, in plays or pictures, you have seen overdressed, disheveled, or awkward girls applying for a position. You may have thought these were overdrawn. It can happen in real life. Anyone who has interviewed young women for any length of time will tell you that some of them do not understand the importance of a good personal appearance for the interview.

You may have to borrow a hat or a coat for the occasion, but do look like a businesswoman. If you look the part, your self-confidence will get a lift. Don't worry about how you should act. *Be your best self.* Your attitude and manner during an interview should be the same as when visiting with any older person whom you have just met.

When you are called into the office, take a few deep breaths and *smile!* Walk in without haste, so that you are at ease. Do not offer to shake hands. If an employer offers to shake hands, then be prompt to extend your hand and give a firm clasp. The *dead fish* handshake is enough to earmark you as a spineless individual. Of course, the *bone crusher* handshake and the *pump handle* movement are never used! In business concerns you shake hands and mean it (even though some books on etiquette insist that the well-bred woman does not indulge in this greeting).

In a large city, gloves are a "must."

If you are in doubt about the personality of your handclasp, test yourself with your family to see how expressive you are.

If you are wearing gloves and someone offers to shake hands, do you stop, fumble, and take off your gloves? No. To do so emphasizes an otherwise routine gesture. You need not remove your gloves during an interview until you are asked to write something, or are invited to remove your hat and coat or to have an informal chat with a junior member of the department.

Unless you have been announced by a secretary, state your name and that you have come for an interview. (The employer may not remember you even though you wrote a letter.) Wait to be seated until you are invited to do so. Sit naturally but do not lounge or lean on the desk. It is not necessary to move your chair close to the employer's desk unless you are asked to do so.

Wait for the employer to begin the conversation, then listen attentively and answer questions promptly. Look at the employer. Keep your hands still. Relax. Speak distinctly, naturally, and confidently. (If you have rehearsed your answers, you are ready for questions about your training, experience, and abilities.) If you have not sent a data sheet, you may wish to have one with you to hand to the employer.

Give complete answers to the questions but do not give too much detail. Avoid family histories and any attempt to be humorous or worldly wise. Avoid slang and high school or college chatter. Do not refer to subjects you had in school as *Math, Psych, Home Ec,* or *Chem.* If you feel you are mature enough for the position, remember that you should talk like an adult.

Good manners are of first importance. Affectation will show that you are not certain of yourself.

When you speak of your training and experience, avoid criticism of persons, schools, or companies.

Have a notebook and pencil ready to use if instructions, references, or names are given. If you have a folio of writings, drawings, or examples of your work, you may offer to leave it now with the employer or send it later.

Do not ask to use a personal telephone. If you must make a call, ask if there is a pay telephone.

Test yourself with your family . . .

Do not mention your influential friends in the company or infer that you can bring pressure to secure that particular position.

Do not ask about salary, working hours, or vacations. If the employer is interested in your ability, these questions will be discussed in their proper time.

If an employer asks what salary you expect, you may say you do not know about living costs and comparative expense, or you may state a fair range of salary. The salary paid by one company for a type of work is usually about the same as that paid by another company in the city for the same type of work. Salaries are based on the importance of the position to the company and, in some degree, on the supply of qualified applicants. The cost of living in different cities influences salaries. Some companies have a scale of salaries within the organization, although allowance may be made for unusual experience and education.

If a salary is unusually high, you should be aware of the insecurity of the position or the company, unusual features about the work, or demands for experience greater than is indicated.

If a salary is lower than standard, the position may be less than it seems, or the company may place a low value on that type of work and may not encourage advancement.

If the telephone rings or someone comes to see the interviewer, you should try to busy yourself with notes, or at least appear to be disinterested in the interruption. If the message seems urgent, you may ask if the employer would like to have you leave the office. Usually, however, the employer is adroit at handling these situations.

Some employers will keep you only ten to fifteen minutes. Others will visit with you and try to help you even when there is no vacancy. And you may be invited to meet other members in the department or in another department where there is a vacancy. If an employer invites you to stay for lunch, do use your very best table manners.

Some companies require all applicants to take a physical examination at the company medical center before a position is offered. This may be a very simple test but it can be time-consuming. For that reason, do not schedule your interviews too close together.

Avoid making dates with family or friends which might interfere with a complete interview. If you want the position, give your attention, your time, and your best effort to securing the right answer to your request for work.

If the employer says there is no vacancy or says you are not qualified for the position, do not show impatience or defeatism. You may wish to ask for suggestions of other business concerns where you could look for work. Show your appreciation for these suggestions and for any other guidance or help, even though you may not see the value of some of the advice at the time. Make the most of every scrap of information and experience gained at every interview, even if you do not get an offer of a position.

Watch for an indication that the interview is finished. Do not show haste to end the interview, but if the employer looks at the clock, rises, or suggests that you fill out the application blank and mail it in, do not prolong the meeting. Thank the employer for the courtesy of an interview and then leave.

After you have left, think back over the interview. Decide if you have given a good performance and a true picture of your personality, education, training, experience, interests, and abilities.

Expense-Paid Interviews

An interview at a company's expense is often suggested by an employer. This must be answered within 24 hours, either by wire or letter. State the day and time of your arrival. Keep an accurate account of your expenses: transportation, meals, tips, and other essential expenses. Do not take a plane if train fare is cheaper. Do not count magazines or other personal expenses as business expenses. See Chapter 13 for travel information.

On arrival in the city, you may telephone the employer to set a definite time for the interview unless a time has been set previously. *Be prompt.*

Wait for the employer to ask for the expense account. Some may ask you to send it in after your return home. Others may have you estimate your return expenses. You may discuss the expenses listed to be sure these are in line with company policies.

Some companies require all applicants
to take a physical examination . . .

Payment may be made at the time of the interview or it may be mailed to you later, so be prepared to finance your return, if necessary.

The ethics of an interview at the expense of a company demand that you give your full time to the company. Do not show impatience at delays. Do not express a wish to go shopping or visit a friend. Above all, do not make appointments for interviews with other employers unless the paying company gives you permission to do so. Incredible as it may seem, some young women have used a free trip to the city as a means of making other contacts!

Do not charge overnight expenses if you could leave at an earlier time.

In other words, *your conduct on an expense-paid trip will show how you would spend company money if you were employed.*

In some cases, a company will pay expenses of an interview trip only if the position is not offered to the interviewee. In this case, if the position is offered, no expenses are paid even though the position is not accepted.

Always write a note expressing your appreciation for the courtesy of the interview. If no offer has been made to you, you may again indicate your wish to be considered for the position.

If you are offered the position, you may accept at once or, if you have a definite reason for delay, you may ask for a few days to give an answer. It is more gracious to give the reason for the delay. But be sure to say *yes* or *no* within the time limit you have set. Do not keep an employer waiting, for that employer might be able to hire someone else in that time. It is not complimentary to infer by your delay that you are taking the offer lightly or that you will accept the position only because this is your last hope.

If you accept the position, let the employer see you are pleased. An employer appreciates an enthusiastic response rather than a half-hearted acceptance as if you think, "I might as well take this and give it a try for awhile."

Before you leave, be sure you understand when and where to report for work, what equipment is needed, and any special arrangements that must be made before beginning the position.

Chances are that you will be inquiring about more than one

position, and will be contacting more than one potential employer. If you receive one offer but still are interested in another company you have contacted, it is perfectly proper for you to check by letter to see whether the second company is considering you. Don't try to hurry the employer, and always be perfectly honest in your inquiry. You may spoil your chances at either place by sending an inquiry which is only a bluff.

If you accept the offer made to you and do not send an inquiry to the other company in which you have been interested, or even if you may have sent the inquiry but have accepted the first offer before a reply came to you, stick with your decision. Have faith in that decision — even though you later receive the other offer. Never play fast and loose with an offered position. Aside from the ethics involved, you also want the reputation for being stable and fair with any employer.

At that point, however, immediately notify the other company so that your credentials may be removed from their active file. Also notify the employment office or the person who told you of the position. It is especially important to keep any placement office you are using informed about your employment.

Remember that each contact you make in your campaign to get the right position builds up a record of your character and ability. Sometimes employers exchange information on applicants. You might be recommended to a position by one of the employers who had no vacancy in his or her own department but was interested in you and your ability.

You can learn a great deal through each contact and you will become more proficient in stating your case effectively and in evaluating the opportunities offered by a company.

A New Start

When you have had some experience in business and wish to change positions, your letters of application will be easier to write and your personal interviews will be more interesting. You will probably have some definite ideas about what kind of work you want and what you can do most successfully.

If you are employed but want to change your work, you should give your reasons for wishing to make a change when you apply for new work. Use good judgment and do not show a critical attitude of your present employer. Even in a personal interview, you will be wise to avoid comments about your former or present work that might make you sound temperamental or difficult. Of course, you should be very careful not to put into writing any criticism of an employer.

There are many good reasons for wanting to change positions after you have worked long enough in one place to know more about yourself and to understand the requirements of the work.

With the many kinds of people and the many kinds of positions, it isn't surprising that some people get into the wrong position. You may find you didn't know what you really wanted. Have you been unable to produce the work required? Does your personality conflict with your co-workers or your supervisor? Is your health such that you can't do the work? Do family demands interfere with your work?

If you have not found the right work, you should recognize the reason and accept your share of the responsibility. But one mistake need not ruin your career! Even a failure is experience which can prove valuable if you learn by it.

Perhaps you are in the wrong company, in the wrong field of work, or in a position requiring too much for your present ability.

If you find yourself in the wrong position, how do you make a new start?

Talk with the head of your department to help locate the reason for your trouble. Ask advice about how and where you can start again. Be sure to notify your college placement officer or department head of your interest in changing jobs. If you leave the company, it is wise to have an understanding about using the employer as a future reference.

Many times, the best procedure after being in the wrong position is to take a course of study to gain a new skill or greater proficiency in your present skill. If your health needs attention, take care of that first. If family conditions are at fault, try to adjust them so that these will not interfere in a new position. Perhaps a new start in a different part of the country will be best. But you can't run away from mistakes. The only way to success is to face the cause of your mistakes and build a future on what you have learned by this experience.

Now more than ever, it is important for you to decide what you have to sell an employer and what kind of work you are really able to do.

When you apply for the new position, you will gain the respect of the employer if you give a fair statement of the reason for your desire to change positions. Your new employer will have confidence in you if your reasons for leaving agree with the statements from your former employer. Do not place the entire blame on the former employer. Admit that you erred, but never admit that you are beaten.

Any employer who has had experience with many employees will understand that a person may not succeed in one position yet be very successful in another position.

It is up to you not to dramatize your ill luck but to take a new look at yourself and get the position that is right for you.

If you are looking for your first position, do not be disturbed by this discussion of how to make a fresh start. No doubt, you will be one of the 99 per cent who find that first position both stimulating and challenging. A year from now, you, too, can look at yourself and recognize a successful businesswoman.

CHAPTER 5

Work Days Can Be Made Easier

So YOU have been accepted for the position! Are you nervous? Of course you are. You wouldn't be a conscientious, normal person if you didn't worry a bit about the terrible mistakes you are liable to make on your first day. Actually, the first few days in a position are the very easiest because no one expects you to know very much or do very much. These are get-acquainted days. Just relax your tenseness, stop thinking about yourself, and be gracious to everyone.

Remember how you worried about going from grade school to high school! It is true that this change moved you into a new period of your life, but you soon adjusted to the new outlook. So, too, going into a business position is a new experience. You'll find there a new code of behavior and you will make new adjustments in your values of objectives. But isn't that a challenging idea! Have faith in yourself and say, "I *can* succeed in this work!"

Dress the Part

Now for that first morning. Get up a bit early and take time to bathe and dress with

Are you nervous?

care. Businesswomen take pride in personal cleanliness and good grooming. Wear your tailored best, just as you did for the interview (*see* page 47). It is true that small cities are less formal than large cities, yet it is best to play safe and follow conventional rules for *what the businesswoman wears.* After you have been working a while you may find that sweaters and skirts are worn, but these are not appropriate the first day.

Dress for work, not for a party. Your shoes should be well fitted for comfort in walking because you may be taken on a tour of the company.

Look at your make-up in daylight, if possible, so that you can meet those first glances. Are your stocking seams straight or, better yet, seamless? Is your slip a safe length?

Give your purse a final inspection for money, notebook, pencil, and handkerchief. It is well to carry an identification card in your purse at all times, in case you lose it or in case of an accident. Don't forget your keys.

Take time to have a good breakfast. You may think you are too nervous to eat, but you may have to wait until an hour later than usual for luncheon. This is no time for a hunger headache.

Don't Lose Your Way

You're off to work. Buy a morning paper and look at the funnies! There's nothing like a newspaper to take your mind off yourself and to make you realize how simple your problems are in face of world affairs. You may have to watch for transfer points, so don't read too much that first day. Look at the many young women going to their places of work. Aren't they gay? Of course they are, and you will be, too, in a day or so.

Now as to transportation: You have inquired about this beforehand and have written down the directions, but *when in doubt, ask a policeman, trainman, or busman.* If he is brisk, it isn't personal. He answers millions of questions about routes and yours is just one of many. Don't ask directions from fellow travelers. They don't know the answers! Well-meaning souls may try

Are your stocking seams straight?

to help, but few of them can give you accurate information about routes other than their own. You'll find that employees of public transportation systems give you better directions than chance fellow passengers.

You're on the Job!

Report to the place and person designated in your interview. If in doubt, ask for the Information Desk or the Personnel Director. There you will find a friendly person who will start you in the right direction.

Of course you are on time! Even if you are early, you have that morning paper to read.

For the next hour or so you are likely to meet a great many people. Repeat the names and start right then to learn them. There are many trick ways to remember names. Whatever your system, put it to work. Do your best to remember the important names, at least. If you make a concerted effort to connect the name, title, and face, you will find this an invaluable aid all through life.

A notebook (a small one to tuck in your purse) can be used to jot down names and titles of the office manager, the person who handles the payroll records, the people in your department. Your special guide that first morning will be helpful and understanding. If you are bewildered and a bit nervous, say so. Don't miss an important direction or suggestion just because you hesitate to admit you don't understand.

There are many trick ways to remember names . . .

First Things First

You have your own place to hang wraps, your desk, your name on the payroll. You are in business!

You'll learn more in that first week than in any previous week of your life. But how interesting and exciting it is! Every company has its rules and regulations that are designed to make work easier. In some companies you'll be given a Manual of Information for Employees and other booklets telling about the company, the officers, the organization, the policies, and many other interesting facts. You won't be expected to learn everything at once. But the sooner you learn the facts contained in these booklets, the quicker you will feel you *belong*.

If you aren't given a Manual of Information, start your own. Your notebook is your best friend. Write down names of people in other departments, as you learn them. Write down assignments. When you get home, (the first day won't last so long) take out the notebook and rearrange what you have written. Have you questions? Write those down and be on the lookout for the answers.

Information Please

The name of the officer to whom you report is Number One on the list. Spell and pronounce the name correctly. Everyone appreciates that courtesy. If your immediate superior is a woman, is she *Miss, Mrs., or Doctor?*

List the names and titles of your co-workers. Practice these. You'll feel you are one of the team when you can say "Good morning, Miss _____." That's a good sign.

Learn the names of the officers of the company. You may meet one of the topflight officers during your first days, and it will help to recognize the name.

Learn all you can about the company, its purpose, products, services, and scope of activities. Be alert to all bits of information.

How is the company organized? Is it by departments, divisions, services? You'll find your work more interesting when you know what all the activities are about, what goes where, who does what, and why. Does this mean you are to ask questions of everyone? No, you could soon become a pest. Look, listen, and read, and ask only what you must. Make haste slowly. If you show an alert interest in the people with whom you work, you'll find a flood of helpful suggestions given to you.

You'll need to know: the lunch time and the best place to eat; where to get office supplies; how to use the files; what reports you are expected to keep; how to answer the telephone; who will train and guide you in your work; and many special organization details.

This won't all come in the first day, but your first week will be a bombardment of new faces, new names, new ideas, new activities, new horizons. It will be confusing, no doubt. But by that first week end you'll look back to the first day and say, like the old lady in the nursery rhyme, "Lawk a mercy on me. This is none of I!" You are a woman in business, with your foot on the professional ladder.

Still I Am Learning

One company has a famous motto, *Still I Am Learning*. It's a fine guide for all of us, and very apt for your first days and every day you are in business.

The first position is almost an apprenticeship where you can learn while you earn. The first year you should learn more than in any year of your life. That is, you will if you have the desire to learn; if you are alert to opportunities around you; and if you have the will to become a professional woman.

You will find it easier to learn while you are working because you will see the reason for learning. Everything will have a meaning. Economics, English, History, Journalism, and all the textbook subjects take on new meaning because at last you see the answer to the question, "What of it?" You'll discover that facts tucked away and almost forgotten now come alive and become real in this new world of business.

How's Your Attitude?

You will be more successful in business if you accept the responsibilities as well as the benefits that come with the position. Some of these responsibilities may look trite in print, but here's some good old-fashioned advice. It may save you from learning the hard way.

You have agreed to work for the company in return for money paid you for your services. *Give more than you are paid for!* Start now to utilize your capacities to the fullest. The difference between a day laborer and a career woman is that the career woman has an ideal and a plan to grow and move up the ladder of success. She doesn't try to just get by or do the least possible work. She gives her best effort every day to her company.

LOYALTY to your company is your first responsibility. Take pride in your association.

The policies and code of ethics established by your company should become your code. Take pride in the products and services offered by the company. Be loyal to the people with whom you work. Don't listen to gossip. Look for the best in people.

Loyalty means that you don't discuss troubles and problems with outsiders. Some people may try to lead you into controversies about your work and your co-workers. But remember that no one admires a disloyal worker. You hurt yourself when you are led into anti-company discussion.

Loyalty is so essential to your happiness and success that if you find you can't be loyal, you had better look for another job.

COOPERATION is another key word in business. To win, a team requires cooperation from everyone. You have learned to work with people in your home, your school, and in your associations in many groups. In business, this cooperation takes on more intense meaning. You, the individual, are important because of, not in spite of, your relation to the department or other unit of the company. Only as you pull together as a team is it possible for you, as a member of the team, to succeed. The prima donna has no place on a business team. She will be miserable and frustrated or will disrupt teamwork by her star performances.

In business, you are expected to have ideas and opinions, and to be creative. However, you must appreciate the fact that each one with whom you work must also have ideas and opinions. It is by a pooling of these ideas, by analysis, discussions, and revisions that the *best idea* develops. This becomes, then, the idea of the team. If you have contributed to this idea, you are fortunate in having been able to help a bit. But whether it was your original idea or contrary to your idea, you are expected to join wholeheartedly into putting the idea into effect and to remember that it is the *we,* not the *I,* that succeeds in business.

If you must be a prima donna, by all means go into work for yourself. Then you alone accept the credit and the blame for your actions.

HONESTY is the keystone of your work in business. This is not an idle platitude to be taken lightly. Personal integrity and real honesty of thought and action must be the final tests of every decision.

SINCERITY is a phase of honesty. Pretense and insincerity in your loyalty to your company or honesty in your attitude are bound to be reflected in your work. A sincere attitude toward your co-workers and your company will win friends who will lend a hand throughout the adjustment period in your new position.

PLAY THE GAME FAIR AND SQUARE. This is another phase of honesty. Company equipment, supplies, and funds may be entrusted to you for use in your work. Treat this property and money with the same consideration you would if these were your own. Keep company secrets, promotions, plans, and conferences confidential until a public announcement is made. You would feel very unhappy if thoughtless conversation on your part gave away valuable information to a competitor.

Play the game square with your co-workers. Since you are part of a team, you must consider the other members and not expect anyone else to carry your work. Accept responsibility and assignments cheerfully without questioning as to fair distribution of the work.

Play the game square and don't ask for personal favors, such as time off to go to a wedding or to meet a friend. Your health, an emergency in your close family, or another critical need may make it necessary to request a leave of a few hours or days. If you abuse this privilege, you may not be granted time off when a real need arises.

Play the game square and give your full time on the job to your employer. Working hours are not the time for personal letters, telephone calls, shopping trips, manicures, and other personal services. You may not be censured or reprimanded for slight lapses of this rule, but the habit grows. Soon you may find you are expecting to be paid for several hours each week when you were not producing or earning for the company.

Play the game square in your attitude to your teammates. Give credit generously. Be sincere in expressing praise to your co-workers and avoid jealousy for the success of others. Recognize the ability of others and do not try to reorganize routine or to rework the department to your ideas. No doubt there is a good reason for the present methods. As you become accustomed to the work, your ideas can be tossed into the melting pot of discussions to be evaluated and used or discarded. Make haste slowly. Stop. Look. Listen.

AMBITION is a worthy attribute. Without ambition, no one can succeed. Continue to improve your standards of work and contribute to the success of your company. Sometimes a woman is classed as indifferent; a time-marker and clock-watcher who doesn't care to move out of her little niche. Then again she is classed as a ruthless, overambitious person who tries to climb to the top at the expense of her co-workers, because she considers that her goal justifies any methods. Of course, the success stories of real leaders among women prove that true ambition has motivated these women to earn advancement and recognition by loyalty, cooperation, honesty, and fair play. They have set high standards of professional ethics and have worked and lived by these standards.

HUMILITY should go hand in hand with ambition. Too often the young businesswoman becomes fired with the spirit of ambition, competition, and power. Then is the time to look around you at the army of fine women who are working efficiently and honestly in many kinds of positions. These women are never too busy to be gracious, helpful, and kind.

Any success you have is due in large part to the work of many others. No one succeeds alone. You cannot afford to disregard the debt owed to many men and women who have helped you succeed. Humility without meekness is the attribute of the woman who combines a professional attitude with the gracious charm of womanliness.

Humility should not be confused with activity. You don't want to become the kind of a person who tries to win favor by fawning on supervisors and ignoring lesser employees. You'll be wise to respect the ability of all loyal employees. Don't

. . . and don't underestimate the help they can give you.

ignore those in lower positions and don't underestimate the help they can give you. Such a person may be a real friend in need and may, in fact, carry more weight than a newcomer in a higher position.

Watch your professional attitude. *Develop a professional point of view.* Be tolerant. Don't get stuffy. Truly "big" people are often the most humble. Too often, the young businesswoman takes onto her shoulders the cloak of authority, with a liberal trim of hauteur and snobbery. Don't be like that!

Your Personality Is You

Your attitude is, of course, part of your personality. Let's look at some of the other personality traits which you as a businesswoman want to acquire and foster.

Success in your work and in your life is up to you. Never underestimate your potential power. But never underestimate the thought, time, and energy required to develop the real you. You have certain personality traits of which you may well be proud. Guard them. You probably have other traits of which you are not proud. Correct and overcome them. Perhaps you would do well to write out your idea of the woman you want to become. Set your ideals high and look to the stars. Start now to develop your latent talents and to build your personal habits of thought and action.

FRIENDLINESS requires a real interest in people. Too often the young person has had a narrow point of view. She has not tried to look for and understand the best qualities in the people around her. In business, you work *with* and *for* people. Friendliness and a kindly consideration for others will bring you great satisfaction and happiness.

Don't think always of yourself. Take an interest in others. Sincere friendliness, not affectation, is required. You will not be expected to seek close friendship with everyone, but you can find a bond of interest in your business associates. Each associate has his or her personal problems and attitudes. Try to be understanding and appreciative of the best traits in others. Be tolerant of their faults and avoid making their mistakes.

Say "Good morning," and smile. That can be a big help in your daily contacts. Say "Good morning" to co-workers, to superiors, to everyone who gives you half a chance. In business, you don't wait for an introduction. When someone comes to your office or department, rise and greet the visitor at once. Introduce yourself, "I'm ————. May I help you?" Put out your hand for a friendly handshake if you wish.

Learn to introduce your associates or visitors easily. Just remember which name to say first. Keep in mind the phrase, "may I present," and present the less distinguished, younger, or less renowned person to the distinguished, older, or more renowned person. The phrase may be said or implied.

For example, "Dr. Nelson, may I present my co-worker Jane Bly," or, "Dr. Nelson (raising voice as in a question), Jane Bly, my associate in this department." In business it may be wise to give a word of explanation about the persons you introduce. As an example, "Dr. Nelson, as you know, is professor of economics at the University of *Y*." Or "Jane Bly has just joined our staff as a design specialist."

. . . rise and greet the visitor at once.
Introduce yourself . . .

Try to give a lead to a topic of mutual interest but avoid needless details or a recital of personal history. It is discourteous to both guest and co-workers to overlook or forget introductions unless, of course, these interrupt a conference or important activity. When in doubt, do the friendly, kindly thing.

Show a friendly interest in people and you will like them. They, in turn, will like you.

Learn the power of *you* and *we*. Submerge the use of *I, my, mine, me.*

Look directly at a person's eyes when you speak. It is human to like to be the center of interest and to have the center of the stage. Be a good listener, also.

Good manners are the same everywhere, although forms of etiquette vary from country to country, city to city, and company to company. Good manners require only a few minutes yet make life so much more pleasant. *Thank you, Please, I'm sorry* — such little words mean so much.

The Golden Rule is your guide to good manners. It is not the formal gesture or the phraseology that counts. The sincere, tactful, helpful act is the mannerly act.

Good manners guide you in omitting long recitations about your family or personal affairs to new acquaintances. Avoid, too, topics that are controversial when you see the other person does not agree with you. What do you expect to gain by the argument? You can't erase the spoken word.

Avoid crude habits, slang, colloquialisms, gossip, and any hint of *off-color* remarks. In working with men and women, you cannot afford to be misjudged by careless words or actions.

Avoid controversial topics when you see the other person does not agree with you.

EMOTIONAL STABILITY is so important for the businesswoman that you will find this is a real test of potential success.

Some women are apt to be too easily hurt. They take criticism as a personal affront, they hold a grudge, and they brood over mistakes and hidden meanings.

Tears are not for the businesswoman. You must learn to control your emotions, your disappointments, your hurt feelings, and your fears until you get home. But don't go home! Go to a movie, a concert, or a ball game. Have fun. Look at other people and see how foolish you are to brood. Give yourself a talking-to later. Admit you were, at least, partly wrong. Say it out loud. Then say, "I'll change my attitude. I'll profit by this experience." Learn to say, "I'm sorry. I was wrong." There's nothing quite so refreshing for your taut nerves as a free and honest confession of an error. Even though you are not the only one who erred, take your share of the blame. Never pass the blame on to another. This doesn't mean you should become the scape-goat for all errors. But do admit your own mistakes and *never make the same mistake again!*

Fear destroys your will to succeed. Too often women "tilt at windmills" and borrow trouble.

Are you predictable? Dependable? Calm? Even-tempered? These are attributes of the emotionally stable woman. Take the rough spots slowly — in low gear. You're sure to have more smooth roads than bumpy. You grow in stature as you are tested. You grow as a woman, not a weakling.

A SENSE OF HUMOR will carry you over the rough roads of experience. Learn to laugh at yourself and with others (never *at* others). Learn to enjoy the funnies, the cartoons, the good jokes. But never try for a laugh at the expense of others. Be kind, not cruel.

The cheerful woman who hides her fears, her hurt feelings, her troubles, who smiles and enjoys her co-workers finds that her circle of friends becomes legion.

Don't be a prude, yet keep your self-respect. Never tell a story that will lead to one which may embarrass you. Women in business must uphold standards of conduct.

THE ADULT VIEWPOINT is soon acquired when you enter business. You will find the little-girl ideas and habits are out of place. Boy friends, and all those other gab session topics, should be kept for out-of-work hours.

Men in business are becoming accustomed to women in business. Here's a guide to your actions: Your conduct and attitude should be such that *men treat you as if you were a man but never forget you are a woman.*

Men and women work together for the common good of the company. Each contributes certain essentials for success. These men usually have wives, sweethearts, or outside interests. They work with you. They are friendly and enjoy the association, but they are not courting you nor do they expect you to misjudge their interest. A safe rule is to keep these contacts impersonal and strictly business. There is no reason why you shouldn't date an eligible man who works for the company. But never carry this friendship into office hours or let this become company gossip. In fact, you should lead a normal social life — but don't bore or amuse your co-workers with a recital of your conquests!

As a businesswoman you should expect to pay for your own transportation, meals, and other expenses when you are in a business meeting. Don't confuse business and social affairs. A chance meeting, after-hour work on an exhibit, a plan of work does not mean that a man co-worker should pay any of your expenses.

DISCRETION is an important guide. Your work in business does not permit you to acquire a new set of morals. In fact, as a company representative, you should consider the reputation of the company, as well as your own. To the public, *you are the company.*

GOOD JUDGMENT is not a question of age. As a beginner, your good judgment becomes an important guide in your decisions during the hours at work and away from work.

Learn to differentiate between essentials and nonessentials. A light touch is a protection against the bombardment of conflicting ideas and personalities. When should you say *yes?* When should you say *no,* gracefully and without anger or resentment? Avoid an attitude of prim, unyielding insistence on little things. Arrange your thinking in terms of broad, realistic principles.

Don't fail to see "the forest for the trees." This is a common fault of women. You'll find men often think in terms of long-range plans. You'll be apt to see details and impossible hurdles. Yet if you stop, look, and listen to discussions, and try to get the broad picture, you'll usually discover that the cooperative thinking of the group finds a way to reach the objective. This means that your good judgment should train you to go into conferences with the idea that "it can be done. Now, how shall we do it?"

Your whole sense of values will become oriented on a new level with the beginning of your first work. Accept this challenge and be alert to the motivating ideas of business. Even though you are a beginner, your good judgment can contribute to new, original, worthwhile and successful ideas.

Moderation Is a Virtue

Any discussion of temperance is difficult because you are apt to think in terms of drinking. Yet you can be intemperate in eating, exercising, smoking, late hours, and in many other things.

Should the businesswoman drink and smoke? Not unless she wants to. *No,* if her company frowns on this practice. *Yes,* if there is no company policy against it, if there is no social objection to it, if she wants to, and if she uses moderation and good judgment.

You do not have to drink or smoke to be socially desirable in business work. It is true that at many luncheons, dinners, and

Should the businesswoman drink and smoke?

other social affairs connected with business meetings, cocktails and cigarettes will be offered to you. Unless you are accustomed to these practices, you should feel free to decline gracefully and with no indication of censuring those who do accept. You don't need to explain your reasons. You certainly should not moralize. You as a woman, in business or out, are in no way penalized by your refusal to drink or smoke. You as a woman must accept the responsibility of using *moderation* if you do drink. Even those jolly companions who urge you, "have another," "don't be a piker," are the first to start a rumor at any sign of intemperance or indiscretion. Never think you can be the exception for it is all too true that *people love to gossip.*

At the convention, at the cocktail party, at the banquet, you'll have more fun and will make more of the right friends if you avoid drinking or drink very moderately. This is not a moralization or an evaluation of the use of cocktails. This is good judgment for you as a woman in business. You'll learn that women who are worthy of admiration and respect are good company, good guests, good personalities because they understand the importance of moderation.

Protocol

Protocol is a word used to mean a body of official formulas or rules prescribing the etiquette in ceremonies of state or procedures of business. These procedures are based on company policies as to the line of authority. To whom do you make reports? To whom may you go for advice or to discuss complaints? What positions carry certain privileges and demand a certain amount of deference?

Each company has its own company protocol and etiquette. Some companies are very formal, others are informal. You will have to learn the code for your company.

You may find your company has written or unwritten rules for correct attire. Do you wear a uniform at work but not in the dining room? Do you wear hose even in hot weather? Do you wear a hat when eating in the main dining room? These and other rules of dress are established by company tradition or etiquette.

Do you ask an executive's secretary for an appointment with him or do you just go to his office and ask to see him? Rap on the door? Walk in?

You'll be safe to address your associates by the proper titles of *Miss, Mrs., Doctor, Mister,* etc., until such time as you find that the more informal use of the first name is accepted. Avoid the use of nicknames which may be permitted by established members of the staff but frowned on for beginners. Show respect to those in authority. "Yes, Mr. Jones," or "Yes, Mrs. Adams" is expected. *Yah, uh huh, OK, sure* are flippant and adolescent.

Courtesy to top management is not bootlicking. You can't be censured for having a respectful attitude toward those of a higher rank. You can be criticized or misjudged for having an attitude of familiarity or disrespect.

When in doubt, tell your troubles to or ask your questions of the one to whom you report as your immediate superior. Never go over her head in the organization unless she gives you permission. But don't bother her with petty details simply to gain the spotlight.

When you have a question, think through the problem and how you will state it. Go to the conference with a notebook and pencil. Ask to see your director when she isn't involved. State your problem briefly and concisely and give your idea of the possible solution. Then ask for guidance. Listen and do not interrupt. Be sure you understand her answer. Write it down, if possible. Restate it to be sure you have the right interpretation and can proceed in the right direction. You don't want to have to say later, "I thought you said," or "I didn't understand what you meant."

Take constructive criticisms, corrections, and suggestions graciously. Sometimes your director will not give the reasons for these instructions. Usually she will explain the reasons. Do not be like the new employee who commented, "You have some good ideas but I wish you would let me do it my way." Only an understanding, patient woman who maintains her self-control would be likely to keep you on the payroll after such a remark!

You may find the protocol is loosely defined in your company. If so, set your own standard based on the line of authority. Ask

Don't interfere, with questions, suggestions, or chatter.

direction from the one immediately above you. Otherwise you may rely on someone who *assumes authority* but is not informed or qualified to guide you.

Courtesy to those who rank above you? *Yes.* Equal courtesy to those lower than you in line of authority? *Yes.* Protocol and business etiquette cut up and down as well as across the strata of employees.

Businesslike Workmanship

Business is run on long-range plans, with each day's plans laid to achieve a segment of the over-all objective.

You, too, should have a long-range plan for your professional career. Where are you going? What is ahead of you? Do you strive for the satisfaction of accomplishment and the real joy of work? Your first day is none too early to set your goal even though you must know that you will revise your ideas of a goal many times. Set a goal and work step by step toward that goal. Don't try to hop over obstacles, short-cut experience, or perform a miracle of achievement. A good solid beginning is the safe base on which to build a substantial, enduring future.

At work, respect the privacy and work of others. Don't interfere, with questions, suggestions, or chatter. Listen when those with experience speak, and avoid interruptions. If you have questions, wait until you can ask them without breaking the thought of the speaker.

Yes, you'll make mistakes. You won't be worth much if you aren't aggressive enough to try. But if you err, admit it, and try to correct any harm that may be done. And don't make the same mistake again.

Be factual, accurate, truthful, and honest in your spoken and written work. Learn to organize your thoughts for logical steps of action. Those daily plans will help you rewrite a better long-range plan.

An *idea book* is a trademark of the businesswoman. This is your small purse notebook in which you have jotted down names and assignments. To these add *do's* and *don'ts,* references, or just hunches. You'll get these at the queerest places! Write them down. Many of them won't be worth a thing when you come to analyze and study them. One may be priceless.

A daily plan of work will clear your thinking. In the evening or on the way to work, jot down the work jobs you hope to do during the day. "Finish report to R." "Look up references on _____." "Consult G on new problem on _____." At the end of the day see if you can check these off. Or have you let nonessentials clutter your actions so that you haven't accomplished

You'll get these hunches at the queerest places!

any tangible results? A daily plan of action will help you eliminate waste motions and *circle thinking*. A daily plan helps you tackle a problem step by step rather than wonder about the result and procrastinate about beginning.

Businesslike workmanship means using outside as well as inside hours to increase your fund of knowledge contributory to your advancement. Start the habit of reading magazines and books related to national and civic affairs as well as those dealing with your own professional interest.

In your business association you'll find the conversation often turns to current events, business, new books and magazine articles, current plays, musical events, art exhibits, or sports. You'll be able to understand and enter the conversation if you make a practice of reading a good current-events magazine such as *Time* or *Newsweek*. The *Wall Street Journal* keeps you informed on day-to-day happenings in businesses of all kinds. The Sunday supplement of the New York *Times* and many other newspapers give reviews of books, plays, and musicals. General abstract magazines such as *The Reader's Digest, Life, Harper's, Atlantic Monthly, The Saturday Evening Post,* and *Look* will give a background of conversational subjects and will broaden your interest in the conversation of others. Make a habit of visiting the periodical room in the public library to browse a bit. Possibly you'll decide to buy one or two magazines regularly for general interest. You'll find certain magazines devoted to your special interests will be a part of your continuing education.

You'll soon discover that worthwhile reading along many lines enriches your outlook, increases your powers of conversation, broadens your interests, and helps you find interrelations of ideas. The arts and sciences do truly have "a common bond, and stand interrelated as if in kinship."

Take time to think. Perhaps you'll find yourself so busy each day that you can't arrange your thoughts in an orderly fashion. Crowds are confusing. Take a walk. Go to a movie. Go to your room. Get away by yourself and enjoy the relaxation of thinking through your plan. Where are you? Where are you going? How well are your daily plans leading you along the professional road?

Those periods for thinking about your personal and professional progress can be most helpful and profitable.

Have you become more alert to new ideas and new concepts? Have you learned to explore these new ideas without prejudice and to judge their value for the company?

So many ideas are presented to you. So many conflicting viewpoints are given. In your *think-it-through* periods ask yourself, "What of it?" Your good judgment, training, and experience will guide you in the evaluation of your daily and long-range plans, if you take time to analyze and think all by yourself. In the rush of business, never overlook the importance of these periods of being alone to look at yourself, to talk to yourself, and to advise yourself.

Learn to acquire habits of businesslike workmanship so that you can use your work time and energy efficiently, and leave your leisure time and energy free. We'll talk about enjoying your leisure time in Chapter 6.

Professionally Speaking

Any woman who sets her goal on a career can be called a professional woman. The attitude about the goal is the thing!

The transition from school to business isn't very painful. In fact, you'll find that people in business are really just like your neighbors, the folks at church, the men and women you have known all your life. People in the East and the West aren't very different these days. People from the North move South, and vice **versa.**

How about you? You've grown up enough to earn your living. You are in business. You have pride in your work and faith in yourself. You are stepping out and up into a fuller life, and you are broadening your outlook.

In business you will find competition is a healthy force for progress. Jealousy and petty rivalry are weakening influences. Loyalty to your company does not include derision of competitors. You will go further by selling the goods and services of your company and your own work on their individual merit rather than by spiteful or malicious comparison with rival companies or other professional groups.

Don't let glitter and froth influence your judgment. You'll meet other girls in business who spend their salaries all on clothes, who talk in terms of powerful influence in their company and in their profession, or who hint at fabulous salaries and many honors. Very few salaries are as large as you think they are! Women with great influence and authority don't have to spend their time impressing others with their worth.

Add the Score

To succeed in business requires a heap of common sense, a generous sprinkling of imagination, a will to succeed, and a balanced sense of humor. Don't expect to be pampered because you are a woman. Surprise your supervisor and co-workers with your ability to *roll with the punches*. You'll need good health and a planned observance of the health rules. You will learn the value of alertness to ideas and of good judgment to evaluate ideas. You will set your code of ethics on honesty, honor, and an abiding faith in the rewards of fair play. You will develop a philosophy of living and grow professionally as you establish your aims and set your goals to be a womanly woman first, last, and always in your chosen work.

CHAPTER 6

Live While You Work

IF YOUR WORK takes you away from home, your release from parental influence may be a bit heady at first. Because of the desire to show your independence, you may be tempted to effect foolish habits or choose companions with extreme views and ideas. But whether you work in a large or small city, you will discover within a short time that unless you decide what you want to do with your spare time, the days will flit past without giving you much in return.

Why do you work? That may seem like a foolish question, but is it? The fact is that some people go through life without a clear idea of what they really want. Of course, you work to buy food and clothing, and to pay for a place to live, and for such other expenses as are necessary. You probably hope to save something toward a vacation. Is that enough?

Why not set up the goal you hope to reach and give thought to making each day take you a bit nearer your goal?

Happiness means different things to different people. But the person who postpones the day when she will *cash in* on her ideas of happiness usually finds she has lost the ability to

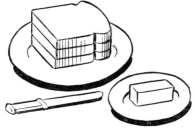

Why do you work?

enjoy her good fortune when it arrives. Happiness is cumulative. If you follow a constructive plan to broaden your capacity for happiness, you will find each day is more pleasant and you will become a more interesting person.

You'll probably work only 40 hours a week. How will you spend the other 128 hours? Why not set up a plan to make the most of those other hours, too, and really live while you work?

You may not believe it until you begin work, but working can be fun! Each day brings new experiences and a chance to try your wings. The hours on the job may seem long at first, and the eternal *up-and-at-it* spirit of business may be quite a change from your former way of life. In a city, the hours spent in travel to and from work, the care of clothes, hair, shoes, and all the little repair jobs will seem to take too large a share of your extra time. Some girls do spend all their time getting ready to work, working, eating, and sleeping. That's a dull routine you will want to avoid.

If your work takes you to a strange city, those first weeks can be lonely unless you make a plan to use your time effectively. If you stay at home to work, you may find the adjustment of work, family, and former friends keeps you in a whirl that leaves no time for all the things you hoped to do.

So let's face the fact that when you start to work you'll have to *make time* by setting up a schedule. Perhaps the idea of a schedule sounds limiting, but if you try it, you'll find you actually get more into each day than you ever did before. Why not try to plan a week in advance and see how much you can do?

To set up a plan of the week, set aside hours for work, and for transportation, meals, and sleep. Then list all the recreational activities that interest you in the order of importance to you. Fit the most timely and important ones into your current schedule.

A Place To Live

If you are off to a new city, plan to arrive a few days early. That gives you time to find a place to live and to get acquainted with some of the mechanics of living in the new city.

The YWCA is an excellent starting place to go for overnight or a temporary stay. This organization will make room for you if at all possible or, at least, they will direct you to rooming clubs which are on their approved list. Unless you know the city, it is unwise for you to take permanent living quarters without getting advice from someone whose judgment you can trust.

Perhaps you have a relative or friend who will take you in for a few days. Be wary of deciding on a fixed plan before you check on transportation to work, to entertainment and educational centers, to shopping districts. An hour's ride on public transportation without too many transfers is not unusual in a city. More than that is too much to add to your working day. Are the streets well lighted so you won't be afraid to be out after dark? Will you have a room of your own? You may enjoy this *at home* feeling for the first week, but avoid entanglements in a family or friend arrangement that may be difficult to stop. Wait until you have time to look at yourself and your friends in terms of your new business experience. You may find that even your closest friend has found new interests and that the old school ties aren't strong enough to make her the best roommate.

During the first adjustment period, the YWCA or a good rooming club are friendlier places than a room in a private home. When you've become adjusted to your work and the city, you'll be better able to decide on more permanent living quarters that are suited to your income. Even though that beginning salary looks big, it is not wise, at first, to sign an agreement for longer than a month at any living quarters.

The Strange City

Of course, you will need to have a bit of a nest egg to see you through until payday. But don't carry much cash with you or leave it in your room. Travelers' checks or postal money orders are a security you'll appreciate. The first payday may be one, two, or even four weeks away. You won't feel so lonesome or lost if you have enough money to see you through this period.

Be prepared to spend considerable time by yourself, outside of working hours. Find out where there's a movie theater and a lending library.

Go to church. Even though you don't know anyone, you are sure to find friendly folk with whom you can chat a bit. Get a church calendar of activities and go to the meetings that interest you. Churches in a city have organized groups for young people like you, but you must go to them, not wait for the church to come to you.

Use these days before you begin your work to get adjusted to your new life so you will be ready to give your thoughts and energies to the new work. Peace of mind about your living conditions is a great saver of nerves.

This is a good time to get folders from the Chamber of Commerce on the interesting sights of the city. Get to know the city in which you will live. If you are in a large city, go to a good bookstore or the book department in a store and ask for the best small directory of the city. You'll want a book that contains a map showing transportation facilities, lists of streets, and an explanation of the street numbering system. Every city has a basic plan for numbering streets. In those first days, you can learn how to find your way around.

Take a bus ride to get the feel of the city. Or better yet, take a conducted tour on a sight-seeing bus. Information on city tours is available at the transportation desk of the large hotels. You can do a great deal of sight-seeing in a short time. Later, you can go back to explore the spots that interest you.

If you are a stranger in a city, you will be wise to plan interesting activities to do when you are alone. The public library will have some books on the interesting background of the city you have chosen. With a little reading it soon becomes "your city"! Also, make a definite effort to join a group where you will meet congenial people. You don't want to be the restless type who can never stay home and amuse herself. Neither do you want to be a stay-at-home who becomes so set in her ways that she is indifferent to and intolerant of other people.

Observations of girls who work show that those who have fun in their extra hours do better work than those who do not have fun. If you look forward to bowling, to a church party, to a sewing class, or to any group activity, the day passes more quickly because of the anticipated pleasure. The next day goes more smoothly because of remembered pleasures. So plan to live a full life while you work.

Balanced Recreation

Your physical health is not to be taken for granted. Health is a prized possession which requires intelligent thought and real planning. When you were at home, your parents talked to you of the need for the right food, sufficient sleep, and adherence to other rules for good health. When you are away from home, you may think you can throw off these parental restrictions and live as you please. But health is a premium asset in business. In school, you could stay home if you didn't feel well. When you are working, you are expected to feel well and be on the job.

Look around you at the many people who are paying for not taking care of their health. Your body is a wonderful machine that accepts much abuse before it complains and falters. But it is poor judgment to try to see how much punishment you can give yourself before you begin to pay in tiredness, headaches, and other signs of ill health. Today, the smart businesswoman follows the basic health rules so that she won't miss out on the many things she wants to do.

Use good sense and moderation in deciding what you do and when you do it. Then you can enjoy your work and play, and show the sparkle and pep that contribute so much to your personality.

Good Food

Good food of the right kind and in the right amount builds good health. If you haven't learned the importance of three balanced meals a day, read a book on nutrition. *Food Becomes You* by Ruth M. Leverton (Iowa State University Press), is an easy-to-read food guide highly recommended by professional nutritionists. Or ask the librarian at the city library to recommend the right book for you. Unfortunately, there are many foolish diet fads that get publicity. Some people seem to actually enjoy eating unpleasant foods and omitting the foods they like. Some people make a fetish of queer diets and bore everyone with their extreme ideas.

The Number One rule is to eat three good meals a day. Avoid the no-breakfast and snatch-and-gulp lunch with a

. . . and you won't have pep for after-work fun.

candy bar or soft drink between times. You won't save money by such a plan and you definitely won't have the pep for after-work fun.

Start the day with a breakfast to see you through until lunch. If you get hungry in midmorning, you haven't had enough breakfast. Good food before you go to work pays off both in physical health and in mental alertness. Try it. Then take time for lunch with a congenial friend. You'll be sure to find co-workers who will invite you to join the group, if you make an effort to be good company. Many girls carry a sandwich and then buy something extra at work. So you won't be conspicuous if you want to save a bit by a make-your-own-sandwich plan. Do eat with the others, even if it costs a little more, because this social contact helps build friendships that make work more pleasant.

A good lunch may consist of sandwiches, with milk, cream soup, or cocoa; or, perhaps, a salad, roll, and dessert. You need fresh greens, vegetables, and fruit each day. Don't forget eggs, and meat, fish, or cheese. Learn the four basic classes of foods and choose your breakfast, lunch, and dinner to include some of each class. You'll not get fat if you eat sensibly at mealtime. It is the between-meal snack that seems so insignificant, yet brings up the calorie count. A bottle of soft drink means 100 to 150 calories. A candy bar or a bag of peanuts may be more than 300 calories. A glass of whole milk is only about 100 calories, skimmed milk only 85 calories, and an egg only 75.

It's really more pleasant to eat the right foods for good health than to take pills to try to regain the health you have lost.

Sleep

Sleep takes a portion of those extra hours. Of course you need sleep and rest. In fact, when you first start to work you will need extra sleep because you'll be under a strain. Nervous tension is fatiguing. Often a change of climate, as from one section of the country to another, makes you tired and sleepy. So, during the first few weeks, plan to get extra rest. You'll soon become adjusted to the climate and work. Then you can determine how much sleep you really need to keep awake and alert.

A few late hours never hurt any healthy young person, but you can't cheat on sleep too long without paying for it. Try a quick nap before dinner, or lie down for 10 or 15 minutes even if you don't sleep. You may find that city transportation systems are not only exhausting physically but irritating and exasperating; too many rude people, too much noise, too much crowding, too much of everything!

Of course, you will be tired when you first start to work. There are so many adjustments to make. But if you are healthy, you should be ready for an evening of vital living after you have had a short rest and a good dinner. As for week ends, these are bonus days to catch up on a dozen of the *extras,* with some planned time for your favorite recreation.

A healthy body and an alert mind make your days much happier and more productive.

The Doctor

Your family doctor was a definite part of the pattern of your before-working life. If you're in a new city, you'll need to get advice about a dentist and, perhaps, a doctor. If your company employs a physician or nurse, they can help you make your choice. Get an estimate of the cost of the dental work, the office call, and other medical services, before you engage these services. You may be surprised at the fees charged, as compared to those you have known. Find out, in a large city, about the cost of neighborhood charges as compared with those downtown. It may be worth your while. But above all, be sure to get sound advice on whom to select. Do not put off consultation with a good doctor if you need that service. Check to see if your health insurance covers this charge.

Your Feet

Do take care of your feet. You may have to change the type of shoes you wear and even the size of your shoes. Be sure your stocking feet are long enough to prevent cramped toes. Give your feet a chance to rest by changing shoes when you get home. Foot trouble can make you feel ill all over and keep you from after-hour recreation.

Exercise

Exercise should not be limited to the *one-two-bend* type! Work-tiredness often is dispelled more effectively by the right kind of exercise than by extra sleep. You may find that you miss some of the kinds of exercise you formerly enjoyed, such as tramping through the woods or riding horseback. Most cities offer a variety of kinds of exercise if you look for them. The YWCA, church, youth centers, city parks, and other organized recreation groups charge very little for dancing, swimming, bowling, tennis, golf, basketball, and other group sports.

Sports

Try to balance spectator sports with participation sports. You may have to search for the group you want to join, but group activity is more than physical exercise. You'll also get a lift in morale and a change of viewpoint.

Social Life

Social enjoyment is essential to happy living. Most young girls want to meet young men and enjoy the activities of mixed groups. It is smart to join groups where you'll meet both young women and young men. A chance acquaintance on a bus or at a movie isn't always a good beginning. You'll be much more apt to meet young people who like to do the things you enjoy if you start with your church group. Don't be stampeded into changing your sense of values or your standard of morals.

Most cities offer a variety of kinds of exercise if you look for them . . .

There are many kinds of people in a city. It may take a bit of time, but you can find your kind of friends. It is better to stay to yourself for a few weeks rather than to become involved with a person or group with standards of behavior other than yours. Good morals are the same wherever you live but in a city you are more apt to meet some people who have a weak code. You are the judge of the price you are willing to pay for a date. It may not be worth it!

Plan a campaign to have fun socially. You may find that the young men in the group have no more spending money than you have. Offer to go *Dutch treat* when you bowl, go to a movie, or have a snack after a group meeting. Young men often are more alone in a city than young women because they can't afford to date a girl. If you recognize this problem, you can suggest going to lower-cost movies, or buying second-balcony seats for the theater or concert. For the snack, suggest a hamburger counter rather than a night club. Social life in a city can be costly without being fun or fun without being costly.

What museums are open to the public? What of the parks, conservatories, free concerts, art galleries, public beaches? Make the most of civic facilities for entertainment and education.

Movies

The movies can be time-killers or selected entertainment. Watch the papers for the shows that are booked at different theaters. Try to vary your movie diet with films about foreign travel or historical episodes, as well as the usual boy-meets-girl extravaganzas. Watch your planned-activity chart and your budget for recreation. It is easy to form the movie habit to the exclusion of other activities. And while movies are all right in a plan, they shouldn't fill the entire time given to recreation.

Theater

Keep informed about the theater, concerts, lectures, and other good entertainment. Read the reviews and try to plan a treat once a month or so. There are usually tickets that cost only a little more

. . . watching and listening to a discussion on world affairs, current labor problems . . . is a worthwhile way to spend some of your time.

than the movie. If you are in a city, you should take advantage of the good plays, music, and lectures that are available.

Television

Watching television can be stimulating as well as entertaining. Many splendid programs present a wealth of cultural and educational information. Specialists in many fields can share their knowledge with you in a direct and effective way. World travelers make faraway places seem familiar to you and thus promote a better understanding of the peoples of the world. Certainly time spent watching and listening to a discussion on world affairs, current labor problems, or a new method of treating health disturbances is a worthwhile way to spend some of your time. Watching a well-written and well-directed play will bring enjoyment at a lower cost than attending the theater, or a movie, for that matter. News and weather reports on television give up-to-the-minute information in capsule form, and an occasional variety show is fun for pure relaxation. But watching television to the exclusion of reading and participating in community and church affairs lends little mental stimulation.

Thus television should be considered as one of several media from which you must choose the best way to spend your precious hours or minutes of leisure.

Intellectual Growth

Intellectual growth is as important in rounding out your plan of activities as physical health and social enjoyment. Balanced recreation means planning some time for activities that stir your intellect and expand your mental horizon. Bridge, knitting, dancing, movies, and other forms of recreation may have a place in your program, but these aren't enough if you want to become a socially-adjusted adult capable of advancement in a chosen work.

Read the book reviews in the Sunday paper. Stop in at the book section of a department store to look through the many kinds of books and the free listings. Get to know a librarian at the public library and chat with her about a course of reading. This need not be exclusively the classics, for there are so many good books that leave you with a message, a philosophy, or a new outlook.

And while you're at the library why not browse through the periodicals and watch the bulletin board for special exhibits and events?

Also notice the new books in your related field and in allied fields. You may develop an interest in an entirely new field. Make a list of the books you want to read and read something worthwhile each day. Perhaps you can use your daily travel time for reading, or keep a good book by your favorite chair or by your bed. Reading is a free activity. Make it an easy one for you.

How fast can you read? Today there are so many things to read that you'll get lost in the confusion unless you learn to discriminate among types of reading material. In this regard, learn when to read critically and slowly. Learn how and when to *skim read* to get the gist of the idea. Countless hours are wasted if you don't learn to skim a table of contents, analyze the introductory paragraph, skim a page, then decide how much time the remainder is worth to you.

If you are a slow reader, perhaps you could profit by a course in fast reading. Some new methods can speed up your reading skill as well as your comprehension. There is so much good current reading and there are so many treasures of the past, you will want to avail yourself of every opportunity to improve your reading skill.

Don't forget study groups, night classes, and planned education courses. Such an activity will be a mental stimulation to carry out your plan for intellectual growth. It may give you an incentive, too, for a good program of home reading. Try to select a group with good leadership and lively discussion periods so that you become a *participating* member.

A Hobby

Get a hobby. Then watch your circle of friends grow and your interests expand. This may be a low-cost or no-cost hobby of collecting information or pictures about travel, music, or people in the news. Perhaps you can afford a hobby that develops a creative skill, as photography, sketching, writing, weaving, or some other art or craft. Maybe you'd like to do little-theater work and can find a group that reads or acts plays. In a city, you'll find many kinds of classes, clubs, and organizations for people with kindred interests in many, many fields. Learn to do something well that is not directly associated with your business.

In a city, you'll find many kinds of classes . . .

Perhaps you'd like to learn to sew by the new, quick method. Inquire at the fabric section of a department store about classes. Some girls join classes in millinery and have great fun making their own hats. Each of these hobbies can be both pleasant and profitable.

There is so much to do in those out-of-work hours that only a plan of recreation and a selective choice can give you enough time to spend wisely.

Friends

Increase your circle of friends and acquaintances as you increase your interests. Your teammates at work may suggest that you join an office group, but don't restrict yourself to those with whom you work. It's too easy to talk shop and personalities if you keep in your own business group.

Whatever your choice of work, you'll probably find a professional society or organization with similar professional interests. Membership in such an organization is your responsibility.

You may be invited to join several groups. Go slowly and be selective. Investigate the purposes and objectives of each group. Attend a meeting to see if you can gain help, meet congenial friends, broaden your interests, and contribute something to the group.

Ask about the dues, assessments, and total cost of membership. Unless you are cautious, you'll find yourself burdened with dues and your evenings booked with meetings.

Join groups in which you'll associate with those who have succeeded and learn from them. Keep your eyes open and learn what *not* to do as well as what you hope you, too, can do. Keep on learning and growing in your chosen work if you want to be a success.

If you belong to a sorority or social organization, look up one

Some girls join classes in millinery and have great fun making their own hats . . .

of the alumna. Watch the social and club pages of the papers for meeting times. Then try to contact someone with whom you can attend a meeting and increase your circle of friends.

Your Home

How do your living quarters suit you now? Have you enough privacy so as to be by yourself when you want to? At first you may not mind dormitory-crowding, but later you may find the need for both the time and place to be alone. The tension and pace of business is such that you cannot do your best unless there is peace and quiet at home.

Perhaps you'll look for an apartment. If that means taking a roommate, choose your companion carefully. The division of expenses, work, and company; the compatibility of temperaments; a comparable income; an agreement on manners, morals, and attitudes toward men — these and other factors that make for a congenial home atmosphere are essential if an apartment companion is the answer to your better living.

Should you live alone in an apartment? This is expensive, and can be lonely until you are established in a planned recreation program.

Should you live at home when it is possible? *Yes,* if your financial help is needed; if you are given a chance to assume an adult responsibility; and if you keep your interests and activities on a broad plan. *No,* if you seek protection from meeting the challenge of new experiences that promote mental and emotional development.

. . . and attitudes toward men.

City Trips

If you work in a small town, no doubt you'll plan week-end or vacation trips to a large city to visit the shops, theaters, museums, restaurants, and other places of interest as part of your live-while-you-work plan. Often the out-of-town visitor sees and learns more about a city than those who live there. Trips can be educational as well as fun, and not too expensive if you plan ahead. It may be worth while to buy a Sunday paper published in the city of your choice so that you can make the most of these sight-seeing trips.

Dining Out

When you visit a city or if you work in a large city, dining out can be part of your education. You'll find that a city offers many opportunities to increase your general knowledge and to broaden your experiences. No doubt you'll have to budget your money as well as your time. But you can get a great deal for your money in the time you have if you plan it right.

Why not plan to visit an interesting eating place now and then? Try new foods and become acquainted with different customs and services.

You don't have to spend a great deal of money to dine at most any place, if you know how to select food and are willing to ask about prices when you are in doubt. Perhaps you'll be able to afford only a cream soup and melba toast. But you can always eat a peanut butter sandwich when you get home!

Here are some tips on gastronomic exploring. Get a booklet on eating places from the local newspaper or Chamber of Commerce. Read carefully the description of each place and note the price range listed. Places with dinner-dancing and a floor show charge a tax and fee to pay for this entertainment. The food usually is expensive, too. It may be you can have a luncheon there, if you insist on seeing such a spot. A dinner and evening is rather certain to be expensive. Be on guard against paying more than it is worth to you.

When you go to a new eating place for dinner with other young women, plan to arrive before seven o'clock. In some places an escort is required, but usually two young women can dine anywhere they wish so long as they make no attempt to attract attention by loud talk or conspicuous actions. Some places may require a reservation but often, at this hour, you can be served. Wait at the door for the headwaiter or hostess to seat you. If you are uncertain as to whether there is a cover charge or a minimum charge, ask the headwaiter before you are seated. A *cover charge* of several dollars may be made for special services or entertainment. A *minimum charge* means you must pay at least that amount.

Many eating places have a list of main dishes at a price ranging from moderate (fish or eggs) to expensive (steaks or game). Read the menu to see what is included with the price of the main dish. Don't order a first course or dessert unless you know whether these will mean an extra charge.

Some eating places have an *à la carte* menu only. That means each food has a separate price. When you select your meal, you must total the cost of each food and be prepared to pay a goodly sum if you have ordered a complete meal.

If you have a descriptive booklet of eating places, you can find out about these charges before you go. But do not be too timid to ask. You wouldn't buy a hat without knowing the cost. Why buy a meal without knowing you can afford it? You may have enough money, but you may n o t choose to spend it that way!

Wait at the door for the headwaiter to seat you.

Do not hesitate to question the waiter when you cannot understand the menu charges. Be sure before you order. Never be intimidated or spend more than you should because you are afraid to ask. Only the timid and the extravagant order blindly. The experienced person selects the food she wants and can pay for.

Sometimes it is wise to ask about the specialties of the house. Perhaps you've chosen an Italian, Chinese, or French restaurant. Try the specialty rather than chicken à la king or hamburger. You can always eat these at home. The reason you came here was to learn about something new.

Remembering the edicts of your junior high days — eat slowly, enjoy your food, and refrain from playing with your silverware! Likewise keep in mind that a fork or spoon in one hand and bread in the other is never correct. One hand should remain in the lap except when bread is spread or broken, or when food is being cut with knife and fork. If food is served in side dishes, it is quite correct to eat from these. When in doubt, use your fork instead of a spoon. The main dish usually is served onto your plate by the waiter or arranged for you to serve yourself. Fortunately, it is no longer necessary to leave some food in order to be polite.

You don't have to order cocktails, wine, or liquors even though the waiter suggests them. These are expensive items.

The cost of a dinner in the general dining room of a hotel is usually less than in the dining room that offers a floor show. Exclusive, high-priced restaurants may be best left on your list for a later time when you can afford to spend without sacrificing more important activities. Many interesting small restaurants are not costly if you select your food with care.

Never be intimidated . . .

When your bill is presented, take time to read it and to add the total. This is a sign of experience, not of inexperience. You may be asked to pay the waiter or a cashier at the door. Always make sure of the denomination of the money you give in payment for the bill, and always count your change. Take time to be sure, and ask the reason for any item you question. It is good business to pay for what you get, but no more. Everyone makes mistakes. Be gracious and assume that any error is unintentional. In most places this is true and the personnel will wish to correct any mistake.

Be prepared to leave a tip of at least 15% of the price of your meal. The more expensive the food, the larger the expected tip. But don't be foolish and overtip, so that you have to cut lunches for a week to make up for your display of extravagance.

Vacation

Your first vacation can be part of your planned recreation. It is fun to save for a trip you really want to take. You can find the right one at the right price if you plan properly. Read the travel section of the newspaper or browse through the travel department of a bookstore or the public library for ideas about where to go. Write or call the airlines, railroads, or bus lines for travel folders. Or stop in at a travel agency and pick up free folders on the part of the United States or the world that interests you.

A reliable travel agency, and there are many in most cities, can give you valuable assistance in planning your itinerary and making transportation and hotel reservations for you. Get information from them on ready-planned tours with or without escorts. The travel agent can tell you the approximate cost of the trip you have in mind. You do not pay the travel agent a fee for his service, rather he receives a commission from the transportation companies, hotels, or resorts after he makes the arrangements for you. That is, plane, train, and bus tickets are the same price whether you buy from the agent or directly from the transportation company. The same is true of the cost to you for hotels and escorted tours. What's more, most travel agents have traveled extensively themselves and can give you firsthand help.

Will you go by bus, train, plane, or boat? All-expense tours are offered on all these transportations. If you go on a conducted tour, there is no need to wait for a friend to go with you. In fact, the wrong traveling companion too often spoils a trip. You can always find congenial people on one of these tours, even though you are alone. Go where you want to go, but do plan to meet new people, see new sights, and learn something worthwhile. Get a fresh outlook. Then you can come back to work with a refreshed mental attitude and start to plan for the next vacation!

After all, vacations are granted to give you a change of viewpoint. You owe it to yourself and to your work to have the fun of planning a vacation, the thrill of enjoying a vacation, and the pleasure of telling your associates about your vacation. This is all part of the fun of working and of living while you work.

Then, you can come back to work . . . and start to plan for the next vacation!

CHAPTER 7

Bon Voyage—East or West

TRAVEL is a form of continuing education. Seeing other people and their countries broadens one's cultural background and one's professional outlook. It can give you new interests and hobbies. When you return, you may read different types of books, and magazine and newspaper articles, and they will mean more. You will develop new professional interests related to your present job. Foreign food and fashions in your locality will become more interesting to you. The local art institute, art show, symphony, or operatic offerings will take on new meaning. You may make new friends. You will be a more interesting person.

The local art show will take on new meaning.

Before-You-Go Suggestions

Before your plans are developed, stop and answer these questions:

How much paid vacation are you entitled to?

If you have only a two-week vacation, a trip abroad is extravagant unless you can take advantage of special tour rates in "off-seasons" of the year. The transportation, a major expense, is the same whether you are gone two weeks or two months. It may be frustrating if it is your first trip unless you limit the area you wish to visit. (On the other hand, two weeks in one country may be quite adequate to give you old-world experience.)

Can you take a leave of absence?

Talk this over with your supervisor. One large company grants a leave based on the length of employment. For example, you may be permitted a two-week leave with less than five years employment, one month with five to nine years, and two months with ten to fourteen years. Some will grant a reasonable leave but you may lose the advantages of continuous service for vacations, retirement, and other benefits. Others consider the job terminated and reserve the right to employ another in the position if a qualified person can be found. On the other hand, some may consider travel a benefit to your position and will even pay a part of the travel bill. At any rate, no harm is done by inquiring about company policy concerning leaves.

Can you afford a leave of absence?

A leave of absence means no pay will be received while you are away. Still, your expenses for apartment rent and services usually continue and expenditures for transportation, food, and travel expenses involved in sight-seeing must be paid.

Do you have good health?

Sight-seeing anywhere is tiring. It requires good health, especially if your time is limited so that the schedule is cramped. Being ill away from home and in a country where you may not understand or speak the language may be a shaking experience. Furthermore, going on a trip abroad in poor health will limit the value of the trip and make it seem an extravagance.

SOURCES OF INFORMATION. Assuming you have no specific source of information on the country or countries you may wish to visit, your first stop should be at the public library. Here you will find interesting books about the history, geography, culture, and climate, telling you almost more than you really care to know! Check the travel section of the Sunday paper, too. If your local paper does not carry articles and advertisements on travel outside of the United States, stop at the newsstand and buy the Sunday edition of a nearby city newspaper that does. Travel agencies and tourist bureaus will give you brochures with a good deal of information.

The public library, bookstores, and book departments of large department stores usually have a section on travel. Browse a bit until you find one book that seems to offer the information you seek if you are buying. Helpful information includes a brief historical outline of the country, current events and things to see, a list of hotels with street addresses rated according to service and price, currency, transportation, food specialities, restaurants, and sometimes, things to buy.

Most countries interested in tourist trade will have tourist bureaus established in the major cities of the United States. A postcard addressed to the Tourist Bureau of France (or Spain, or Mexico), New York City, N.Y., will bring an avalanche of travel brochures containing valuable information for you.

The consulate of each country maintains offices in New York and Washington, D.C. A letter addressed to those that interest you, requesting travel information on each of their countries, will bring you reliable material.

Airlines and steamship companies will be glad to send

. . . . a postcard indicating your interest will be answered quickly.

travel information on the countries they serve. Many have travel consultants who will give you individual help. A telephone call, a postcard, or letter indicating your interest will be answered quickly.

How MUCH DOES IT COST? The brochures from transportation companies usually list basic travel costs. They may have package tours that include transportation, lodging, and sight-seeing tours. For specific costs of a trip, it's wise to seek the assistance of a travel agent or you may sharpen your own pencil and figure transportation, hotel fees, approximate cost of food, sight-seeing tours, and shopping allowances. Remember that tips for service in foreign countries take a considerable share of your travel money. Most first-timers feel more secure with cost estimates figured by travel experts who have up-to-date price lists at their finger tips.

Don't let the seemingly astronomical tab frighten you if you sincerely wish to travel. A self-planned saving program and stay-at-home or low-cost vacation for a year or two may well bring that dreamed-of travel abroad without too much sacrifice.

THE BEST SEASON. The best time of the year to travel depends upon you and your pocketbook. Most of the music festivals, outdoor dramas, art exhibitions, fairs, races, and some sight-seeing tours, are held during the spring and summer, April to October

Don't let the seemingly astronomical tab frighten you if you sincerely wish to travel.

. . . some countries have very definite rain or snow seasons
which you may prefer to miss.

or November 1st. However, transportation and hotels may have
lower rates during the so-called "off season." If every dollar
counts, investigate the savings enjoyed by traveling between
October and April. After all, the scenery, historical sights, art
galleries, cathedrals, shops, and markets will be the same and the
crowds will not be nearly as pressing.

Even though weather is unpredictable, some countries have
very definite rain or snow seasons you may prefer to miss.

ONE, A FEW, OR A GROUP? Will you go alone, with one or two
friends, or will you join a group? If you have traveled very little
you may feel more at ease with an organized group. This will
let you develop confidence in your ability to deal with im-
migration authorities, transportation agents, and hotel representatives, and to read maps of foreign cities. Check with the pastor
of your church, the YWCA, any social club you belong to, or a
travel representative in your locality. They may know of tours
that are being planned or will be able to tell you whom you
should contact.

Teaming up with a friend should be carefully considered before plans are definite. Does this person have some of the same
interests and about the same amount of money and energy to
spend that you have? What about patience, adaptability, and
temperament? Traveling together is a constant association and
plans once made may be difficult to dissolve on foreign territory.

Traveling alone may mean that you will meet more people than you would by traveling with others. Although it means you may have some lonesome moments, you may also have some priceless, quiet times enjoying great views, people, statues, works of art, and architecture. You'll have no misgivings about hurting another's feelings, nor will you be troubled by disagreements. Only you know yourself and your friends, so only you can decide whether you should travel with or without them.

LET'S GET STARTED. First there is the matter of a passport. A passport is needed as you enter and leave all countries except Bermuda, Nassau, West Indies, Puerto Rico, Virgin Islands, Uruguay, Guatemala, and Mexico. If you live in or near the port cities of Washington, D. C., New York City, Boston, Chicago, New Orleans, Los Angeles, Miami, Seattle, Honolulu, or San Francisco, apply in person at the Passport Division of the Department of State. The address will be found listed in the telephone directory under United States Government, State Dept., Passport Agency. You may get an application form from a travel agent and fill it out in advance if you wish. Take with you two full-face photographs ($2\frac{1}{2}$ by $2\frac{1}{2}$) inches with a white border, $10.00, and proof of citizenship. A birth certificate, naturalization papers, or a baptismal certificate is proof enough. Within a week or ten days, the passport will be mailed to your home address.

If you cannot go to one of these cities, simply pick up a passport application form at your post office. Fill in the form and make a personal application to the clerk of any United States Circuit Court. Here, too, you will need photographs, $10.00, proof of citizenship, and a person who has known you for five years. Allow six to eight weeks for the processing.

A passport is valid for three years and may be renewed once for $5.00. Take good care of your passport. It is your most valuable possession when you are out of the country, for it is your proof of citizenship. The passport is requested when you check into hotels, when you cash traveler's checks, and when you enter and leave a foreign country. It gives you the right to re-enter the United States.

Also needed for re-entry into the United States from most other countries is a smallpox vaccination certificate less than

three years old. It is a wise traveler who has the vaccination six
to eight weeks before the trip begins. This gives plenty of time
for any reaction to subside. It also allows time to send the certificate which has been signed by your doctor to the city or state
health department for validation. Often your doctor will advise
additional shots to fend off diseases common in the countries you
plan to visit. It's better to be safe than sick.

Before leaving the United States, it is wise to write to the
customs office in the port cities mentioned to find out how many
and what foreign purchases you can or cannot bring into this
country. If you organize your purchases and your receipts for
easy inspection, and if you are honest in your declarations, you
will find "going through customs" abroad and when you return
is neither difficult nor trying.

THE QUESTION OF CLOTHES. First, look through your current
wardrobe. Pick out dresses, suits, or skirts that are wrinkle-resis-
tant, comfortable to sit and walk in, and fairly dark in color so
they won't show soil easily. Constant packing, unpacking, and
wearing is hard on clothes, so you are wise to take old favorites
rather than new ones. For fall, winter, and early spring, firmly
knit suits and jersey dresses are excellent for wear in cool climates.
For summer weather, choose fairly dark clothes that wash and
drip dry without ironing. A travel iron is excess baggage in most
foreign countries since the current and plug-in outlets differ from
ours and vary from one hotel to another, even in the same
country.

Limit the number of outer garments to two or three daytime
sight-seeing outfits and one or two dresses suitable for dinner in
the hotel dining rooms and better restaurants. A sweater or two
will be handy to wear in place of a blouse, as a light wrap, or
even to bed during chilly weather. A plastic raincoat with a hood
is indispensable, and some travelers recommend plastic boots for
rain or snow wear. A light or heavy coat, depending on the season you plan to travel, is a must. If the seasons change as you
travel, a coat with a zip-in lining makes you master of the temper-
atures. Remember that a coat takes a real beating, so leave the
good one at home.

You will save space, weight, and packing time if you can use
the same lingerie and accessories with all of the clothes you take.

Here's a list of items you may want to consider taking with you, depending, of course, upon your own personal requirements:

adjustable clothesline
heavy cord, 1 or 2 yards
a few rubber bands
facial tissue
toilet tissue, cardboard
  removed
cosmetics, if you insist
  on a special brand
facial soap
shampoo
laxative
headache tablets
band-aids
instant coffee
instant dry milk
camera and film
cigarettes and lighters
address book

spiral-backed notebooks or
  shorthand notebooks for
  travel notes, at least two
ball-point pens and fillers
sunglasses
extra pair of eyeglasses, if you
  wear them
sewing kit
safety pins
packets of granular detergents,
  or cold water soap
travel alarm clock
plastic bags for laundry, hose,
  shoes, plus extras
large manila envelopes, to
  mail things home
evening or clutch purse large
  enough for traveler's checks
  and passport

Tuck in enough hose for the entire trip; often the quality and fit of the hose you can buy will not be the same as you are accustomed to at home.

Even though many of these items may be purchased in the countries you visit, shopping takes valuable time. Furthermore, it may be very inconvenient, to say the least, to be hunting for a shop that sells aspirin when you are suffering from a headache and would prefer to be in bed.

. . . often the quality and fit of the hose you can buy will not be the same as you are accustomed to at home.

"If your feet hurt, you hurt all over." A greater truth was never spoken. Well in advance of your departure, decide on the walking shoes you will take. Whether you buy new shoes or take some you have, be sure you have walked for miles in them. Do forget the appearance of the shoes and take flat or medium heels. Rubber-soled shoes are a joy for walking on cobblestones. Take the style of shoe that gives your feet the best support. You'll be glad you did. Then take a pair of semi-walkers, the kind you could walk in for an hour or so and finally, take one pair of real dress-up shoes to wear in the evening when sight-seeing and shopping are over and you are out on the town.

BAGS TO PUT THEM IN. Checking on and off planes, trains, buses, or ships — and through customs — gives luggage hard wear. If you have reasonably lightweight, sturdy luggage, by all means use it. New luggage won't fend off the bumps any better than the old. But if you must buy new luggage, seasoned travelers recommend bright-colored, lightweight canvas bags that can be located easily. Luggage tags of a uniform red, green, or blue, for example, will make your baggage stand out in a crowd, too.

Those who travel by plane must be more conscious of free weight allowance than those traveling by ship. An economy flight allows only 44 pounds, while first class permits 66 pounds of luggage on overseas flights without a charge for excess baggage. One good-sized suitcase and a flight bag are convenient to handle with or without assistance at ports or stations. Folks who travel by air usually plan to go light in order to have space and weight allowance for purchases made abroad. Even though you are sure your shopping will be limited you are bound to find a darling wood carving, Parisian frock, beaded evening bag, or antique plate rack that you simply must take home.

WHERE TO STAY. Many of the first-rate travel books list the hotels according to the price and class in these or equivalent terms, *deluxe, first-class, medium priced,* and *inexpensive.* The hotel rate usually includes a "Continental" or light breakfast, that means rolls and coffee or tea. In some places it also includes the noon or evening meal.

Pensions are especially popular with travelers who enjoy the friendly atmosphere of a small hotel or boarding house. The rate may include full pension (all meals) or partial pension. People who are staying in a city for several days or weeks, often take advantage of the lower price as well as the comfort of the pension.

Youth hostels in European countries are convenient, cheap, (often rugged), and very popular with travelers under age 30. Dormitory or room arrangements are available in most of the hostels. Here is a wonderful way to meet people of similar age and interests from many countries. Check the local phone directory for an office of the American Youth Hostels in your town. If there is none, write to American Youth Hostels, Inc., 410 S. Michigan Avenue, Chicago, Illinois, for more information. Hosteling may mean that the travel budget can be stretched to cover months rather than weeks.

Having advance reservations for lodging in the cities during the height of the tourist season is recommended, especially if you wish to stay in the popular hotels. Reservations are not so important at the pensions, especially during the off season and in the villages. No advance arrangements are necessary at the hostels, making planning very flexible.

Having advance reservations for lodging is recommended

Those who arrive in a town without advance lodging reservations find the local tourist bureaus of infinite help. Usually located in the railroad stations, they have lists of approved hotels, pensions, and hostels grouped by price and location. Do not ask for or accept advice on hotel accommodations from any stranger. At some railway stations and terminals there may be agents who get a commission for getting people to go to a certain hotel. Maps of the city and information on current tourist attractions are available at these authorized tourist bureaus and some hotels.

A LAST WORD — MONEY. How much money you take with you is a personal decision. But you will need enough United States currency to get to the port of embarkation and on your return to get from the port of entry to your home. In between times, carry your money in the form of traveler's checks that can be changed into the currency of the country after you arrive. Traveler's checks for $10.00 are handy to use for checking out of hotels and for shopping. They help you to limit the amount of local currency you carry. Some $20.00 checks or larger denominations are good for long vacations and for trips where hotel and travel expenses are not prepaid.

In the major cities, many of the hotels and some shops will accept personal checks, so it is a comfort to leave some money at home in a checking account to draw on in case of an emergency. You may also want to have some one-dollar bills tucked away to use as you are checking out of the hotel so that you do not have foreign money left over as you leave one country and enter another. Unless you plan to visit many countries, it is convenient to get $5.00 to $10.00 worth of the money of each country from your bank before you leave the United States, or you may depend on currency exchanges in the terminals. This assures you of having money for tips, bus, or cab fare to your place of lodging before you have an opportunity to get to a bank or currency exchange in the new city. Some travelers have found it handy to keep the money of each country separately, using several envelopes. Keeping extra money, transportation tickets, and any other valuables in the hotel safe provided for the use of guests brings a real feeling of security.

A computer or conversion table that can be obtained in large department or bookstores before you leave home, will help you know the types and values of local currency in terms of United States money. In this way, you will know what you are spending.

After-You-Arrive Suggestions

When you are in a foreign country you are an ambassador of the United States. What you do, say, and wear become part of the image people of other lands build up about Americans. That is a sobering yet challenging thought. But it is true that the United States needs friends abroad and we can do our part to help make them. It may be that you will find some foreign people have an exaggerated impression of us based on lurid movies and headlined scare or strife stories. Sometimes this is accentuated, unfortunately, by the thoughtlessness or crudeness of some of our touring countrymen. Perhaps if you think of yourself as representing a typical American, you can help build an image of which you and all of us will be proud.

Money. One way to make friends is not to belittle the foreign money. And don't show extravagance or indifference to the money values of the local people. On the other hand, you should not be indignant if a store or a service does not want to accept United States money, especially silver coins. There may be gov-

What you do, say, and wear become part of the image people build up about Americans.

ernment regulations about use of foreign currency, or there may be difficulty for the recipient in exchanging our coins into their spendable coins.

Shopping. You may not find fabulous bargains in shopping in reputable stores for goods of similar value to those found in stores here. Look for trade-marks and signs of origin of the goods. Consider, too, the total cost of shipping purchases home. Usually the tourist association of a country will give you booklets listing reliable dealers of items that are typical of the country's crafts or customs. Keep all receipts for your purchases. For your convenience, translate the cost of these purchases into United States money for easy reference later. Know the foreign government rules and regulations about shipping goods and carrying items into and out of the country.

Tipping. Travel folders, tourist agencies, and travel agents in a country usually will advise you, on request, as to the range in tips expected in a country. Many foreign restaurants and hotels add a 15% (or more) service charge to a bill. This may be adequate. Of course, you are expected to tip for special services such as packages delivered to your room, errands you may request, or room service of food and other conveniences. Many tours of two or more days include in the total price the tips for luggage, meals, and guide service. This should be indicated on your ticket or on the descriptive folder for the tour. It saves annoyance and misunderstanding to know what you should and should not be expected to pay in tips.

Travel. On arrival or a week before your planned departure from a country, recheck on the correct departure time of the plane, train, or boat you expect to take. Travel schedules change. You should not blame American agents if you have been given incorrect information at home.

It is unfair, too, to expect to get the accommodations you want if you make last-minute changes in your plans.

When traveling in a tour group, it is courteous to try to keep to the time schedule. The straggler, the "just-one-more-picture" camera fan, or the late sleeper may upset the entire group as well as the tour director or guide.

Dress. Be moderate and modest in your dress. Respect local customs for street wear and for visits to churches, temples, museums, and other places open to visitors. Shorts and brief sport clothes may be accepted at resort spots but such clothes for travel and street wear make women conspicuous.

Talk. You'll find that many people in foreign countries understand some English. You will embarrass them if you make discourteous remarks to or about people just because you think you won't be understood. You might remember, too, that your actions may make your words understood or misunderstood. Avoid loud talk and loud laughter. Dining rooms, art galleries, and other public places are open to guests of many countries. It is unfortunate when young (or older) folk from this country attract attention and give unfavorable impressions of boldness, thoughtlessness, or crudeness.

Try to learn a few words of the native language. You may make a friend by saying "Thank you," "Good morning," or some other friendly phrase in the language of the land. Perhaps you can carry with you a phrase and pronunciation leaflet so that you can practice and try to learn a few foreign words. Most guides can speak English. However, do not expect all taxi drivers or all people in out-of-the-way places to understand your English. It doesn't help to shout or become irritated if the native people cannot understand you.

Appreciation. Your sincere appreciation of scenery, customs, products, history, and accomplishments of people in the countries you visit will win friends. Avoid making comparisons with people and things "back home." Of course, foreign countries and peoples are different. That is why it is fascinating to go abroad. It is a sign of immaturity and colloquialism to criticize, complain, or belittle what you see or hear on your trip.

Information. Do try to refresh your memory about American history and be as up-to-date as you can on current events before you visit another country. You will be surprised to find how much many foreigners know about our history, our government, and our educational institutions, as well as facts about our important people, cities, and scenery. At times you may be able to correct false information about customs and practices in the United States. That is, of course, if you are sure of the facts!

Do not try to settle political, religious, or moral differences with casual acquaintances you meet. You seldom have time to convince them and you seldom have time to understand the heritage responsible for the opinions of the other persons.

Of course, you will enjoy your trip more and the people you meet will be more interesting if you have studied about the countries and their people. In most countries, you will be given descriptive folders and maps which you can study as you travel to get the historical facts and special features of the land.

Photography. Abide by the rules of the foreign country, city, village, building, or park concerning taking pictures. Some national regulations permit confiscation of your film if rules are violated. Regulations in some places make picture-taking a punishable offense. It may cause you needless trouble if you try to "sneak a shot." Do not take a picture of a person or persons without asking permission of the persons, a guide, or a guard. You would not like to have a foreigner snap a picture of you in your home town, especially if taken unaware in an awkward moment.

Smile. A smile is a universal language. Most people understand the friendship shown by a smile, a cheery "hello," a wave of the hand or perhaps a handshake. Children love to wave and smile.

Regulations in some places make picture-taking
a punishable offense.

Your friendly attitude while traveling and living among people of other lands can make your visit so much more pleasant. It can help them understand you and other Americans. You can help establish a picture of the United States citizen as one who is friendly, and one who is eager for friendship with citizens of the world.

CHAPTER 8

Master the Mechanics of Your Job

D O you remember, when you first entered high school, how many rules and regulations there were? Some of them seemed rather foolish and troublesome, no doubt. Yet soon you began to take these rules for granted and found that most of them really made your work easier and more orderly.

So, too, a business organization has to establish procedures and policies to make the work move efficiently, to prevent repetition and confusion, and to equalize the benefits and penalties among employees.

You will save yourself possible embarrassment and disappointment by learning your company's policies and office practices. If these are not in written form for employees, you can start your own listing and add to it as you find mention of new rules of procedure.

A questioning attitude may be a sign of an alert mind, but the person who questions the wisdom of established rules of procedure and rebels against office policies is apt to become an unpopular worker. She wastes her best energies in *negative* work. Your work will be easier if you learn the rules and follow instructions pleasantly and willingly.

The Manual of Information

If your organization is small, you will meet almost everyone in the first few weeks. This may be a very informal unit of workers with rather elastic policies. But the larger the organization, the more defined and specific are the policies.

There may be a great gap in rank between top management and you. Thus the policy makers may seem remote and unrelated

. . . you will meet almost everyone in the first few weeks.

to your work. The company policies and regulations may seem involved and burdensome. Actually, you'll soon learn that the larger the organization, the easier it is to know what you should and shouldn't do, how you should do it, and when.

Who is *top management* in your company? There may be a board of directors, with a chairman, that establishes broad policies. Learn their names and build up a reading acquaintance with them. No doubt you'll read or hear many interesting things about these policy makers which will personalize them for you and foster a better appreciation of your company.

Other officers may include a president, vice presidents, comptroller, treasurer, secretary, and others. Learn these names, too, and try to be able to identify them and their special company duties. In many companies you will have occasion to see and meet some of these top management people even when you are a beginner.

You'll want to learn how your company is organized and what variations in services are offered. Today, most business concerns have far-reaching operations. You'll understand and appreciate the policies and procedures established for your work when you become acquainted with the broad operation of your company and the people who direct these activities.

Your happiness and efficiency will be affected by your attitude toward the policy-making members of your organization. Even though, as a beginner, you have a minor position among thousands of employees, you can be an intelligent contributor to the total effectiveness of the organization. An understanding of your company and confidence in your ability will help you do the little routine jobs that are part of most assignments.

Before you came to this position, you may have had some general information about company policies toward employees. Now that you are an employee, you'll want specific information as it applies to you and your future.

What are the hours of work and what are the regulations about overtime? Each state has laws affecting the hours that women may work. These may vary for different vocations. What are your company's policies about payment for overtime work?

How are raises awarded? Some companies have a set scale of advancement. Raises may be granted in six months, one year, or at no set time. Sometimes general cost-of-living raises are given as distinct from merit raises.

Should you ask for a raise? You shouldn't expect an increase in salary until you have completed a year of satisfactory work. You have been learning at company expense this first year and probably have gained more than you have given. Talk with the head of your department about a raise. Don't be emotional or demanding. Your personal troubles and financial obligations are not reasons for an increase in salary. Only your ability to produce effective returns to the company merits consideration.

Perhaps your request will have to be put into written form, so that this in turn may be discussed with the executives of the organization. This is for the head of your department to decide. Go first to her with your problem, so as to avoid any ill feeling that might result from side-stepping an immediate superior.

Vacation policies are established by company rule. The length of the vacation and the choice of time are usually determined by the length of employment. Do not ask for special favors, such as an extra day or a split vacation. Find out the rules concerning allowance for a legal holiday occurring within your vacation period. Find out how payment is made for your vacation time. Is it given to you in advance, if you fill out the required form and have it signed by the proper person?

The special services offered by your company to employees are part of your payment for work and are arranged to make your working conditions happier.

What is the company policy about sickness? Is there free medical help? Are you paid for a certain amount of sick leave? Does your company insist on prompt treatment of an accident or illness as a protection to yourself and other employees? What are the facilities for X-ray examinations, dental care, nursing service, and advice on the selection of medical and dental service?

What is the company policy about sickness?

Does the company give legal advice or require you to sign legal statements about assignment of patents and participation in outside financial ventures? Do you hold a position in which you must be bonded as a protection to the company?

Many companies have facilities to help the employee avoid legal entanglements in case of law suits, collections of damages for personal injuries, or loss of property. Ask your department head about these services if the Company Manual of Information does not clarify this point. The company wants to protect you against trouble and fraudulent claims.

As a businesswoman, learn to read every document before you sign it. If in doubt, get expert help. Don't sign petitions, contracts for purchase of goods, leases to rent, or any paper, unless you are sure of the liabilities which you assume. As a member of a company you cannot risk involvement in any situation which brings adverse publicity to the company or disturbing trouble to yourself.

In some companies, personal counseling and advice are services offered by experts in several fields. You may need help in deciding on insurance, investments, savings, loans, and other matters that influence your happiness and your effectiveness as an employee. Do not hesitate to ask the experts.

What educational services are available to you? Is there a company library? Are education classes offered to employees, or is there an allowance given for educational work in a recognized institution? Some companies encourage employees to continue their study and formal education. Is additional pay given for completion of further education work?

Today, modern businesses assume the attitude that it is not only good business, but part of their moral obligation to help their employees retain good health and lead normal, happy lives. Such companies want to help you and want you to use the special services for employees.

Sometimes you may be entitled to repayment for money spent on essential company business. Find out the company rules. If you take a company guest to luncheon, can you be reimbursed, and how do you proceed? When can you buy needed supplies, and how can you be reimbursed? What are the accepted procedures for getting new equipment and supplies? It is wise to ask before you act, or you may find you have overstepped your authority and have no redress for the expenditures.

Is the company responsible for your loss of money or other property while you are working? Usually you are expected to assume this responsibility. You cannot afford to be careless.

Does your work require the use of a company car? This situation is covered by a chain of rules as to your responsibilities and liabilities. Be sure to understand these regulations. When you are entrusted with expensive equipment you should take full precautions to protect the company and yourself.

Do you travel on company business? You will find definite rules for expense money, limit of expenditures, when and how to report the expenses, and adjustment of expense payment to any advance of money. Some women are very careless about understanding exactly the privileges, responsibilities, and limitations of traveling or working on an expense account. Do not expect special favors. Do not act without knowledge. Ignorance is no excuse in law or in business. Chapters 7 and 13 deal with problems of travel.

Salaries may be paid in several ways: cash, check, credit on a ledger account, or in other ways. Some companies will mail your check to a designated bank. Some companies have offices to cash your pay checks or to make out company checks for you to use in payment of certain bills. Some have other arrangements to help solve your money-handling problems. Do not carry much money with you or leave it in your desk or in your room. Loss of money is not only your loss but is apt to cause embarrassment to others. Get advice from the experts and use company facilities or other businesslike methods in your money affairs.

Does your company allow a discount to employees for purchase of goods produced by the company, or give credit cards for discounts at other companies? This can be a helpful service to you, but do not abuse this privilege. Your sense of fair play will guide you in determining what you can buy honestly on such a plan. Remember this company service is not intended to include your family and friends.

Telephone Etiquette

The telephone is an essential part of business. You may find that your company has policies governing the use of the telephone, the proper etiquette for telephone conversations, and your responsibilities for information given in these conversations.

Company telephones are for company business. The number of phones is determined by the amount of business. These phones are not planned for personal use so do not abuse this service.

How is your telephone voice? Did you ever stop to think how much your voice tells about your personality? When you use a company telephone you are representing your company policy of friendliness, courtesy, and dignity.

Respect the time of other people. Decide what you want to say before you telephone. Keep a pad and pencil handy to jot down names and facts so that you can accomplish your purpose. Do not prolong the conversation, yet avoid an abrupt termination. Learn how to end a long conversation tactfully. Always close the phone call with "good bye," and do not bang the receiver.

The use of intercompany telephones requires the same etiquette as outside phone service. Of course you will be as courteous to your co-workers as to your public.

Be sure of the right telephone number. Dial carefully or give the number distinctly to the operator. Ask to speak to the correct person before you begin to talk. If the correct person is not there, you may ask if someone else can give you the information or ask to have the original person return the call.

If you ask someone to place a call, be ready to speak as soon as the connection is made. Never keep anyone waiting. Everyone is busy. If you must interrupt a conversation, ask if the other person will excuse you a minute or if it would be convenient for you to call again. Do not imply that your time is more valuable than that of the other person.

Be courteous. Listen and do not interrupt. Be sure you understand the message. Do not shout. Speak distinctly. Do not disturb others in your office by long, loud chatter. Speak to the person on the telephone — don't address the office force! Don't say anything in a telephone conversation that you would hesitate to say in a face-to-face conversation.

As a company representative, you must uphold the company policy of public relations in your phone calls. Do not ask someone to wait while you get information. Get the name and telephone number and say you will call back or send the information.

If you answer a telephone, use the proper response, "Y company, Miss Z speaking," or "Y company, Personnel Office." Identify yourself so that the caller can give the message to the right person. If you must call someone to the telephone, explain your absence and be sure the person answers the call. You are responsible for the completion of the call. If necessary, ask if you can take a message. Write down the facts and be sure the correct person gets the memo. Most companies have special forms to record a phone message. Do get the name right.

Learn how to transfer a call. Tell the person to whom you are speaking that you will try to locate the other person so that there is no question about the silence or delay. Say, "Please transfer this call to 318, or to Mr. Jones."

You will learn that there are many irritating mannerisms in using a telephone. There's the shouter, the whisperer, the person

Never keep anyone waiting.

who doesn't give a name but expects you to guess, and the one who goes into details that should be given in a letter or conference. Then there's the person who says, "Who's calling?" — to see if you are important enough to rate an interview! And there's the abrupt, officious person who barks out a message and gives you no chance to speak. You can set your own standard of telephone etiquette which is, after all, *good manners*.

Long-Distance Phone Calls

Company policies determine who, when, and how, long-distance phone calls may be made. There may be intercity telephone service or direct wire service for company business.

Telephone service is expensive. Some companies are very liberal in allowing long-distance calls. Usually, however, this method of transacting business is limited to those in executive positions. If you have permission to use the long-distance service, ask what record you must make of the call so that the bill may be charged correctly.

When you must make a long-distance call, have your notes organized, state your message, take notes on the information received, and do not waste company money. Sometimes it is wise to confirm the conversation by a follow-up letter.

Use the same precautions in long-distance telephone calls made at company expense as you do for those calls you must pay for personally.

Incoming Mail

Mail should be opened and sorted promptly. Clip the envelope to the letter to keep the address with the letter.

Read each letter carefully and circle or underscore important points. Make notes in the margin to help you answer the letter.

Sort the letters as to types. Then when you answer them you will be able to dictate more easily, and the stenographer will be helped in selecting stationery and reading her notes. You may want to arrange the letters according to ease of answering, or by importance and urgency, or by the audience: intercompany, consumer requests, applications, invitations, acknowledgments, professional communications, offers to sell, and complaints.

Answer letters promptly. If you must collect information that causes a delay, send a note saying the complete answer will be given at a certain time. Then be sure to fulfill this promise.

Memos and Letters

Company policies are usually very definite about the form used for intercompany memos and for letters.

Large companies have an instruction book for stenographers indicating proper headings, salutations, margins, punctuation, and other rules. Some companies object to handwritten notes without a file copy, or communications other than through the prescribed channels.

If you dictate to a stenographer or use a dictating machine, learn to organize your message, to be definite, to speak clearly and slowly enough to avoid confusion. Give accurate data so the typist can write the letter correctly. Read all letters carefully before you sign them. Queer slips can creep in unless you are observant! Some are just funny, some may be costly.

Plan, think, and take it easy. If you can use a dictating machine, you can play back the record and hear how you express yourself. Do you stumble? Do you suggest punctuation and paragraphing? Do you spell names or technical words? Until a stenographer becomes familiar with your style and technical terms, you will cut down on the need for rewriting if you help her get your meaning.

Use the prescribed method of signing letters. Some companies insist on the company name, with your initials. Some want the name of the department head, with your initials. Learn the rules and follow the policies.

Learn to write a good letter that is friendly, informative, concise, and inclusive. Letters are a form of public relations.

Know what you want to say. Say it. Use correct English. Avoid stilted phrases. Personalize your remarks but don't be dramatic, too clever, or trite. Read the letter. Are you willing to be judged by it?

Companies have definite rules as to who gets copies of letters as well as who may send letters without submitting them for supervision. When in doubt, ask your supervisor to read the letter. You may find that you have violated a company policy or given a wrong impression.

The art of writing letters is real and very important. Study good examples of letter writing. Learn to write the kind of letters you like to receive. A business letter expresses the philosophy and the policies of the company. You'll find more about letters in public relations in Chapter 11.

Files and Other Items

Each company has rules about the use of files. There may be special file clerks who take care of filing. If a message belongs in a file, do not keep it in your desk.

If a letter is marked for several persons, read it at once, check off your name, and pass it along. This is not your personal property.

If you have promised to send certain booklets or enclosures, be sure to see that these are sent.

Postage

Company policy probably dictates whether the letter should go airmail or special delivery. Should supplementary material be enclosed or sent at a lower rate? The relative value of special service must be weighed against the extra cost incurred. In any company operations, *little expenses make big totals at the end of a year.* That's why company postage should go only on company mail. Your personal letters should carry your personal postage.

Telegraph

You may have occasion to telegraph a company message. What are the rules? Does the company have a wire system between company plants in different cities? Is the message urgent enough for a straight wire or can it go at the lower rates of a day letter or night letter?

Make the message clear. Avoid unnecessary words, yet do not confuse your message. Consider the wording *without punctuation.*

Be sure to keep a copy of the wire for your file. Sometimes it is wise to mail a confirming copy of the wire, to prevent a misunderstanding, and give the receiver a file copy.

Parcel Shipments

If you must send a package as part of your company business, ask the proper official as to the correct way to handle this shipment. Does the shipping department do this? Are there record forms to fill out? Should the package go parcel post, express, air express, registered or insured? Consider the urgency and the expense.

The cost of shipment depends on the weight, size, distance sent, and sometimes the content of the package. Do not enclose a letter or written instruction unless this is within the regulations of the shipping media.

If you receive a package for business reasons, should this be registered at a receiving office before you accept it? Perhaps registration is required to check the receipt against the order.

In large companies, there are definite rules for all shipments and receipts of packages. Why not learn the mechanics of this procedure?

Out-of-country shipments require special forms and handling for duty payments and to comply with national regulations. You aren't expected to know all these rules, but you are expected to consult the person who does know.

Visitors

Visitors to the company should be treated with courtesy, and in conformity with regulations. Avoid personal visitors unless you are sure this is permitted by company policy. You want your family and friends to see where you work, but does your company permit this interruption?

Never permit solicitors of any service or product to take your time during working hours. Most companies prohibit solicitors except on authorization from the proper company official.

Visitors to a company are usually under the direction and care of a specialized department. If strangers visit your department, be sure you are authorized to visit with them and to show them the department operation. This may cause difficulty. Be courteous, but get advice from the head of your department. Perhaps it will be necessary to call the guide service or a messenger to take the guest to the visitors' office. Do not assume the authority to judge the right procedure in extending information or permitting inspection of work by any visitor.

Conferences

Conferences are an integral part of business operation. These are usually set up by an office memo stating the purpose of the meeting, the time and place, and probably the others included. The conference may be set up by telephone or personal call.

Be sure your superior knows about the conference unless you are authorized to act without this notice. Determine what rights you have to express your opinions in the conference if you represent your department. A newcomer can save herself embarrassment and avoid looking ridiculous if she will refrain from talking at meetings on matters about which she knows little. Of course, a good idea should be expressed. But it is a wise policy to talk over your suggestions with someone who knows, before presenting an idea to the group.

If possible, try to collect data and information which will help you understand the subject to be discussed. Perhaps you can take along records or reports which might help you if you are called on to speak.

Be on time! Do not keep others waiting. Give your undivided attention to the subject under discussion. Do not whisper or talk to others. Do not introduce unrelated subjects. Listen. If you are called on to give your opinion, do so (1) as your personal opinion, (2) as a representative of your department, if you have that right.

If the conference includes out-of-company people, be very careful not to violate company secrets. Be sure you know how much authority you have to speak as a representative of your company.

Take notes on the main points of the discussion. Be exact and complete, but to the point.

Discuss the conference with your immediate superior. Then write a report to her, with copies to others, if necessary. Always ask her to check your reports before they are sent to others in the organization. See Chapter 9 for further details on reports.

If you call a conference, be sure to include the right people.

Have a clear plan of action and consult your superior about your plans. Many companies have an established form to use for conferences. The subject or reason for the meeting is usually set as a title so that subsequent reports and meetings may be given the same title and filed together. Keep notes. Write a report of the meeting and follow through on your responsibilities and assignments. Show your report to your superior and determine who should get copies.

Forms, Blanks

Companies have forms, blanks, and record sheets to minimize the time spent on records and to make identification of certain information readily evident. Use the right form for each office assignment, as telephone message, package shipment, expense account, and time sheet. These are all mechanics of a job. Regardless of what you may have done on another job, you will save yourself work by mastering the mechanics of the present job.

Duplicate Messages

Duplicate messages can be made several ways. Companies differ in their need for various methods; one may have elaborate equipment, another, one or more simple machines, inexpensive and portable. You can adapt to your company's policies regarding processes and formats.

Carbon copies of a letter are seldom legible for more than seven or eight copies. Unless the message is easily read it may be necessary to have the letter typed several times or use another method.

Copying equipment, such as thermofax, verifax, and xerography, can copy letters, reports, drawings, and in some cases, even photographs, directly from the original. Such equipment is a quick and convenient way to make one to ten or fifteen copies. On some machines, the page to be copied must be in black type,

Carbon copies . . . are seldom legible for more than eight copies.

black ink, or in lead pencil. Other photocopiers can copy, in black and white, any mark on paper, including ball-point pen, colored inks or crayons, or rubber-stamped copy. Such equipment makes it possible to send information on to others without either retyping or sending the original piece. This eliminates the possibility of errors that may occur in retyping. A special, coated paper is necessary for these photocopying processes.

Hectographing is a method of reproducing seventy-five or more messages. Methods differ so that you should ask how many legible copies can be made.

Planographing is a more expensive method of reproducing messages. This is a photographic reproduction of the original copy and requires special typing, paper, and specialized equipment. The result looks like a typewritten letter. Several hundred copies can be made.

Multilithing equipment may be owned by a company needing to turn out several thousand copies of a piece per hour. This operates on the lithographic principle. It is a process that involves transferring a photographic image of the original copy to a flat metal or foil plate. The image is etched into the plate by acid. The finished plate is wrapped around a cylinder on a press. Then a roller applies ink to the plate. The rotation cycle brings the plate into contact with a rubber "blanket," transferring the ink to the plate to the blanket. The blanket, which is another cylinder, rotates and comes in contact with the printing paper. *Xeroxing* is a similar process but uses a sensitized paper plate instead of the metal plate.

Mimeographing is an inexpensive method of making many copies. Most stenographers can cut a stencil for mimeographing. Be sure the stencil is clear and accurate. Keep the stencil in case you should need more copies.

In other types of reproducing letters and bulletins a person's name and address can be used, just as in typing. Investigate the facilities available for multiple messages before you ask for any one kind. The head of the stenographic department can give you this information.

Printing is, of course, the best method of making many copies of a message. This is a more expensive method for small runs but may prove to be a low unit cost for large runs. Consult someone who knows the answers before you have anything printed. Provide *clean copy.* Don't expect the typesetter to guess at your meaning. Changes after the copy is set are expensive. Proofread carefully. Mistakes are costly.

Company policies will determine the method used for multiple messages. If you are responsible for the copy, be sure you have organized your message, said what you mean, stated the facts clearly, and presented a complete story. Would you be proud to have people know you wrote the copy?

Sometimes, of course, it may be desirable to have each letter an original, addressed to the individual. The importance of the message and the company policy must determine the value of the method for the occasion.

Order out of Confusion

When you first begin to work in a company, you may feel that you will never learn all of the many regulations. You will, if you keep a record book and organize your information for future reference. Start a policy and regulation file for forms, copies of good examples of notices, and data on procedures. Make haste slowly.

Company policies and procedures are planned to make your work easier. Aren't you glad you don't have to set up an entire system of your own.

Systems of procedure make for efficiency, impersonal action, and prevention of errors.

In a large company you will find experts on so many phases of the business that you won't have to guess or hesitate. Look in the company telephone book to see how many functional departments

You aren't supposed to know how to run the company.

are listed. Just as you are hired to learn to do specialized work, so too, other specialists have learned to make the mechanics of some phase of work more efficient. You aren't supposed to know how to run the company. You are supposed to know how to get advice to save time, money, and energy.

Give your wholehearted support to the policies, procedures, and practices established by the company. Master the mechanics of the job and you will find your work more pleasant and effective.

CHAPTER 9

Look at the Records

WHEN you are in a business position with a future, the subject of records and reports becomes very real and very important.

What did you do a year ago today? What plans do you have for a month from today? Records of work accomplished, plans for work to come, hunches, ideas, quotes, and appointments — these are the basis of constructive, progressive plans for accomplishment in the business world. In school, you took notes on lectures and reference readings to summarize and crystallize the points you wanted to remember. In business, your notes and records are even more important and should be more inclusive. In fact, they should be so complete and usable that one of your co-workers could understand them and carry on any project you have started.

Good records make for continuance of work. It has been said that the real test of an efficient worker is that she records her work and outlines her plans so exactly that another person could pick up this work and go ahead with it without loss to the company. Cooperation and teamwork are keynotes to success. The lone worker or prima donna doesn't belong in most business positions. If you are ill or called away from work, your work must go on. You can't afford to be careless about good, clear, accurate records.

The type of records required by your work may be suggested

by your immediate superior or left to your discretion. But you'll be wise to keep a record for your own protection against forgetfulness; to help you analyze your work; to make plans for improvement; and to make reports.

The Daily Journal

Some positions call for a record of each activity of the day, with the amount of time devoted to each one. This may be essential for the office manager to make charges to departments or projects, or it may be required as a check on the effectiveness of your use of time.

Other positions do not require a time-action record, but do require records of data, sales, contacts, programs, and major activities.

You may be bored with this detail work at first. You may spend too much time in writing records. But it is well worthwhile to form the habit of jotting down plans for daily work, names of people, titles of books and magazine articles, quotable sayings, facts, hunches, and pertinent data and happenings. Your daily journal can become an important tool for your work.

A desk calendar for appointments and extra duties may be used as a reminder for the records in your journal. Each notation on your calendar probably deserves a record of *what? why? who?* and, perhaps, *what of it?* Ten minutes at the end of the day may be enough for your day's record or you can keep a running account directly in your journal. Keep your record book handy and use it.

Work Sheets

Some positions require work sheets or forms to record specific information. If these are separate sheets, plan a systematic filing system to use until you compile the data and important facts in a permanent record. Loose record sheets are lost easily and may spoil a long project.

Research Records

Research work requires definite, accurate records, with nothing left to chance memory. Anyone who is trained to do research work

Loose record sheets are lost easily . . .

appreciates the importance of keeping a permanent record of each fact and figure as it occurs. It must be kept in such an organized form that each notation is incorporated into the over-all plan for the project. Dates, details of method, techniques, observations, results, and references are not only essential for progressive work but may prove invaluable in establishing patent rights and claims of monetary value.

Records are the basis on which reports are made.

Reports are evidence of accomplishment.

The Purpose of a Report

The purpose of a report is to present facts, plans, and suggestions in such a way that future action may be taken wisely. The purpose may be:

To assemble facts for a review of the problem.

To state facts to show the need for a program or project.

To present the progress made on a program or project.

To report on contracts and activities which have a significance to someone in the business.

To condense in logical, classified form the work of a designated period (day, week, month, or year).

The purpose of different reports will vary, but every report should be clear, concise, and correct.

WHEN: Be prompt in sending a report. The time element in business is so important that a delay may make the report worthless. Few people enjoy writing a report, but procrastination doesn't make it easier!

WHO: A report is made to a definite person or group of persons. Keep that person or group in mind as you write, so that your report has meaning.

WHY: Before you start to write, review the subject and decide why the report is important.

WHAT: Think through what you want to say, what facts are essential, and what details may be omitted.

HOW: Organize your report so that the reader gets the purpose and impact of your report at once and can follow the organization of your presentation.

Test the organization of your report. Be sure the person to whom it is written will get a clear and concise picture of the subject. Make your statements give the correct meaning and proper emphasis.

The length of the report is important. If you visualize the purpose of the report, the persons who will read it, and the importance of this report in terms of company business, you can judge whether this subject deserves a half-page memo or a 20-page detailed report. Try to answer the question, "What of it?" This may help you give proper emphasis and balance.

Write the report when you are enthusiastic. *Check it over later* when you are analytical and critical. *Rewrite* it when you are calm, objective, and impersonal.

Are you willing to be judged by that report?

Some Don'ts

Avoid criticism of another person in the organization. When it is necessary to register a complaint or criticism, think about it, then discuss it with your superior. The written word is limiting and may cause trouble you wish to avoid. There is always the chance that you may not understand all the circumstances.

Avoid taking credit for work done by others. Be generous in giving credit to co-workers.

Avoid half-statements or implied statements you can't substantiate. Be explicit and correct in limiting the statement to a specific time, place, person, or fact.

Avoid unnecessary details. Don't detour! Reserve little asides for your personal records. Perhaps you can use these in a conference or an explanation, if required. Your main points can be lost in the little items.

Avoid opinions on subjects you are not qualified to judge. Keep to the facts in your field of work.

Don't send a report until you have read it for clarity, conciseness, accuracy, and emphasis.

Don't send a report unless it does credit to your perception, organization ability, efficiency, and good judgment.

Don't send copies of your report to anyone until your superior approves and authorizes you to do so.

Are you willing to be judged by that report?

Mechanics of a Report

The *appearance and form* of a report should invite quick reading. The form for the report may be given to you or you may be expected to organize it and set it up. This is a test of your organizational ability and shows whether or not you are a clear thinker. Give your best effort to every report. Forms for reports vary according to the purpose or type, company policies, and importance of the report to your company.

Use good English, spelling, and punctuation. Use the third person when possible. Avoid *I*, (*we* is a form of *I*). Use names when necessary to make the point clear. Avoid indefinite *it, they, some, many.*

Select headings for important divisions, with subheadings for lesser points. Keep all headings parallel in construction. Underscore important words and use other devices to make points clear and reading easy. Keep the tense of the verb consistent. "The meeting *resulted* in . . . , action *was* taken to. . . ."

Use charts, graphs, diagrams, or tabulations of figures or facts if these clarify points. A tabulation of figures gives, at a glance, facts that would take pages to explain less effectively.

Check or mark in margin the particular point of interest to each person to whom a copy of the report is sent. In this way, one report of a meeting may be sent to several persons with different paragraphs checked for each person. A short memo may be sent with each report calling attention to the checked statement.

Keep reports as compact and short as possible to give the facts. Avoid too much detail. Stenographic help may not be adequate to handle unnecessarily long reports. Files are always crowded.

A Plan for a Report

From whom: Write your name and department in a top corner.

To whom: Be sure to send the report to the right persons. Usually the report is made to your immediate superior. She can tell you if copies are to be sent to other interested persons.

Title: Give the report an explicit short title that is a definite clue to the subject and that facilitates filing.

Give the report an explicit short title that facilitates filing.

DATE: Give complete date of meeting or time of report. If the report is for a period of time, give inclusive dates, as June 19—— to Jan. 19——.

PURPOSE: Give a statement of the purpose of the meeting, data, or other reason for the report.

REVIEW: This usually comes after the purpose. This may or may not be necessary to set the stage for the report. If a review of literature, previous events, or circumstances is important, state this briefly.

BODY OF REPORT: Use headings and subdivisions according to subjects, chronological or other logical sequences or activities. Begin each section with a topic sentence. Follow this with a sentence related to the topic. Use this same plan throughout the body of the report.

EVALUATION: Give your evaluation or summation of the report. This may be placed directly after the purpose to save the time of the person who receives the report. Remember that those in management positions receive a mass of reports which take up many office hours. Your evaluation and summary will indicate whether a follow-up conference on your report is important.

RECOMMENDATIONS: Make constructive suggestions for future action, changes, etc. Weigh these statements carefully to be sure you have a sufficiently broad experience to express this opinion. Do not overstep your position.

FOLLOWUP: List action that remains to be done to complete or follow up the report.

Kinds of Reports

There are so many kinds of reports that no attempt is made here to cover all variations. Many companies have certain forms for writing reports. You will find it helpful to check the method your associates have used in writing similar reports. As a beginner, you can learn from filed reports of others the best form to use for different occasions. You'll find that some of your associates are experts in giving facts in a clear, quickly read style. Others may include details and extra words which confuse the reader. You may have to decide when a subject or project requires a short memo, an informal note, a brief report, or a formal presentation or working plan. You may be asked to give an oral report as part of a group activity.

The kinds of reports you are most apt to make include:

Oral report.
Memorandum (Memo) on a conference, idea, or observation.
Report of a meeting of a committee or group in the company, trade association, professional society, or consumer affair.
Report of a trip, a new program or project, of progress on past work, or weekly, monthly, biannual activities.

Avoid taking credit for work done by others.

Oral Report

Never underestimate the importance of an oral report. Plan it, organize it, think it through, and outline it. Even if this is just a 5-minute conference with your director, know what you want to say. Stick to your subject. Have a pencil and notebook handy to write down her comments or directives.

You may be asked to give a report in a group meeting. This is a real test of your clear thinking.

Be sure you understand the purpose of the meeting and your part in the over-all plan. How much time are you allowed? Never take more than your allotted time. This requires careful selection of facts and clear organization.

Visualize your audience as you plan. Select statements that have meaning to that particular group. Keep to your subject. Do not take credit for the work of others. Plan the presentation to suit the size and character of the group. Don't be overdramatic. The tone of your report to a group of 6 should be different than that used for 600.

Plan and organize your facts. Make an outline of the major points. Limit the number of points to the time allotted you. Write out an opening sentence that tells what you plan to report. Don't be historical or take time to review the case, but if necessary, review past events briefly after you have stated the main purpose of your report. Develop each point sufficiently to make it clear, but do not belabor it or overwork a particular subject. Write a summary. You may write out your report, *but don't read it!*

Practice your talk, but do not give the impression you are reciting a piece. Speak from your own experience and prove that you know what you are saying.

The old advice is still good: Tell them briefly what you are going to say, say it, and tell them in summary what you have said. Time the report and keep to your time.

Notice whether other members of the group stand or sit to give their reports. Often, in company meetings, the group sits around a table or in an informal circle.

Face the group. Remember the protocol of your company, and address most of your report to the person of highest rank.

However, do not exclude others in the group. Talk *with* the group, not at them.

Relax. Speak clearly so that everyone can hear. Keep the tempo of your report lively, but don't race through it. Try to speak naturally and sincerely. Do not orate.

Be factual and be sure you can explain or expand the facts if there is a discussion period. Because oral reports are followed often by a question period, keep reference data at hand to give details if necessary. Charts or figures may be typed and handed out later if necessary. Be sure everyone can see any illustrative material you use.

If charts or illustrative material are helpful, plan these to suit the type of group. Overelaborate charts may be out of place. However, illustrative material may make your points easily and clearly and give the group a quick understanding of your presentation.

Avoid passing samples around; this distracts the attention and you may lose your audience. Watch the reaction of the group. If you are sensitive to the reception of your report, you may find it good practice to omit some portion of it. Learn a summary statement and give it. Stop on time.

Mannerisms in giving a report may detract from the forcefulness of your presentation. Dress the part so you won't feel self-conscious. Watch your posture in sitting and standing. Try to be at ease. Listen to the reports of the others. Forget yourself

Watch the reaction of the group.

and get into the spirit of the meeting. Remember, you are just one of the group and you aren't expected to give a stage performance. You are expected to give a clear, understandable report on the subject assigned to you.

Office Memo

To: Date:

From:

Subject: (*Example*: Booth, Wisconsin State Fair, August 12, 19——)

An office memo is usually an informal communication on a subject or portion of a subject. The subject may be used in subsequent memos or reports so that a file can be built up.

Some companies have forms for use in memos. Sometimes these forms state:

From the desk of . . . .

Memos are usually interoffice communications. They should be kept short, concise, clear.

Report of Business Meeting or Conference

Copies to: Name:
To: Date:
Name of meeting:
Purpose of meeting:
Attendance:
Main points of discussion:
Special points of interest to others in company:
Summary and evaluation:
Recommendations and follow-up:

Report of Consumer Meeting

Copies to: From:
To: Date:
Activity:
Name and title of contact:
Address of contact:
Attendance:
Summary:

(State important points in short paragraphs. List name, title, and address of speakers. If you were on the program, state your subject.)

These meetings may be called to explore a subject, to assign work, to set up a plan. Be sure to take notes on who suggested what, and get *accurate* statements. When in doubt, ask for a restatement, to be sure you understand. Report essentials only.

Always end your report with:

Evaluation:

(*Was meeting worthwhile?*)

Followup:

(*List statements to check, to report, to cause action, to send material, etc.*)

Progress Report

To: From:
Title: Date:
Review:

(*Give former work or report in brief paragraph.*)

Progress:

(*Give a brief statement of work since last report.*)

Remaining work to be done:

(*Give a brief statement.*)

Summary and conclusions when complete:

(*Try to indicate value to company, suggested use of whole or part of work, other projects suggested by findings.*)

Convention Report

Copies to: From:
To: Date:
Name of Association:
Place:
Dates:
Good Talks
    Speaker, title:
    Subject:
    Good points made:
Contacts
    Name, title, address:
    Subject of discussion:
    Followup:

Exhibits
    New or unusual features:
    Names, addresses:
Evaluation or worth to company:

Travel Report

(Forms to fill in each evening save time and act as reminders of important facts.)

Name and address of superior:

                              Name of reporter:
                              Dates included in report:
                              Monday ————————————

Activity:
Name of contact:
        Title:
        Address:
Attendance: (Number)
Evaluation of contact:
Material requested:
Activity:

(A summary page for entire week condenses report. The right kind of forms for your work minimizes time for you, for the stenographer, and for your superior.)

Project Report

Presenting a project or plan of action is a real challenge to your ability. Do not underestimate the importance of this presentation. Make it clear, concise, and complete.

Before you write your first project report, ask to see other reports that have been submitted so that you can see the style that is acceptable. Different departments in a company use different styles and forms. The form used to report a research project is different than that used to present an advertising campaign, a plan for a sales meeting, or a proposal for an employees' open house.

The project report may be for a proposed project or for a finished project.

Think it through. Try writing your ideas as they come to you. Then reorganize and rework the plan. Let it rest a day or so in order that you can look at it critically to be sure it is logical, complete, and essential.

Keep the style consistent — either formal or informal. Watch the sentence structure to avoid long, involved sentences.

Outline your report. Use strong sentence subjects with explanatory sentences under each heading.

Use complete direct sentences that are easily and quickly read.

Give enough detail to inform the reader, but omit unnecessary details.

Develop the subject in logical sequence of time or importance of points.

Analyze and check your report.

What is the project?   (Title)
Why is it important?   (Purpose)
Who is involved in work?   (Cooperation)
How will you proceed?   (Method or plan)
When will you begin and finish work?
What is the estimated cost?

Rewrite your report until you are sure it sells your idea. Talk with your immediate superior about it, to make certain you haven't presumed too much or underestimated the project. Ask for suggestions, help on certain phases, and guidance to make the project complete. It is good judgment to get the best possible advice before you write the final report.

If this is a proposal, ask yourself, *what of it?* Is it worth the time and money?

If this is a report on a finished project, give an evaluation and state any suggestions that may be helpful for future work.

Weekly and Monthly Report

Some companies ask for a weekly or monthly report of work. These reports are usually set up according to a definite outline to give facts and figures. Reference may be made to project numbers or titles. These time-unit reports can give a condensed picture of activities and can act as an index of work for future reference. If you have kept a good daily record book, you will find it is easy to compile a weekly or monthly report.

Annual Report

What did you accomplish during the year? What do you want to accomplish next year?

An annual report is one of the best methods of checking your progress and charting your future. Whether you are required to make an annual report or not, you will profit by making a report for yourself.

If you have made monthly reports, you can tabulate results, figures, and data under activity headings. Look through your daily records, your file of memos, project reports, and all other reports. Take time to analyze and evaluate these.

You may find that a project that seemed important at the time does not seem to be as valuable in the light of the entire year. Weigh each activity in relation to the value to the company.

Group your activities into units so that similar projects are reported together, even though there was a time lapse between them. Plan your report by activities rather than by dates. Condense the facts to give a clear but concise statement of results.

Remember — this report may be sent to top management. Give enough explanation to make each activity clear, but do not give unnecessary details.

Give figures of cost and profit, number of items, minutes on radio or television, and total contacts. Chart data when possible to give a quick, complete picture.

Begin the report with a strong statement of the scope of the work, trends of increases, decreases, and changes. The first paragraph should set the stage for the report.

The organization, planning, analysis, writing, rewriting, checking, revision, and final writing will make use of all your skill in writing reports, your objective interpretation of values, and your comprehension of your ability to serve your company.

Condense the facts to give a clear but concise statement . . .

CHAPTER 10

Whose Money Are You Spending?

THE DREAM of most newcomers to business is to have an expense account. The very idea of traveling, dining, and entertaining without paying your own money for these pleasures sounds intriguing.

Remember that a business is run for profit. A company that does not make a reasonable profit cannot continue in business.

Actually, anyone who spends the money of a company has a grave responsibility to make every expenditure return a profit. You can be rash with your own money, if you wish, because you have to account only to yourself. When you spend the company's money you have to account to someone for every penny you spend.

In most companies there is a very definite policy about who can spend, for what, and how much. If you ever have an expense account questioned and are asked to explain some item, you will realize that one or several people check these accounts for accuracy of figures and established practices for expenditures.

The policy of allowable expenses varies greatly from company to company. Naturally, some types

. . . you have to account to someone for every penny you spend.

of work require more use of an expense account. An executive position is usually permitted a more liberal allowance than a lesser position.

The cardinal rule is to know whether you are allowed to spend company money and *what limitations* are placed on these expenditures.

Office Equipment Is Worth Money

Essential office supplies, work tools, and equipment usually are supplied by a company to make work more efficient. These are the property of the company and should be given the care and attention necessary to produce the most good. Too often, workers are careless with company equipment and do not appreciate that replacements cost money and cut down profits.

In large companies the cost of pencils alone runs into a staggering figure. The cost of stationery and all the many forms, clips, pins, erasers, and a hundred-and-one little items mounts up into real money. Then there are the large items of furniture and equipment that are very expensive. It's so easy to expect a private office with movie-type fixtures, but some of the best work is produced in very modest surroundings. Some companies consider a *front* and expensive equipment as a legitimate expense. Others are keyed to modest furnishings. Whatever the policy is, the operation costs are weighed against returns in profits. As an employee, you should operate on the level of necessary costs and avoid waste of supplies and destruction of equipment.

This is not a grim picture. It is just good business. Usually the more definite the policies of allowable expenditures, the easier it is for you to abide by the rules and not be embarrassed by having your expenses questioned.

Petty Cash

Your work may necessitate a petty cash fund to be kept on hand for the payment of minor items. For this, keep a running account of withdrawals or keep receipted bills in the cash box so that you can give a report on the uses for which the money was spent.

Purchase Slips

Some companies allow certain persons to buy special articles. The receipted bills, together with a request form for money spent, can be okayed by a designated person so that payment may be received. Usually, there is a rule as to the type of article which may be purchased and a price limit for such a transaction. A purchasing agent often gets a discount on certain items. Therefore, it is not economical for individuals to buy these items at retail prices. Occasionally, you may be allowed to shop for items and get a description, price, and other data to make it possible for the purchasing agent to put in a confirming order.

It is best to learn the company rules before you order supplies or spend your own money for supplies or equipment needed in your work.

Transportation

Transportation on company business is usually considered legitimate expense, but the cost often is weighed against the need. Should you use public transportation, a company car, a rented car, your own car, or a taxi?

This question of how you travel is answered by company policy. If a company car is provided, you should know your responsibilities in regard to general care and in case of car trouble or accident. What is covered by company insurance? Must the car be parked in a garage? Is there a rule that requires registration of destination and type of business, as well as authorization for use of the car? Are you permitted to let someone ride with you? Will you be allowed to buy repairs, have towing service, and buy gasoline? It pays to find out first, rather than after the emergency arises.

Under certain circumstances a company may approve using a car rental service. Check on the company policy and procedure before accepting the responsibility of a rented car. Is there a company identification and credit card for you to use? What records will you need in reporting the expense? What about insurance?

The use of your own car for business purposes may or may not be allowed. Some companies allow a certain mileage cost, with payment for oil and other operative costs. Certain requirements for insurance usually are made. Whether you drive your own or a company car, you will usually be required to keep a record of mileage — an accurate record, too!

Taxi service may be required in your work but this is not to be taken for granted. Ask before you spend your money for taxi fare.

Train, plane, and boat transportation may be ordered through a company transportation department and the most economical service chosen. Your business needs and your rank in the company will influence the kind of transportation provided. You may want to go by the way of (via) a certain city, but be sure the company agrees to this route before you order or buy the ticket. Few companies expect employees to *see the world* at company expense. Do be reasonable and fair. Do find out what is expected and accepted as reasonable transportation costs.

When you are planning any transportation expense, consider how you would travel if you were paying for it yourself. Usually your company will allow as good, if not better, accommodations because they want you to do an efficient job. You will be expected to guard your health, to make the best use of your time, and to be a good representative for your company.

Traveling Expense

Expenses allowed when you are away from your headquarters are different than when you are at home. Before you leave on a trip, find out if you are allowed complete or partial expenses. Is there a form for filing expenses? Is your report due the day you

Your business needs and your rank in the company will influence the kind of transportation provided.

return, each week, or at the end of a trip? To whom is the expense report given?

Most important of all is a clear understanding of what is considered *reasonable expenses.*

Some companies allow a certain amount per day (per diem) for room and for meals. Others allow a set amount for each meal. Again, some companies ask that the actual cost of each meal be given and the tip included. The allowable room rate and cost of meals usually is explained to an employee. So, too, there must be an understanding as to expenses of telephone, telegrams, and business supplies.

Some positions require entertainment of customers and other business guests. What is expected of you and how much can you spend for entertainment? If you are entertained, should you indicate no charge for the meal or are you expected to make a reasonable repayment with a courtesy gift?

Are you allowed laundry and pressing service? Are you permitted to hire an assistant for some work? Be sure you understand

There is considerable difference in company policies concerning gratuities . . .

about deduction forms and regulations for social security payments.

How about tipping? Are you expected to include the cost of tips for meals? for taxi service? for the doorman at the hotel? There is considerable difference in company policies concerning gratuities for services.

Your company expects to pay for legitimate expenses but not for your entertainment or personal pleasures. Magazines, theatre tickets, meals for personal friends, gifts, and the many other tempting purchases which traveling may suggest are *personal* expenditures.

Whose money are you spending? Your code of ethics need not and should not make you unhappy in deciding what is right and justifiable company expense. To save embarrassment or out-of-pocket losses, know ahead of time the legitimate expenses the company will reimburse you for.

If your company provides a form for use in submitting expenses, keep up the record each day. Perhaps a small notebook in your purse will help. You'll be surprised how easy it is to forget little items and to find you can't account for several dollars you know were spent for business reasons.

Keep receipts for expenses such as transportation, hotel bills, and other sizable bills. Find out what receipts are essential so that you won't have to make an excuse for an item that is justifiable.

Is it fun to have an expense account? It is bothersome unless you are a methodical person who is trained to keep a record of what you spend when you spend it. It is a responsibility to use someone else's money and to get full value for it. You have to use judgment in deciding what is right to spend and what is extravagant or even dishonest.

Budgets

Some types of work may require you to operate under a fixed sum set up as a budget for a specific period or for a specific activity. Knowledge of the scope of the work and of accurate costs for each phase of the work are essential in setting up a budget. Planning a budget for any job requires experience. Too high a projected budget may result in cancellation of the project. Too low a budget may hamper the effectiveness of the work.

If you must set up a budget for your work, consult your immediate superior. Discuss every phase of the work before making a definite plan. Consider the cost of all supplies, labor, overhead, and those specific activities related to the work.

When the budget is accepted, you should keep an accurate account of all expenses, commitments, and projected costs. Watch your arithmetic. A misplaced decimal point can be a tragic error! Most things cost more than you expect. It is not good business to spend too much too soon and thus penalize your work toward the last of the budget period. Management seldom accepts without investigation and question any request for a new budget to cover a deficit.

If you have an opportunity to work on a budget, you gain excellent experience. The higher you climb on the professional ladder, the more certain you are to have to project a plan of activities, to estimate the cost, and to weigh the value received against the money spent.

It is excellent business training to get a good return on all sums of money you spend for your company.

CHAPTER 11

You Are in Public Relations

YES, you are in public relations as soon as you accept a business position. Of course, you have been a part of the public relations of several groups even before you entered business, though you may not have realized it. That is to say, your conduct as a part of your school, your church, your clubs, your community, and even your country has helped to determine the public's opinion of those groups or organizations.

It has been said that the most important factor in determining our lives is our relation with the people with whom we come in contact.

In business work, the term *public relations* takes on new significance because public relations has become a motivating force throughout every modern business organization. Your company may have a Department of Public Relations which carries on a company program, but each individual on the payroll is a contributing member to that program.

What Is Public Relations?

You'll find many definitions of public relations. In fact, one hears this term and reads about it frequently in connection with a business or trade association; industries such as banking, insurance, or motion pictures; a philanthropic organization such as the Red Cross; public services such as the public library or public transportation; and government services such as the armed forces or the United States Treasury savings bond program.

A public relations program for a business concern tries to establish for the company a good reputation based on high moral standards and ethical principles.

Who is this "public" that determines the reputation of your company? It is all the people who have contact with the company or who hear about the company and who, by word or action, affect the company. That can mean a great many people! This is especially true when you realize that your company is not just a name or a group of officers. Your company is made up of people, including all the employees from the chairman of the board to the part-time worker. In this way, every employee of your company helps determine its reputation. Therefore, when you are employed you contribute to the public relations of your company.

The importance of people is a relatively recent concept of modern business which places an extra responsibility on each employee as well as on management. As an employee, you not only assume responsibility for your own reputation but you contribute to the reputation which the public attributes to your company.

Publicity and Public Relations

Public relations is not to be confused with publicity, which is just one of the tools of the public relations program. Publicity means acquainting the public with the goods, services, and policies of the company. Publicity is a word that has been abused by stunts and extravagant devices to get public attention for many kinds of products, affairs, and people. Use of good publicity to interpret the company to the public will be discussed in Chapter 12.

As part of the company public relations program, you should understand your relation to management, your co-workers, and the company's public.

Management and Public Relations

The management officers of your company have established policies to guide the public relations program. If your position is one in which you sell goods or services to the public, you are taught the fundamentals of salesmanship in terms of good relations with your customers. Even if you do not meet the customer-public in your work, you do influence public opinion in your outside contacts.

The company reputation is your Number One business. Learn all you can about your business organization through company magazines, publications, letters to employees and to the public, and through advertisements and personal contacts with company personnel. Then you can speak with authority and confidence.

You and the Public

You are an ambassador of good will to make friends for your company. How often can you perform this assignment effectively?

If you are in a position of direct contact with the public, you should make a conscientious effort to study and practice the art of salesmanship. You may think you are selling just products or services but, always, you are selling the good will of your company. If you can, take a course in salesmanship. This has become a highly skilled profession in our competitive system of free enterprise. You can get books and magazines on salesmanship from the public library. Learn to be a good salesman.

Personal contacts represent an important method of establishing good public relations. These contacts may be during business hours or in your association with people outside your work. These contacts may be person to person, or in small or large groups. Wherever you are known as an employee of the company you can build good will.

This responsibility can be most stimulating and helpful in developing your personality. You may be timid and hesitant about selling your ideas, your accomplishments, or your successes. But if you are convinced of the quality of your organization's products, services, and ethics, you will find it easy to sell ideas, accomplishments, and the success of your company. You will learn to think in terms of *you* and *we*. You will become more interested in people, how they think, what they need and want, and how they react to suggestions. Human relations take on new meanings when you represent a company instead of just yourself.

You will appreciate readily the importance of personal contacts if you stop to think why you shop at one store instead of another. You often go to the store to get a brand of goods you can trust. But if two stores sell the same brand, *you shop where you like the people.* Sometimes your choice of brands is decided by the reputation of the company or the people who represent the company.

You can directly and indirectly influence the financial success of your company by your good public relations.

Criticism and Complaints

All of us like to receive praise and approval of our work. Generally, however, we learn more by conscientious analysis and appraisal of criticisms and complaints. Your work would be easier if everyone agreed with you, but personal opinions, needs, and wants differ.

In your work, give serious consideration to every complaint received from a customer. This is not an easy task. A natural reaction is to defend the company and to belittle the judgment of the complainer. But stop to think, "How can I win a friend?" If the complaint is received when you are talking to a person, you can establish a friendly attitude and try to understand that person's viewpoint. What are the facts about the product, the service, the causes for the complaint? Perhaps the complaint is justified. Mistakes do happen.

If the product is wrong or the service faulty, follow the company policy in correcting this situation, or get advice from the company on handling this case. Always make sure the customer understands that this is an exception and that you are glad it was reported to you. The confidence of the customer is of greater value than the cost of the product.

Often you will find that your company gives very definite instructions on handling complaints.

A natural reaction is to belittle the judgment of the complainer.

There will be an established rule as to your attitude toward the customer, the degree of authority to make amends, the method of reporting the complaint, and the follow-up procedure.

If the complaint is received in a letter, be prompt in answering. Take time to visualize the sender of the letter. And *always* give the benefit of the doubt to the writer. Be friendly and helpful and make a friend. Letters in answer to complaints will be a real test of your tact and your ability to turn a dissatisfied customer into a loyal customer. That is good public relations.

Friendly Competitors

Good relations between competitors are a part of today's modern business. Associations, institutes, and other organizations of companies with similar interests have established a code of ethics for mutual benefits and for good competitive practices.

In your loyalty to your company you may be overzealous. Never underestimate the value of a good competitor. Competition is the basis of our free enterprise system. You should be able to sell your company, its products, and its service on merit, without resorting to unjust references to your competitors in business. You should become informed on the products and practices of competitors but you will win more friends for your company if you play the competitive game fairly. Criticism of another company, its products, services, or employees is not a socially desirable practice. Good public relations means good conduct in all business relations.

Telephone Relations

How are your telephone relations? Whether you make a call or answer a call, do you show the same friendly courtesy you would if you were talking directly to the person? Do you keep a pencil and pad handy to jot down names and important points? Do you always remember you are speaking for your company? Reread the suggestions for use of the telephone in Chapter 8. Telephone courtesy is often emphasized in company policy because the telephone plays such an important part in establishing a good reputation for your company.

Letters and Public Relations

Do you write letters to your friends when you have some news to tell or when you can be of help to them? Then, you know the person to whom you are writing and can imagine the reaction to your letter. Perhaps you are like most girls and have been rather careless about the stationery you used, the appearance of the letter, spelling, and lapses of good English. You may have excused yourself by saying, "My friends understand me and won't care as long as they get a letter."

A very different situation occurs when you write a business letter to an unknown or slightly-known person. There, the cold facts of appearance and content speak to your public. There is no one to interpret your meaning or to say, "She means well."

When you are in business, you may find that letters become an important part of your contact work with the public. You may have to write many kinds of letters to many kinds of people. Their opinion of your company may be influenced by just *one letter* you write. Isn't that a sobering thought? Isn't it important that you make a conscientious effort to write the right kind of letter?

Although one of the most important ways to build good will is through personal contacts, letters can be almost as effective. Too, they reach a vast audience which you could never contact personally. Each business letter can be an ambassador of good will. Winning and holding good will is a big public relations job.

Your Attitude

You is one of the most powerful words in the English language. We all like to feel important and to feel that a letter brings a personal message from the sender. The *you* approach connects the message from sender to receiver.

When you write a letter, try to visualize the person to whom you are writing. Write to a person, not to a name.

Learn From Letters Received

You can learn many things from the letters you receive. Did the sender misspell your name or send it to *Mr.* instead of *Miss*? Was the company name wrong? A *you* approach in such a letter fails to carry much weight in giving a personal feeling.

Can you get an idea of a need or a desire from the mail you receive? Sometimes a letter points the way to a new approach in messages to the public. When someone takes time to write to the company, this fact indicates consumer reaction. If several letters bring a similar point of view, you will become more aware of the significance of the reaction.

Never underestimate the importance of letters received. Never take lightly the responsibility of reading and answering business letters.

Practice Letter Writing

Learn to write good letters, the kind you like to receive. From your analysis of the letters you receive, you can learn what to avoid as well as what words, phrases, and styles arrest your attention and give you a friendly feeling. Practice writing letters and reading them critically. Then rewrite them. Would you like to receive such a letter?

Sometimes you'll find that a company allows different kinds of stationery for special letters. This means that you may be able to have more personalized and less formal stationery than the standard business paper.

The form of the letters may be set by company policy but leeway may be given for salutations and closings for letters from your department. There is a trend to make business letters less stilted and formal so that the receiver feels the friendly personality of the letter writer.

The purpose or reason for writing the letter often determines the form of the salutation and close. The body or the real message varies in content and form but the spirit of friendliness should permeate even the most routine letter.

The Aim or Purpose of the Letter

Why should anyone take time to read your letter? Most business people are very busy. Today, so many kinds of mail are received in most offices and homes that yours must be distinctive in order to attract the interest and attention you wish.

You may have to write so many letters that you become bored and irked by the task. This need not be so if you appreciate the importance of each letter as a good public relations service. Letter-writing can become a challenging work which requires continuous study and effort to improve your style. If you excel at letter-writing, you have learned the basic points of orderly thinking, clear expression, and personalized presentation, and these will prove invaluable in many other areas of your work.

Every letter should be friendly, sincere, and personalized. Don't try to fool your public by big words that mean little. Short words that express your meaning are most effective. *You* is the key attention-getter. Strong verbs activate your message, whereas strings of adjectives may look amateurish. Strive to invite reading, give information, complete the message, avoid misunderstanding, and make a friend.

Remember that the person who receives your letter should get a mental picture of a company of friendly people.

Your Message

The main part of your letter requires thought. The first sentence gets attention or loses it. The first paragraph sets the stage. Don't *back into* a letter. Give the reason for writing and let the receiver decide whether she is interested in finishing the letter.

Before you start the letter, think, *Why am I writing to you? What have I to say to you?* Think what you have to say and say it. Show the same courteous spirit you would if you were talking to the person.

Avoid stilted phrases like, "Yours of the 25th received." How much better to say, "Thank you for your letter of June 25th . . ." or "How kind of you to take time to write to us about our new . . ."

Do not belabor a point or ramble along without a

The first sentence gets attention or loses it.

plan, but avoid terse and abrupt sentences that jolt the reader or fail to invite continued reading.

Questions are interest-getters. This is especially so if you ask for help or an opinion.

Will you help us decide what kind of booklet will be most useful to you and other women in setting up a savings plan? Enclosed are two ways of giving the same facts. Which one do you like better, number 41 or number 19? (Give a choice.)

Avoid sarcasm, criticism, or any indication that you doubt the sincerity or right of the sender to the opinion expressed in her letter. Praise first before you suggest a different opinion or explain a possible reason for the complaint.

You are very right in objecting to the advertisement if you have had difficulty in buying this lamp in your store. We sincerely appreciate your suggestion and shall contact your dealer to ask him to stock this lamp for you and other good customers. In the meantime, we hope you will enjoy glancing through the enclosed booklet which gives pictures and descriptions of other attractive home furnishings.

* * *

Thank you for taking time to write to us. Of course, we are very sorry you are not completely satisfied with our lamp. We appreciate your telling us about it so we can send one of our representatives to call on you to find the real cause of the trouble.

Some letters you receive may seem unjust and harsh. Your loyalty makes you rise to a defense and you write a letter that sets the person in her place. That's all right. *Blow off steam* if you must but *never* send the letter! Put it aside for a day. Rewrite it. Read it aloud to someone and get the reaction. *Will my letter help to correct a feeling of ill will or will it antagonize the person who receives it?* You never know the many reasons that caused the writing of the complaint letter. Maybe the letter was a release for hurt feelings caused by something not related to your company.

Avoid dramatics. A letter is not a sales bulletin.

Avoid slang, overworked phrases, and *cute* expressions.

Avoid *I* and use *we* and *our*. Also sprinkle *you* liberally through your message.

Leave the reader with a feeling that your company is a good, friendly company, economically sound and socially desirable. That is good public relations.

The Office Memo

To help mail distribution, intercompany letters are usually written on different stationery than letters going to outsiders. If a memo, letter, or report is part of a file, give a title or a subject to the communication to make filing easier:

"Convention, National Association of Advertisers" or "Re: Convention N.A.A."

Re is an abbreviation of the Latin word *res,* meaning *thing. Re* is commonly used in business for *in re* or *in regard to* or *referring to.*

Keep office memos short, to the point, but complete in meaning. Don't neglect courtesies and the friendly cooperative approach. Avoid criticism of co-workers, opinions based on too few facts, or negative suggestions. Remember modern business needs creative suggestions and open minds to work out problems together.

Re: Your Memo June 15.

Your suggestion sounds like a good one, and I'll be glad to chat with you about the plans. I've been thinking about the problem and will bring my notes along to see if you think they have merit.

Set the stage for a good conference even though you can't agree with the proposed plan at the present. Listen to the whole idea. Then you may give your constructive suggestion for a change.

Cultivate good employee relations.

Letters Concerning Legal Affairs

You may receive letters offering to sell an idea or a gadget. Do not attempt to handle these letters without legal advice since they may involve questions of patents and copyrights. You *are* the company when you answer on business stationery. Your letter could prove costly.

Letters for the Experts

Your letter of June sixth asking for an explanation of the shortage of women's hosiery is sincerely appreciated. You certainly have a right to know why this shortage occurs.

We are referring your letter to Mr. L. R. James of Lee Company who is an expert on the many questions of supplies needed for the manufacture of hosiery.

Because of your interest in consumer problems, we are sending you some of our booklets that tell about interior decoration, and include items which our company manufactures.

(Send a copy of this letter to Mr. James of Lee Company.)

Don't attempt to be an expert on subjects outside your field. If someone in your company can answer the letter, send it to him. But if the letter refers to a product or problem outside your company, suggest a person who can give help. If possible, make the connection so that the answer is handled promptly.

You may get questions about everything from battleships to mouse traps.

Letters Giving Reason for a Delay

You may think we overlooked your request for information on our film but we assure you we have not. We are so sorry there has been a delay in publishing this brochure but you'll get your copy just as soon as it is off the press. We hope you'll agree that it is worth waiting for.

(*Delays are understandable, if explained.*)

Letters of Apology

Will you please forgive our error in sending the wrong booklet to you? We misread your letter, perhaps because we have been receiving so many requests for the new booklet we sent you.

(*To err is human.*)

Thank You Letters

Thank you takes so little time to say or write, yet how powerful these two words are.

Thank you for your kindness to me when I was in your city.

Thank you for including me among your guests yesterday.

Courtesies extended to you in a business capacity require the same expressions of appreciation as those of your personal life. Write a note thanking those who helped you on a committee, who asked you to speak to a club meeting, on the radio, or in any other public relations capacity.

Even when a meeting is large and the guest list was selected automatically, write a note of appreciation. You may have been lost in the crowd, but you become a person in your thank-you letter.

Letters of Congratulation

Congratulations and good wishes upon your recent admission to the Illinois Bar. We hope your future will bring you still higher honors and even greater successes. We are looking forward to serving you . . .

(Make a new friend and customer.)

Congratulations to you on completing the planned savings through an endowment policy. To start a plan requires foresight. To complete the plan as you have, requires real strength of character . . .

(Keep a friend and customer.)

Requests for Information

Take time to answer letters asking for information. Read the letter carefully so that you understand the real need. Perhaps you can send additional help in the form of booklets, reprints of articles, or advertisement. Be sure this material goes forward promptly.

Invitations Received

You may receive invitations to openings, exhibits, publicity luncheons, and other business affairs. Good business etiquette is the same as personal etiquette. Write promptly. Show apprecia-

You are the company when you answer on business stationery.

tion for the invitation. State your intention to accept, give a reason for declining, or, possibly, suggest an alternate associate to represent your company. Do not accept for yourself and then request that you be allowed to bring a fellow-associate.

Invitations Sent

Invitations to company affairs may be formal or informal, depending on the nature of the affair and the people to whom the invitation is sent. Formal invitations are written in the third person in a manner similar to a wedding or reception invitation. Informal invitations should give the necessary information in an easily read way. State the reason for the meeting and the name and address or telephone number of the person to whom the reply is to be sent.

Will you have luncheon with us June sixth at one o'clock at the Lowry Hotel? Some of us at Lane Company would like to tell you about a new product we're introducing in this market.
We hope you can be with us. We promise to keep the presentation short so you will feel free to leave at 2:30 P.M. if you wish.

Sometimes novel features are used for invitations. But you had better consult your friends in advertising before you attempt a dramatized invitation. These can be a bit foolish.

Letters to Company Employees

Here's the new booklet we offered in a recent advertisement. We want you to be one of the first to see it because we know you, too, are proud of the progress our company has made in this new work.

(*Strengthen the bond of cooperation and mutual interest.*)

Letters to Business Friends

Your letter was a most welcome one because we were just noting on our calendar that convention time is almost here.
We'll be glad to meet with you to plan. . . .

Accept professional work in organizations without saying how busy you are. If you can't work on a committee, give a better reason than that of being busy and offer to help in another way.

Do not be *high-hat* or formal with those in your line of work. Avoid boring them with talk of your work, your success, or your problems. These associates are naturally a bit critical and analytical of you and others in the same work. Teamwork and coopera-tion help all of you to give better service.

Requirements for Writing Letters

A business letter is one of the most important tools in the business world. A letter can be worth a definite amount of money or can be an intangible, but equally valuable, item to the company as good public relations.

A good letter requires:

Understanding and imagination to know your subject and your public.
Appreciation of and respect for human nature.
Good command of English to express ideas clearly and concisely.
Good judgment in selecting the proper approach to the message.
A refined sense of humor and good balance in treating each person
as an intelligent, honest individual, thereby gaining his respect.
Constant evaluation of its contents as a means of good public rela-
tions.

Talks, Radio, Television

Public relations through appearances before groups requires special skill and thorough planning. Suggested help on these problems is given in Chapter 14.

Commercial Research

Many companies have a Commercial Research Department or employ the services of a research organization to investigate and report on public thinking about the product, services, and good conduct of the company. Sometimes this is called *market analysis* because, by surveys and research, this department analyzes con-sumer attitudes toward products and the business behind the products.

One company's written code states that "to have good conduct, a business must be economically sound and socially desirable." Economic soundness means that the company must satisfy people's wants and must be run efficiently to make a profit. The Com-mercial Research Department makes planned contacts with se-lected segments of the public to sample public opinion and report to management a true analysis of facts.

This is no work for a beginner. Too often, unskilled people attempt to get an expression of public opinion through personal interviews or through questionnaires.

In statistical analysis, it is most important that you have the skill to limit the problem; to select the type, size, and location of the group for *sampling;* to word the questions properly; and to set up the other mechanics of the survey.

In your work, you may want to conduct a small survey to get an expression of consumer likes and dislikes. The best advice to you is, "Don't, until you have read a recent book on the techniques of conducting a survey and can fully understand the mechanics of this work and the dangers of faulty conclusions." If you follow this advice, you will probably conclude that surveys of public opinion are scientific works to be handled by experts. If you are to do this kind of work, be prepared to study and learn the correct methods.

You probably will have occasion to hear and read reports of surveys. You may be asked to help set up a survey. If you wish to advance in your work, you will want to make a study of this important phase of business work.

People's likes and dislikes determine their opinions. It's the little things that count. You receive a letter that sounds stuffy, or unfriendly, or threatening. Your emotions influence your judgment, even though the sender of the letter did not intend to affect you in that way. A clerk in a store seems to treat you with disdain or suspicion. Your emotions cause you to form an opinion not only of the clerk but of the store that hired the clerk.

In this same way, the public forms opinions based on emotions and impressions. The commercial research experts try to determine what the public likes and doesn't like about the products, services, and company. They try to determine what factors influence the emotions, as well as the preferences, of the all-important public.

Management bases many policies and actions on results from scientific surveys.

The Public Relations Department

The Public Relations Department usually handles *external relations,* whereas the Industrial Relations Department is concerned with *internal relations,* as with employees. However, these activities are so interrelated that close cooperation is essential. As an employee, you will want to become acquainted with the people in these departments and their work. Their philosophies and methods of work will be helpful in guiding you in your contacts with the public.

The Public Relations Department is usually a storehouse of facts. Its members act as counselors to management and employees; they direct the written words that go to the public; and they advise those who talk to the public. Do not hesitate to consult with them on facts, policies, methods of presentation, and evaluation of your contacts with the public. Since you are in public relations work, you will increase your efficiency if you learn more about this work from those who have specialized and trained in this science.

Advertising

Advertising has become an integral part of our free enterprise system wherein a variety of goods and services is offered to many people. Each person has a free choice to select the product or service which suits his needs and wants.

The advertising for a business concern is usually handled by a department which is distinct from the Public Relations Department. Advertising plays a vital part in the public relations program in presenting an honest story of company goods, service, and general conduct. Some advertisements may be devoted entirely to telling about policies or services to the community and nation.

You will learn a great deal about your company by making a collection of its advertisements. Study the message set forth in the advertisement so that you can keep up-to-date on recent developments as well as methods used in the presentation of ideas.

You may be called on to help with the background information used in an advertisement or in the evaluation of media such as magazines, newspapers, radio, television, billboards, and car cards. You may be asked to help as a specialist in your field, as a consumer, or as a part of the public to whom the message is sent. Modern advertising is based on skilled work in research, techniques of presentation, and evaluation of results. You will find this a stimulating and fascinating activity of your company.

Whether you work with the advertising department or not, you will, no doubt, have occasion to discuss some phase of the advertisements with people you meet. You will be affected by this method of establishing the reputation of your company. You will want to be able to help interpret these messages in your contacts with the public.

Advertising Agencies

Advertising agencies are established to help companies which may or may not have a department to handle advertising. Many agencies have Commercial Research Departments and Public Relations Departments to further their services to a company. In your work, you may be called on to meet with members of one or several advertising agencies that service your company. Friendly cooperation and an appreciation of the many skills that are required for such a service can make this a valuable association for you. As a reader of advertisements you are familiar with the objectives of attention, interest, and sales behind each ad. If you have an opportunity to work on an advertising program, you will be amazed at the work involved in collecting the facts, in developing the technique to give the right impression to the public, and in helping to influence public opinion in favor of the company.

Industry and Trade Associations

Companies with similar interests usually join together in associations for mutual benefits, such as research, advertising, and public relations. Thus, we have associations for railroads, banking concerns, and insurance companies. You probably are familiar with the names of such trade associations as The American Meat Institute, The National Association of Radio and Television Broadcasters, The Public Relations Association of America, and The Association of National Advertisers. Your company may have membership in many associations. You may have

Your company may have membership in many associations.

an opportunity to participate in some of these associations and learn how these organizations work to set up standards of good conduct and get credit for this good conduct. You will see that these associations strive to improve the public relations of all the members.

Public Relations and Government Agencies

In your work as well as in your personal life, you must assume a responsibility for abiding by the laws and regulations of our national government. You may be asked to sign a statement that you will abide by certain trade regulations and practices between your company and the government. In any contacts with government agencies your conduct will be interpreted as that of a member of the organization for which you work. This is no idle responsibility. Get expert advice on how you should proceed in these contacts. Management of modern business expects employees to be law-abiding citizens and to conform to the spirit and practice of the law. This, too, is public relations.

Community Service

Modern business management accepts the responsibility of community service as part of the public relations program. Whether you are in a large or small company you will find that community relations play an important role in the success of the business.

Your company may encourage participation in the United Appeals, Red Cross drives, and other community services. Members of management may serve as officers on the school board, hospitals, charitable organizations, civic planning boards, and church organizations. This leadership in community affairs has resulted from a growing philosophy that civic activity is a moral responsibility of business.

As an employee of the company you will be expected to be a good citizen, too. The *know-how* gained in your work in business should make you a more valuable worker in community activities. However, since you are an employee, your civic activities cannot be disassociated from the company. Therefore, you may be wise to consult the public relations director before you become involved in the work of an organization, unless there is no question about the ethical purpose and practices of that organization.

Just as management assumes the responsibility of a good neighbor, you, as a member of business, should do your share for the betterment of the community in which you live. That is part of good public relations.

Research

Public relations is not just an activity. It is the motivating force for all activities. Modern business is alert to the importance of research to improve the standard of living through new and better products, greater efficiency of operation and distribution, and refinement and specialization of services. Your company may maintain a research laboratory or employ the service of research organizations. People expect business concerns to provide increasingly better products and services. Pasteur said, "Laboratories for scientific research are sacred places where the future is born."

You may find that your company not only maintains a research staff but also sponsors research programs in educational institutions. Grants-in-aid, fellowships, scholarships, and research awards totaling millions of dollars have been given to these institutions by industrial organizations. The findings of this research work are made available to other research workers and to the public.

This sponsorship of research is another phase of public relations. You should take an interest in the research work sponsored by the management of your company. You may have an opportunity to take part in this program by telling the public you contact about this extra evidence of good conduct.

Professional Organizations

Most companies encourage participation in the professional organization related to your work. This is another evidence of the operative philosophy which your company applies to all activities that promote the general welfare.

Your Co-workers and Public Relations

The loyalty of employees to the company and to their co-workers is not only sound business but is helpful in establishing the reputation of the company with the public.

You have met people who work in many different companies. Have you noticed that some people are intensely loyal to the products, the services, and the ethical practices of the company? Have you noticed the pride with which these people speak of "our company"? Your good opinion of such a company is most naturally influenced by the loyal attitude of these employees. In some cases, the reverse situation occurs. Some employees may not respect the company or their co-workers, with the result that you form a negative feeling for the company based on the complaints and criticisms of the employees.

How you think, talk, and act with co-workers is important in the over-all public relations program of your company. A friendly, cooperative attitude is part of the good conduct which is so essential in internal as well as external relations of a company.

Develop an appreciation of the importance of your attitude and behavior toward management, co-workers, and the public. Put into practice the philosophy that public relations is the responsibility of everyone.

Attending Business Meetings

Attendance at business meetings will become more and more frequent as you progress in your work. These meetings may be short conferences or semisocial affairs such as a luncheon, cocktail party, or dinner. Never overlook the business significance of such a meeting nor the ethics required.

Acknowledge each notice or invitation promptly. Be a good member of the group and do your part to make the meeting a success. Be a good guest. Listen to the message and later write a summation of the purpose and results of the meeting. If this was a semisocial affair, write a *thank you* note just as you would for a social affair not connected with business. As a representative of the company, your conduct at meetings in the company and outside is public relations.

Public Relations for You

Remember that the aim of a public relations program is to establish a good reputation based on high moral standards and ethical principles. This means that you, as an employee, should:

Assume your responsibility for a share in the public relations program for your company.

Do a good job in contributing to the service to the public and the community.

Tell the public that your company and you are doing this service.

Explain how this service is being done.

Form the habit of thinking in terms of good public relations.

Never allow an exception to occur.

Good Publicity Is an Asset

DID you ever see your name in the local paper and find it quite thrilling? If this publicity was due to the fact that you were chairman of a prominent club, helped in a worthy cause, won a contest, or displayed some special skill, your family and friends were proud of you. No doubt your circle of friends increased and even strangers remembered you as someone of unusual merit. If your name was linked to an unfortunate or undesirable incident, you probably wished you could have kept your name out of the paper and could have prevented the act that prompted the poor publicity.

Yes, good publicity is more than getting your name in the paper. Good publicity plays an important role in the success of a person, an organization, and a company. Publicity can be so powerful in influencing opinions that most business concerns make an organized effort to secure good publicity and to avoid any publicity that might be harmful to the welfare of the business.

Publicity and propaganda are often confused in meaning. Both refer to informing and influencing the

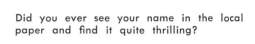

Did you ever see your name in the local paper and find it quite thrilling?

public. The basic features of publicity are names, places, dates. Who said it? Who did it? Is it new? Is it news? Does it interest the public? The responsibility for the statement or act is given specifically to a person or a group. In contrast, propaganda does not carry specific authorship. Propaganda aims to influence people's opinions about an idea, a group, or sometimes a person. It may be for a worthy cause, it may be justifiable, but it is more intangible and indefinite than true publicity. The author of propaganda is usually an indefinite *someone*.

We live in a highly competitive world. In order to be known, to gain prominence, and to gain public acceptance, we must devise ways and means to reach a large public with good publicity.

Personal Publicity

You personally, can become a publicity agent for yourself, for your company, and for organizations to which you belong.

Perhaps you have never thought of working to gain good publicity for yourself. But when you are in business, you will become aware of the importance of selling yourself and your good behavior to your company.

There is a delicate balance between justifiable pride in your work as compared to an overestimation of your importance in the company; between acceptable ways of attracting recognition to your ability as compared to overbearing actions to gain the attention of top management.

Your efforts to do a creditable piece of work can be made known to your superior by your oral and written reports. Copies of letters or memos which you receive containing praise for your work may be sent to her. This is legitimate publicity for you.

There is keen competition within a company and no one is expected to hide her light under a bushel. You should aim to do the kind of work that justifies attention. In your daily contacts within your company, your personal appearance, your actions, and your friendliness can mean good publicity for you.

Do you have a good reputation for being cooperative, sincere, reliable, and competent? Do you participate in company social activities as well as in business meetings? This is good publicity.

In a large company, it is easy to become lost in the multitude. The person who gets ahead is the one who produces results and gets credit for it. But remember the fundamentals of good publicity for yourself as well as for your company. Good publicity must arise from true statements of facts and worthy actions. Remember the old adage, "You can't fool all of the people all of the time."

You might remember, too, that one way to win friends is to work hard, but not bore them by talking about it. To get good publicity you must work hard and let your reports, contacts, and actions speak for you.

Publicity for the Company

As an employee, you can help gain good publicity for your company. In some positions you may play a very important part in publicity programs.

The Public Relations Department of a company usually directs the flow of publicity releases to the public through many channels. You may receive from this source notices of publicity which you, in turn, can pass on to your public.

The life blood of publicity is news, and people are the most interesting news to other people. Your company wants to gain honest, accurate publicity about its people, its products, and its services to the community and the nation.

News is anything that is interesting to the public. Good publicity is giving good news to the public.

In a large company, it is easy to become lost in the multitude.

Kinds of Publicity

There are many ways of getting good publicity, such as personal contacts in small and large groups; planned talks given at consumer and professional meetings; publicity releases sent to newspapers about products, services, or people; radio and television releases and personal appearances; films, booklets, and exhibits; publicity luncheons and other parties.

Personal Contacts

Even as a beginner, you can take part in good publicity for your company. Personal contacts are important means of telling good news to the public about the products, services, and people in your company. If you like your work and your company, you can spread good news. Your good judgment should caution you against repeating rumors or discussing with anyone outside the company any news that might prove to be harmful publicity.

Planned Talks

When you were in school, you gave talks before your class and other groups. Then you probably thought only of your pleasure or suffering at these appearances. When you are in business, you will find that more and more often you will have occasion to talk to groups in connection with your work, your professional contacts, or with some outside activity. Whatever your line of work, you may find that these talks to the public can become an important means of good publicity, not just for yourself but for your company. Whether a talk is for five minutes or an hour, you have an opportunity to influence the public and give a favorable impression of your company. In Chapter 13 suggestions are given for planning and giving talks.

Every public appearance offers an opportunity for newspaper publicity.

Publicity Releases for Newspapers

The responsibility for releases about products, policies, and people may be assigned to one person in your company, or to the Public Relations or Publicity Department. There is a code of ethics and established procedures for contacts with the press.

Before you attempt to send a release to a newspaper, be sure to ask if there is a person or department that handles company publicity. Today, in many companies, no one contacts the press personally or through releases unless trained for this work. That person understands the importance of good relations with the press and the philosophy of good publicity.

Perhaps your talk before a group has news value. If someone in the company writes publicity notices, you should give her complete information so that she can write a newsworthy story. If you handle your own publicity story, you will need to write out the important facts so as to include them in your story.

Here is a form that might be used for the basic information about your talk.

Request for Publicity for a Meeting

Writer of publicity:
Date of request:
Date of program or meeting:
Sponsor (organization) :
Sponsor's representative contacted:
Other newsworthy names:
Type of group:
Is meeting open to public?　(yes)　(no)　　Free? (yes)　(no)
Tickets available from:
Have you appeared before this group? (yes)　(no)　　When?
Place of meeting:
Title and brief abstract of your talk or demonstration:
　　Special points, features, etc.

Publicity desired, type:
　　Suggested introduction for use by program chairman:
　　Release for newspaper:
　　Release for magazine:
　　Photograph:
　　　　Mats (number)
　　　　Glossy prints (number)

Send publicity to:
　　Name:
　　Address:
　　City:　　　　　　　　　Zone:　　　　　　State:

Your name:

The example following shows a typical publicity release sent to a newspaper.

FROM: *Nutrition Department, Johnson Baking Company*
1130 State Street, Evansville, Indiana

"Nutrition for everyone" will be the subject of a talk by Jane Bolton, nutritionist for the Johnson Baking Company, at a meeting of the Lowry Parent-Teachers' Association at 8:30 P.M., Wednesday, January 9, according to Mrs. Adell Wyatt, Lowry PTA president.

Miss Bolton states, "Good nutrition is your business," and it is this theme upon which her talk will be based. The practical aspects of good nutrition and the dividends it pays in good health, good looks and good living will be stressed in her talk. She will show, too, how right foods can be easy to prepare and fun for the entire family to eat.

Colorful booklets illustrating Miss Bolton's talk will be distributed to all parents attending the meeting.

A graduate of Indiana University, Bloomington, Miss Bolton was on the staff of the National Nutrition Council before joining the Johnson Baking Company's Nutrition Department.

A news story must present a fact or series of facts and must give the source of the news. Who did it or will do it? Who said it or will say it? When? Where?

This is the attention-getting feature of the story and must be given in the *lead* or first sentence or paragraph. The five *W's* are the essence of publicity: *Who? What? Where? When? Why?* and sometimes *How?*

The news of next importance belongs in the second paragraph, and so on throughout the story. Newspapers are crowded for space and often cut releases. Keep the release short. Its length depends upon the size of the city. The larger the city and the newspaper the smaller *event* the meeting becomes. Give the news first, so any cutting will not kill your publicity.

Names are news. Perhaps your publicity will be more interesting to the readers if the first names mentioned are those of the club or organization president and the club she represents, with your name and affiliation given later as the guest speaker. This type of release is especially effective in the papers which give a page to news about clubs and organizations.

Your name and your subject may be important enough to

make the strongest impact. Remember, however, that you want publicity for your company, not for you personally. Your name becomes a tool to gain publicity for the company and its products or services.

Be sure to give complete names: first name, initial, last name, with titles and affiliations. Spell all the names correctly. Names are very personal, and misspelled names are irritating to most people. Give the correct title, as Mrs., Miss, Professor, Doctor. Add the address, too, so that the publicity carries authority.

Read the publicity notices in the paper you wish to contact. Note the style, the length, and the emphasis on names.

Does your publicity belong on the Woman's Page, or where? Write the kind of story that fits the plan of that page. If you can meet the editor of this section of the paper, you will be able to write the type of release she likes and will use.

The style of writing is so important that you cannot afford to disregard custom. Be sure of your facts. Keep the style simple. Avoid slang. Don't try to be clever. Keep the sentences short. Don't repeat words. Make the action move. Use strong verbs. Omit long descriptions and unnecessary adjectives. Tell your story briefly and simply. Then, *stop*.

A photograph may be sent with your release if you have a good business picture. This is especially true of smaller papers. If your work includes traveling, you may want to have mats made of your photograph so that you can offer the kind of picture most likely to be used.

Be sure your picture is good publicity. Consult your department head about what to wear, the pose, the kind of background, and the finish. In most cities, there are photographers who specialize in portraits for publicity. It is important to have the right kind for your work. The pose of a Hollywood star is not desirable for a businesswoman.

Some papers like action pictures. If these are used, do not send the same picture to more than one paper in a city. A portrait may be sent to several papers, however.

Send the release well in advance of your talk. Sunday feature pages are made up early; allow two to three weeks.

The Mechanics of Writing a Publicity Release

The mechanics of writing a publicity release should be followed, so that your story looks professional and gets attention.

Use 8½ x 11-inch plain white paper. Do not use the company letterhead. Always use a typewriter. Double-space and write on only one side. Avoid abbreviations.

Put your name, office address, telephone number, and the date at the top of the page. You may mark the release "For Immediate Release" or "Hold for Release . . . (date) ."

Begin the story halfway down the page so that the editor can write a headline.

Leave ample room at the sides for editing.

If the release is more than one page, number the pages and write "more" at the bottom of the first page and "30" at the end of the story.

Most women's and club sections of metropolitan newspapers are prepared well in advance of the publication date. Therefore, for best usage, submit the story at least two weeks in advance of the week you wish it to appear. When in doubt about a closing date, ask the club editor.

Address the envelope to the club editor by name, if you have the name. If not, address it merely to "Club Editor."

Reporter Interview

Your talk may be reported by a representative of the press. Always take time to give a press representative an interview. If questions are asked you, answer them if you are qualified and are sure of company policy. Give the reporter facts about the subject of your talk or work. Spell out names and technical terms so that

You may be surprised to read later what the reporter thought you said.

the reporter gets an accurate account. Be sure of your facts. Always consider what members of your company will think when they read this publicity. Try to avoid too much personal history which may lead to a news story about you rather than the company. Sometimes you may be surprised to read later what you said or what the reporter thought you said.

Action Picture

A newspaper may send a photographer to take action pictures. Try to get a picture that will do credit to the company. If possible, include a package or other item that gives definite evidence of your affiliation. Don't try to be cute or clever. Do play fair with the press and you will get fair treatment in return. The press wants news.

Don't try to be cute or clever.

Abstract of a Talk

Sometimes you may be asked to prepare an abstract of your talk for publicity. This condensed version of a talk is especially desirable for technical papers. Select the facts of interest to the public. Give the main facts of your talk in about 50 words. Omit descriptive phrases. Use complete sentences and make the reading smooth. Try to omit technical words that will not be understood by the public. An abstract of a talk requires real skill in condensation, but it is an effective means of giving to the press an authentic report of a paper or an address.

Here is an abstract of a 30-minute talk given by Jane Robinson, Nutritionist, of the John Day Company.

The Protein and Amino Acid Story

The era of concentrated research for new vitamins, their food source and use in nutrition has been succeeded by an increasing amount of research on the important role played by protein and the different amino acids contained in different protein foods.

Researchers on Biochemistry and Nutrition now agree that at least ten of these amino acids are essential to good nutrition. Meat and other animal protein foods contain these essential amino acids and have a superior biological value. Animal proteins are used in pre- and post-operative cases and for ulcers, severe burns, and other cases where a rapid growth of new tissue is important. Meat is used in the diet of tiny infants. High quality protein is needed for the preschool child, the adolescent, and the adult. Complete proteins are important in diets for older people, too.

A recently established concept is that the essential amino acids are needed at every meal and that animal protein foods best fulfill this requirement for amino acids.

An Introduction for Your Talk

Few people have the gift of giving a good introduction for a speaker. Take with you a prepared introduction or send it in advance to the club chairman to make certain you are properly introduced. The introduction should make clear your association with your company, the field of your work, and the experience or training which qualifies you to speak on the subject.

Example of Introduction for Your Talk

Good nutrition is everybody's business. And an important business it becomes, too, when we consider the dividends of good health, good looks, and good living it pays for each and every one of us.

Our speaker tonight has a key to good eating for all of us. She is a graduate in nutrition from Indiana University. She has been a practicing nutritionist, first with the National Nutrition Council and now as a staff member of the Nutrition Department of the Johnson Company. It gives me great pleasure to introduce Miss Jane Bolton.

Radio and Television Publicity

Radio and television have become important media for publicity. When you enter the business field, you may be given an opportunity to appear on a radio or television program. The types of presentation are discussed in Chapter 14.

Time on radio and television is expensive. Those in charge of programs have a responsibility to the public as well as to the management of the station to police the programs. If you have an interesting story to tell and the ability to tell it, you may contact the person in charge of a special program. However, it is always better if the director of your department or someone in the Publicity Department writes to the person about you. If you are traveling, your visit may be of interest to the public. When you are invited to be a guest, your preparation must be made with great care. Never underestimate the responsibility of such a public appearance. Be sure your talk is good publicity and good public relations.

As Program Chairman

If you belong to a professional club, you may be on the program or publicity committee. In selecting a speaker, consider the possibility of publicity as well as the interest of the group. If your group is small, you may be able to get a sizable audience by opening the meeting to outsiders and by publicizing the speaker.

Before engaging a speaker, find out about her ability to interest the audience and to hold its attention. Unfortunately, some people who are well versed on a subject cannot give an interesting talk.

Write a letter to the speaker inviting her to address your group at a definite time. If she is not acquainted with the organization, give her a description of its aims, purposes, and membership. Be sure to ask what fee is charged or, if your group has no funds, state that the organization has no funds for fee or expenses. Be sure the question of payment is clear.

In these letters the fee and expense costs are clarified:

July 6, 19——

Dr. Vivian Reed

(Address)

(City)

DEAR DR. REED:

Many of us are still quoting from the excellent talk which you gave a few years ago at a meeting sponsored by the Federated Women's Club. Now I'm hoping you can again spare us some time for another inspiring talk.

We are holding our annual Business and Professional Women's Club convention here at the Beach Hotel on November 1, 2, and 3. We would be greatly honored if you would be our keynote speaker on Friday afternoon, November 2. The theme of the convention is "Tomorrow's Businesswoman." We know that whatever subject you choose, you will be an inspiration to these three or four hundred women who are active in many different lines of business.

If you can accept our invitation — and we truly hope you can — will you advise us of the charges?

We look forward to a favorable reply.

Cordially,

(name)
Convention Program Chairman

(Name)

(Title)

(Company)

(Address)

August 1, 19——

Dr. Vivian Reed

(*Address*) _____

(*City*) _____

DEAR DR. REED:

Such good news! We're elated that you can be with us for our convention.

The schedule has been revised, since you indicate in your letter that it will be more convenient for you to have a late date with us November 2nd.

Will you be our banquet speaker that evening? Although the enclosed tentative program indicates the convention theme, there is no need for the banquet speech to carry out this theme. Your talk can be as broad and inspiring as you care to make it . . . along any line you choose. The members of the group will be happy to have you share your recent European trip with them, or any of your other rich experiences. We hope, therefore, that you will suggest your own title for your talk.

May we have four glossy pictures and a sketch about your activities for our newspaper publicity? Your fame is well known . . . but we do want to be accurate!

Your charges are certainly very fair and reasonable for your services. Like most professional groups, we must operate on a budget and therefore would like to have an indication of what your expenses will be. We had originally allotted $150.00 for the banquet speaker, but now wonder if this will be adequate.

Cordially,

_____
(*name*)
Convention Program Chairman

(*Name*) _____

(*Title*) _____

(*Company*) _____

(*Address*) _____

Remember that your letters to a speaker, and your courtesy, should be good public relations for your company, as well as for your club or church groups. You see, a speaker judges you, your company, and your group by the treatment received. Whether there is payment for services or not, every speaker deserves to be treated as an honored guest.

Ask the speaker to send a biographical sketch so that you can write a good publicity release for the newspapers. Ask for the number of photographs needed for all the papers. Signify whether glossies or mats are desired.

Be sure to emphasize the date and place of meeting, and the time and location of your meeting with the speaker. If the speaker is a woman who is a stranger in the city, you may wish to call at the hotel for her.

Publicity for a Guest Speaker

The preparation of a release for a guest speaker for your group should follow the same rules as outlined for writing a publicity release for a talk by you. Give the *who, what, where, when,* and *why.* Give the full title of the sponsoring organization. State whether the meeting is open to the public and the amount of the admission charge.

Avoid personal opinions. Write in the third person.

Be sure to send the release to the correct person on the newspaper, as Woman's Page Editor or Club Editor.

Watch the papers for the publicity. Get copies for the speaker as well as for your report to your club president.

FROM: *Name of person releasing story*
Position, Club
Telephone number

Jane Doe Smith, vice-president, Blank Advertising Agency, New York, will speak at the March 28 meeting of the Los Angeles Women's Advertising Club. The meeting will be held in the Wedgewood Room of the Tower Hotel at 12:30 P.M., May Blake, Women's Advertising Club president, announced.

Mrs. Smith, who has just received recognition as the outstanding woman in advertising for the year, will speak on the subject, "Are Ad Women Here to Stay?" Material for her talk will be drawn from her 20 years' experience in all phases of advertising, both with agencies and private companies.

Following Mrs. Smith's talk, plans will be made for the club's activities to help raise funds for the Woodlawn Summer Camp for Underprivileged Children, Miss Blake stated.

Courtesy to a Guest Speaker

It is good publicity for your company and your organization to treat every guest speaker with courtesy. If you, personally, have invited the speaker, assume full responsibility for his or her comfort from the time you meet until you have taken the speaker back to the hotel.

If the speaker is a woman, your group will probably authorize you to send her a corsage. This need not be expensive, but do select colors that will go with any frock, unless you know what she is planning to wear.

Ask the other people who are to sit at the speaker's table to meet you before going to the table. Introduce the other guests to the speaker. When the audience has been seated, ask someone who is to be at the speaker's table to lead the way to it. Place cards should indicate the seating arrangement. The main speaker should be seated in the center at the right of the person who is presiding. If you are program chairman, you sit at the speaker's right.

Introducing the Speaker

A good introduction for a speaker requires careful preparation and practice.

Study the facts sent to you by the speaker. Select the important items that will be of most interest to the audience, such as present

A corsage
need
not be
expensive.

affiliation, major interest, honors, books written, and other praise-worthy accomplishments. Avoid dates. No woman, and few men, want to be dated! Be sure of your pronunciation of names. Avoid overstatements. Do not give a lengthy eulogy or make your introduction sound like an obituary notice. If the speaker is famous, a long introduction indicates your audience is uninformed. You have heard the shortest introduction, "Ladies and gentlemen, the President of the United States of America."

An introduction does not give you the right to make a speech. Do not try to tell what the speaker is going to say. Do not try to be clever. Do not tell a funny story unless you are expert at this and are sure the story is suitable and new. So many sins are committed in the name of an introduction of a speaker that a good introduction is a real joy.

Plan what you are going to say and practice saying it. Use notes if you must, but do not read your words. Limit the introduction to one or two minutes so neither the speaker nor audience becomes restless.

A really clever introduction omits the mention of the speaker's name until you say, "It gives me great pleasure to introduce _____." Avoid hackneyed phrases like "I give you _____" or "Here she is, Miss _____."

After the talk, thank the speaker, with no attempt to sum up the talk, to add your ideas, or to make a speech.

If you have permission from the speaker, tell the audience that they may ask questions. However, this is usually anticlimactic and often spoils the impact of the talk. It is generally more satisfactory to suggest that those who wish to ask questions come up afterwards to talk with the speaker.

After the meeting, thank the speaker sincerely and briefly. If there is a fee, choose a suitable time of privacy for presenting an envelope containing the fee. See that the speaker is taken back to the hotel. Be sure the speaker receives copies of the publicity that appeared in the paper and notices of radio or television publicity. And always write a thank-you note expressing the appreciation of the group.

Perhaps the best way to sum up the courtesies to extend to

a guest speaker is to suggest that you treat the speaker as you would like to be treated when you are a guest speaker.

Films for Publicity

Films are prepared to gain wide publicity. If you are asked to produce or help in the preparation or display of a film, you will need expert advice on the special techniques of showmanship required.

The preparation of audio-visual presentation of a subject requires sound knowledge of the subject, understanding of the media or type of picture, definition of the audience, and a clear-cut purpose. These picture-presentations may be filmstrips, with or without accompanying sound, or movies. Even the less costly filmstrips represent a considerable investment of money and require expert advice. Today, competition is keen, and so many excellent films are available that a novice should not attempt to produce a film without the help of an expert.

Find out if there is an audio-visual expert in your company. Ask his cooperation and advice. There are film companies which specialize in the preparation of different kinds of films. If you must prepare a film for your company or professional association, talk over your problem with a representative from one of these film companies. Before you see him, have a planned outline of the purpose, the audience to be reached, the subject to be covered listing major points, and the budget. The expert then can advise on the type of picture best suited for your needs at your budget figure. Make a study of many prepared films so you are familiar with different types of pictures, the plot or sequence, and the effectiveness of different methods of presentation.

Do not neglect to consider methods of distribution of the picture to get the best results. Figure the cost of this distribution in your budget. Is there need for booklets to accompany the film? Will there be advertising expense and distribution costs? Will your company or a paid agency handle bookings and mailings?

How many prints are essential to get the maximum number of showings? Are there provisions for replacement and repair of used prints? Is the equipment needed for showing the film available to the groups to whom the picture will be shown, or must you plan on providing screens and machines? Must someone accompany the picture to make the proper presentation or will a sheet of instructions be sufficient to permit good showings?

The actual production of a film is only part of the cost of obtaining the desired publicity through this type of medium.

The preparation of the script, the planning of each shot, the selection of important sequences, and the theme (entertainment or education), require all of the consultation and expert advice you can get.

Before signing the contract for the production of a film, have advice from a legal expert to be sure you know the exact responsibilities you are assuming.

The plan for distribution of the film may include a publicity party, releases to the press, advertising notices, and informative leaflets to be sent to interested persons.

If you help to show the film, be sure that the subject is of interest to the selected group and that careful preparation is made to show the picture to the best advantage. The screen, machine, operator of the machine, and the physical condition of the room are important. Plan the program to include a short introduction of the film, the actual showing, and then a brief summary. This follows the principle of *tell them what they will see, show them, tell them what they have seen.*

Is the showing worthy of newspaper and radio publicity? If the film was planned to gain publicity, consider every angle to make the most of each showing. Be sure the cause is honest and worthy, then capitalize on the investment.

Exhibits for Publicity

Exhibits at professional and trade meetings should be planned to make a dramatic presentation of an idea. Showmanship is at a premium because competition is great and the public wants news.

Study the exhibits at a convention to see what attracts attention, tells a story, makes a favorable impression that will be remembered, and is good publicity and good public relations for the company or association.

Consider first the audience who will see the exhibit, the location of the booth, and the news you have to tell. Confine the theme to a single idea and coordinate all the features to flash the idea to the viewers without need for personal explanation.

Modern techniques and materials for making an effective exhibit are employed by companies which specialize in displays, exhibits, and booths. Perhaps there is a department in your company to produce this type of work. You should be able to discuss with them the story you have to tell, the audience, and the budget for your exhibit. But unless you have training in this work, the planning and production should be left to the experts.

Manning an exhibit or booth at a convention is a real publicity and public relations job. The visitors like to meet the person who represents the company. Good grooming, comfortable shoes, and a ready smile are requisites for this work. You must know the answers or take the name and address of anyone who wants an answer you can't give. These questions and requests for information should be handled promptly so that your company is credited as being a friendly one.

The hours may be long and the throngs large, but if the cost of participation is worthwhile, it is important to capitalize on the investment and get good publicity.

Booklets for Publicity

In many types of work you will be asked to prepare booklets, leaflets, and bulletins for educational and publicity purposes.

The preparation of such material requires special consideration of the purpose, the audience, the budget, the methods of distribution, and the best techniques to use to give the story in the most effective way. Many skills are involved in the preparation of even the simplest booklet if it is to gain recognition among the many publications of the day.

Excellent guidance in the preparation of booklets and films as well as newspaper, magazine, and radio releases is given in the book, *How To Write for Homemakers* (Iowa State University Press, Ames, Iowa), by Genevieve Callahan and Lou Richardson. Although the book is keyed to the home economics field, the sound guidance given by these two experts is basic for directing any message to the public.

Before attempting to prepare a booklet, make a study of those available in your field of work. Get from the library the material on techniques of presentation and illustration of booklets. Competition demands a superior job of workmanship in order to receive attention and the desired publicity.

Publicity Parties

You may have an opportunity to help plan a luncheon, cocktail party, or dinner to publicize a new product or service. Such affairs are accepted as a friendly way of giving news to a selected group of people who are especially interested. These people, in turn, can give wide publicity if the news is worthy and if the presentation is made effectively.

The basic consideration for a publicity party is, *Is the message news?* You cannot buy publicity. The party is given with the hope of publicity, but this fact may not be expressed. It requires a *light touch* to make the guests feel that this is a friendly party without any ulterior motive.

Every detail of such a party necessitates sound judgment and careful planning.

What is the purpose? The purpose may be to introduce a new department head, a new fashion, a new product, a new service. It may be to explain some new policy of the company; to show a new film or new book; or to thank the selected guests for their friendship and past courtesies.

Always test the purpose. Is it news? Is it worthy of this expensive entertainment? Will it be good public relations?

Now for the plans.

When is the best time? The day is important. Investigate possibilities of conflicting meetings, holidays, or special events. Often one day in the week is more apt to be an *easy* day for the special guests you wish to reach.

What is the best hour? Should this party be a luncheon, cocktail party, or dinner? Should the guests be invited for 12 or 1 o'clock? Local custom determines the best hour.

Where will the party be held?

Select the hotel, club, or other appropriate meeting place, on the basis of convenience, type of service, prestige, and cost.

Who should be invited? The guest list is important. Be sure

to invite the right persons from the newspaper, the magazine, radio station, television station, the company, and the association. Be sure of the spelling of the name, the correct title, and the right address. Even though this is a business party, every detail must be as correct as if it were your own personal party.

Who should be the author of the invitations? Since the invitation should be personalized and definite, consider very carefully whose name should be used. If the company name is sufficient, sometimes individuals send a personal note with the company invitation to those persons whom they know well.

To whom should the replies be sent? To what address? If the party is to be held in another city, try to establish the name, address, and telephone number of a person in that city. Include these under *Please reply,* in the lower left-hand corner of the invitation.

Should the invitation be formal? If so, the formal style used for weddings or receptions is correct. Usually a more informal note-type invitation is used. Sometimes a tricky feature announces the party, but these should not be amateurish.

FORDHAM COMPANY
Public Relations
Newberry, Wisconsin

July 6, 19——

Miss Lois Black
(*Address*)

(*City*)

DEAR MISS BLACK:

You are cordially invited to join us for cocktails and luncheon, August 2, to meet a brand name new to the Newberry market.

We will meet for cocktails at 12 noon in the Blue Room of the Baker, and go in to luncheon at 12:30. A brief introduction of the product will follow luncheon; you can count on being out at about 2 o'clock.

We are looking forward with pleasure to seeing you, and do hope you can be with us.

Sincerely,
(*name*)

Please reply.

Before sending the invitation, make definite arrangements with the hotel or club as to the following: the menu; price, including tips and tax; flowers; size and location of room; hour of service and program; and special arrangements for tables, cloak checking, stage displays, showing of pictures. List these before going to see the person in charge of party service. Leave nothing to chance.

You may wish to get prices at two or three places. Check on the total cost to be sure this comes within the budget allowance. You will have to guarantee a certain number of guests. Usually you can give a tentative number. Then, verify the number the day before the party so that you can give a more definite estimate of the number of guests expected.

Strange though it may seem, some people do not acknowledge an invitation to a party given by a business concern. You will never be guilty of such a social lapse if you have had the experience of wondering how many guests were coming to your own party. Remember this when you receive such an invitation!

Plan the program. Who will make the presentation and who will introduce the speaker or speakers? How will the presentation be made? Meetings without showmanship are rather certain to be dull. Dramatize the presentation to make it memorable, but in good taste and suitable to the occasion. Keep the program short

A one-hour program must be very good to be appreciated.

and interesting. Audiences are made up of busy people. They are critical of anyone who wastes their time. Because the meeting must be worthwhile, get the best advice possible on the program. Consult the experts in your company. Plan it, practice it, time it. The best program lasts only 30 minutes. A one-hour program must be very good to be appreciated.

Decide on the plan for seating the guests. If possible, have a member of the company at each table to be host or hostess to the group. Be sure the right people in your company are invited.

What kind of release or informative literature will be given to the guests? Should this be at the table, or be given to them as they leave so they won't know the big news before the program?

Will the guests be given a sample or a gift suitable to the occasion?

Should cocktails be served before the meal? This is usually determined by company policy and by local custom.

When all these details are settled, send the invitations. Then recheck and complete every detail. Try to anticipate every emergency. Check on hotel arrangements to be sure the right food will be served at the right time. Will waiters clear the tables before the program? Will the service and program move swiftly without waste of time? Don't leave anything to chance.

Keep an accurate check on the replies from the guests. Be sure your company guests are properly informed about their part in the party. Ask them to arrive ten minutes early. Are they to wear a flower, name badge, or other designation so the guests will recognize them as company representatives?

On the day of the party, go to the party room early to be certain everything is ready.

Be gracious in greeting the guests and in introducing guests. Say, "I am _____ of Gray Company," and extend your hand so that the timid guest is made welcome. Introduce your co-workers. Try to move from group to group if time permits. Do not stay with your special friends. Bring the stranger or bashful guest into a group. Make it a good party.

After the party, bid the guests goodbye. Pay the hotel bill and make a complete report. What can you do next time to make the party more successful?

Publicity? If the guests were well chosen, the program newsworthy and interesting, and the party thoroughly enjoyable, you will get publicity. Watch for it, and include this with your report.

Good publicity for your company is good news which attracts the attention of the public and causes many people to think or act favorably toward your company.

Contests

Contests have become a popular form of advertising and publicity. A contest requires an expert in this field to set up rules that meet legal regulations, appeal to a wide audience, get good publicity, accomplish the objective, and establish good public relations with those who enter the contest.

Judged on the merits of publicity, the contest rules must be easily understood. They must require a definite action by those competing. They must provide an area of judgment or discrimination on the part of the designated impartial judges, and state how and when awards will be made.

Unless great care is taken to handle every step in a fair and equitable manner, a contest can create unfavorable publicity. Even when the prizes are of nominal value, the losers may claim unfair decisions.

For the sake of good publicity, everyone who enters a contest should receive a card or letter acknowledging receipt of the entry. An announcement of the names and addresses of the winners gives authenticity to the contest.

There are legal considerations concerning contests. Be sure you are protected from legal action. Be sure you have facilities to handle the judging of the contest. And be sure to provide for good publicity throughout the contest and for the announcement of the winners.

Contests can be good or bad publicity.

CHAPTER 13

Travel Like an Expert

M ANY positions require some traveling for business reasons. This may be to see a customer, to attend a convention, or to make a public appearance before a group, on the radio, or before television.

Whether the trip is for a day or a week, certain preparations and regulations can make travel less confusing and can assure more satisfactory results for the company.

Any travel is expensive. Each trip must produce results to justify the cost as well as the time.

The *purpose* of a business trip should be clear and definite. Sometimes you can accomplish several other jobs but you should have a well-defined purpose for going.

Perhaps you will receive a letter from a group inviting you to speak to them, an office memo may come from a department asking for help, or you may originate the request. Analyze the estimated results against the cost before you submit a request to the head of your department for the trip.

Get permission for the trip to a definite city or cities on definite dates. For your protection, write your request and get a written okay, if possible.

Schedules and Tickets

Look up travel schedules for convenient arrival time. Consider night travel as an effective use of your time so as to leave daytime for work time. If there is a Transportation Department in your company, talk over your needs so that you will have the maximum amount of time at your destination. If you get your own tickets, call the airline or railroad offices for advice. All this investigation must be done early to assure reservations. Two to four weeks before the trip is none too early.

Round trip tickets save money, and it is safer to get your return reservation before you leave on the trip. If your plans change, you will have to rearrange your tickets. Then, be sure to cancel a reservation twenty-four hours before departure time in order to get refunds on the unused tickets. Try to have definite plans for your trip before you give the final order for tickets to avoid as many changes as possible.

Mode of Travel

Car travel is used by many business people whose work takes them from city to city, or throughout the country, or who must carry heavy equipment. The company will make an allowance for use of your car on a mileage basis, will furnish a company car, or give approval to rent a car. In any case, convenience, time, and cost are deciding factors for car travel. It costs to operate a car and it may be slower travel, but your work may require this transportation. Most companies are very strict about the use of a company car for other than company business. Proper insurance, good checks for car performance, driving tests for safety, and accurate records of mileage, repairs, storage and other allowable costs are all part of the consideration in using a company car.

Bus travel may have a place in your schedule. It is usually the cheapest, but takes the longest. Sometimes, however, a bus may get you to your destination exactly when you want to arrive.

Train travel is a most accepted form of transportation for business trips. There are several different price ranges of accommodations which you should investigate.

Coach fare is the cheapest train rate, but with crowded trains, this may not be convenient. Some trains have reserved coach seats. These are less expensive than a reserved seat in the parlor car which requires a first-class ticket plus a charge for the seat.

Overnight travel means sleeping arrangements and a first-class ticket. Most modern trains have eliminated sleeping cars equipped with upper and lower berths, and sections (upper not made up so the lower berth has more head room). Taking the place of these is the convenient roomette that is comfortable and private for one person. A bedroom, and other higher-priced accommodations, may be allowed for two or more persons, but seldom for anyone except those in executive positions. Either the roomette or bedroom eliminates the trek to the ladies' dressing room.

Get acquainted with the types and prices of train accommodations. Extra-fare trains, which offer extra service and extra speed, may be allowed if the occasion warrants.

Plane travel is a thrilling experience for the beginner, but to the experienced traveler, planes are judged on convenience of schedule and cost. The price of meals and the tips are usually eliminated in plane travel, but you must add the cost of transportation from airport to hotel. This is usually higher than taxi fare from a railroad station because of distance. Airports may be as much as an hour's ride from the city. Again, if air travel means an extra night at a hotel, this is a cost to consider. If you have heavy luggage, the excess weight will increase your total cost of transportation.

Coach fare planes are lower in cost than first class, but very satisfactory for many trips. Usually no meals are served (or just a light snack). Seats may be closer together with three seats in a row on one or both sides of the aisle. The planes are comfortable and the flying time may be just as fast as for the first-class plane service. On jets and some other flights, the cabin is divided and both accommodations are available on the same plane.

Investigate the total cost of plane travel, the time schedule, and the company policy before deciding on the best way to make the trip.

Boat travel is usually slower than train or plane. There may be several different rates on the boat, dependent on the accommodations. The larger the boat, the greater the price range. Before deciding on boat transportation, know the time schedule and the range in prices. Usually, the slower schedule eliminates this type of travel for the person on business.

Hotel Reservations

As soon as you know your arrival time in a city, make a hotel reservation. Never trust to chance. If your company has a Hotel Department, they may handle reservations for you. Your company may prefer that you use certain hotels for business reasons. Sometimes a hotel which is one of a chain will make a reservation for you at a hotel of the same chain in another city.

Check on what you are allowed to spend for a room before you spend it.

If you write for a reservation, be definite in *what* you want, *when* you want it, for *how long,* and for *how much.*

Letter for Reservation

Your business address
Date

Name of Hotel
Address

GENTLEMEN:

Please reserve for me a moderately priced single room with shower for June 10th through June 12th.

I shall arrive about 11:00 P.M., so please hold my reservation until midnight.

Please confirm this reservation and state the room rate.

Yours truly,
Your name

If you do not get a reply, you can wire the hotel:

PLEASE WIRE CONFIRMATION RESERVATION SINGLE ROOM LATE EVENING JUNE TENTH.

Take a copy of your letter or telegram and the reply from the hotel with you on the trip. Late arrival at a hotel requires special notification to avoid a misunderstanding. Sometimes it pays to send a wire to the hotel the morning of the arrival day.

CONFIRMING ARRIVAL TONIGHT JUNE TENTH. HAVE YOUR CONFIRMATION SINGLE ROOM.

Be sure to cancel your hotel reservation if your plans change.

Hotel accommodations vary greatly, from a single room with a shower or bath to a twin bedroom with parlor (known as a suite). There are different classes of hotels, too, as commercial, resident, and resort. Your company usually will want you to stay at a good commercial hotel located reasonably close to the contacts you must make.

Contacts

Be sure of the names and addresses of business contacts to be made on your trip, and make a notation of the specific purpose of each contact. Know what is expected of you.

If your company has a representative in the city you are visiting, are you supposed to notify him of your proposed trip or telephone his office when you arrive in the city? Should you notify the contacts of your proposed trip and try to set up a tentative schedule? Should you notify the publicity department to try to get publicity for your trip? Are all interested persons in your company informed about your trip so that you can make the most of your time and company money?

Financing the Trip

What is the company policy about advancing money to finance your trip and about accounting for your expenditures? The availability of *credit cards* to cover almost every kind of expense — air fare, hotel charges, meals, telephone calls, gasoline, and other auto expense — has made it possible to travel for extended periods without having to carry large amounts of money. An itemized billing is sent the credit card holder, of course, thus giving a convenient, detailed accounting to the company or individual.

If you travel frequently, you may wish to get a credit card for a chain of hotels or for a hotel in the principal cities you visit. Apply to the hotel manager, give as references your company and your bank, and allow time for the hotel to check on your credit rating and send the card to you. No charge is made by the hotel for this service.

A similar procedure is followed if you wish to apply for a more comprehensive credit card that may be used at many hotels, restaurants, and a variety of shops. The comprehensive credit card usually requires an annual membership fee.

. . . approval
from the
credit manager.

If you do a great deal of driving on company business, *gasoline credit* cards are especially convenient because monthly statements give you records of gasoline, oil, and other operating expenses. Companies maintaining a number of gas service stations have application forms available and issue credit cards free after an investigation of the applicant's credit rating.

Some companies issue *air travel cards* to employees who travel great distances and often must arrange their own transportation while away. The air travel card may be used to charge the cost of transportation and excess baggage. If such a card is issued to you through your company, care should be taken to check with your supervisor or accounting department as to how the card is to be used.

If you and your company aren't using credit cards, you may be allowed to draw advance money for expenses on the trip. Some companies do not want you to spend your own money. Inquire about the amount of the advance.

Play safe in carrying money. Do not carry a large sum. Usually your company is not responsible for your loss of money, so a lost purse means a personal loss.

Several kinds of *safe money* are possible.

You may plan to pay hotel bills by personal check, but you will not be able to cash a check for more than the actual bill unless you get approval from the credit manager of the hotel. This takes time.

A *company check* may be used to prevent carrying too much

money. To cash this at the hotel, you must see the credit manager and must have good personal identification. Again, this takes time.

Traveler's checks are the safest and easiest way to carry more than $100 in cash. Ask at an express office, bank, or your company banking department concerning the use of traveler's checks. These are in denominations of $10, $20 and up per check, in books of whatever number you want. There is a small charge for getting traveler's checks, but you can cash them almost anywhere and anytime. You first sign your name on each check when you buy it and then you must sign it again on a prescribed line in the presence of the person who accepts it in payment for a purchase or in exchange for cash. Never write your duplicate signature on the check until you are sure you can cash it. If you lose traveler's checks, notify at once the office that sold them to you so you will be able to collect repayment for them.

Don't carry over $100 in cash. Don't keep bills in an easily lost extra purse or display a roll of bills in public. If you must carry much money, ask the hotel clerk about the use of the hotel safe.

Some companies have credit arrangements with certain hotels, so that you may be able to sign your hotel bill rather than pay cash for it.

Get Proper Blanks

Be sure to collect a supply of the proper blanks to use for your expense report, activity report, and other forms which make your paper work easier.

Ask your supervisor what are allowable charges for room, meals, tips, taxis, entertaining, telephone, telegrams, and supplies needed while on your trip. Be sure you know how to make out an expense report and what receipts are required before you go on a trip. How often must you send in your report? How can you get more advance money if you run short of cash? It costs to send money by wire. It is a nuisance to someone at the home office if you have to wire for money and ask for special service. Play safe and plan to take enough money to cover your expenses, plus a reasonable amount for an emergency.

Luggage

Luggage for traveling should be planned to minimize the tipping of porters, cab drivers, and bellmen as well as to avoid delays in waiting for luggage checked through on your ticket but which may arrive on a later train.

You'll find, after you have tipped a few times, that your luggage will decrease in size and number. There's many a trick to packing clothes so they won't wrinkle. Some like to use tissue paper to fold along with clothes to eliminate creases. Another way is to use the garments themselves. To do this, first place all of the bulky and small items in the bottom of the suitcase as it lies on a flat surface. Plastic bags make excellent lightweight covers for shoes, gloves, and hose. To pack a suit, button the jacket while it is still on the hanger. Remove the hanger, put the jacket, button side down, into the suitcase with the bottom of the jacket at the far side of the suitcase and the shoulders and sleeves dropping down over the front edge of the case. Next, place the skirt on top of the jacket with the hem at the far side of the suitcase and the waistband hanging down over the jacket shoulders. Next, lay the garment that is most apt to wrinkle on the bed or any flat surface. Stack as many as three or four more dresses on the first one, being careful to smooth out any wrinkles. Arrange the sleeves as though they are outstretched arms. On the top of the dresses spread your slips, gowns, or pajamas. (If you will be overnight on the train, don't put your sleeping garments here.) Fold the sleeves over the dresses as though folding your arms. Then place one hand under all of the dresses and with the other hand at the waistline fold the entire lot in half and lift all into the suitcase. Now fold the top of the skirt and jacket up and away from you over the dresses. Fold the jacket sleeves in the same way as the sleeves on the dresses. See the step-by-step drawings (pages 204, 205) that illustrate this method of packing.

Magazine articles, now and then, give special tips on packing, but you'll have to experiment, since even experienced travelers use different methods. You will learn to select clothes that minimize wrinkles, if you travel much. Remember, however, that clothes acquire fewer wrinkles when the bag is packed full but not bulging.

In purchasing luggage, consider your needs for overnight, for a week, and for a long trip. Is the luggage lightweight? Is it durable? Any luggage used in travel must take punishment, so it is not

1

Put bulky, small items in bottom of case.

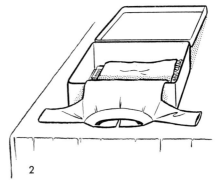

2

Put in suit jacket (button side down) with jacket bottom at far side of case; shoulders and sleeves dropping over front edge.

5

Fold sleeves over dresses. Then place one hand under all the dresses, and, with the other hand at the waistline, fold entire lot in half and lift all into case.

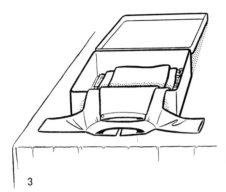

3

Place suit skirt on top with hem at far side of case and the waistband hanging over jacket shoulders.

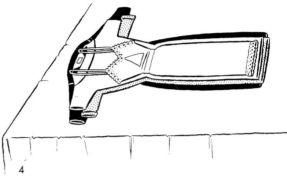

4

Next, lay garment most apt to wrinkle lengthwise on bed or flat surface. Then, stack other dresses on the first, smoothing out wrinkles. Arrange sleeves as though they were outstretched arms. Spread slips, gowns, or pajamas on top.

6

Fold skirt top and jacket up and away from you over the dresses.

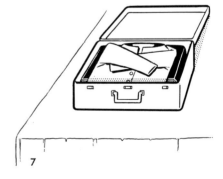

7

Fold jacket sleeves.

wise to buy flimsy bags or very expensive ones that will become marred and scarred.

Don't take everything you own when you go on a business trip. If you are contacting different people each day, your clothes will be new to them. Even when you are with the same people, a different blouse is enough variety.

An experienced traveler learns to plan a suit-blouse wardrobe that provides the right outfit for any occasion. For the two- to five-day trip, you'll want an extra pair of shoes because your feet get a workout on most travel jobs. Nylon underthings washed out each night are dry by morning. An extra pair of hose will meet an emergency until you can get to a department store and recoup your loss.

As to cosmetics, fitted cases are heavy. You may find an all-purpose overnighter is more suitable since you can use midget-sized tubes of tooth paste and lightweight plastic cosmetic bottles and containers in place of heavy jars and bottles.

Remember that you pay for weight in excess baggage on planes and in the extra tips to a groaning porter. Perhaps trunks and big packages should be sent by express.

Matched luggage looks smart. If you start on a piece-at-a-time plan, ask how long that style or pattern will be available. Luggage makers drop styles and introduce new ones just as the silversmiths do.

Specialty bags, like the make-up bag, hat bag, and shoe bag, may be all right, but not necessary.

The two-suiter bag with hangers may be fine for the short person but impossible for the long-skirted gal. As a rule, the fewer folds at prominent smooth-surface places, the better the results. Notice how your suits and dresses are packed when they are delivered from the dress shop. You'll get ideas from many sources and get your own ideas, too.

One more word. A hat box carries hats well unless you use it for a catchall for shoes and forgotten articles. Better give your hat a break and keep it in tissue paper in its own box with no interfering heavy articles.

Is the luggage lightweight? Is it durable?

Few coats pack well . . .

As to an extra coat, you'll be wise to carry this. Few coats pack well enough to be worn without pressing.

Off to the Terminal

Trips out of the city should not require time-off from regular work to put your personal effects in order. The beauty shop appointment, the bit of extra shopping, the repair job on shoes, and the last-minute dry cleaning, require management of your out-of-work time. Daytime departure hours may be such that you can leave from work rather than stay home or go home early to pack. Ask your supervisor what arrangements to make for a good start.

Take time to check on your ticket dates, departure time, and station. Put the ticket in your purse where you can get it easily. Have you ready change for the taxi driver and porters? They never have change! !

Allow time to get to the terminal even in traffic jams, to check in, and to get settled. One minute late is *too* late.

You can carry your bag if you wish. Porters are there to help you if you need help, but you pay for this service. If the porter takes your bag to be delivered to you at your seat on the train or at a designated spot, be sure to get an identification tag or check.

Put it where you can find it! You'll see many women, and men too, who go through an extensive search for baggage checks and tickets, to the amusement of passengers and the boredom of transportation personnel.

Plan a safe and accessible place for your ticket and claim checks.

Check-in Time

All transportation stations have good direction signs. Take time to read these signs and see how much you can learn without asking questions. *Pullman Passengers, City of Denver, Check in Here, Taxis, Baggage, Passengers With Tickets, Passenger Information, To Planes, To Trains, Departure Time.* These and many other signs tell the answers to the questions most often asked.

Never stay in doubt because you fear to ask, and do ask the right people, the transportation employees — not fellow passengers. The information desk is there for your convenience, too.

Have you something to read? Almost every station has a newsstand, in case you haven't a book or magazine. Trip time is wonderful for catching up on your reading.

One minute late is **too** late.

Don't take everything you own . . .

For plane travel, check in at the desk at least 15 minutes before departure time, to have your ticket stamped and your baggage checked. Listen to the announcement of your flight number and departure gate. When your flight is called, go to the right gate, and be prepared to show your ticket there or on entering the plane.

For train travel, arrive at the station at least 15 minutes early. Often reserved-space tickets must be checked at specified stands before you board the train. The tickets must be shown at the gate. The trainman at each car entrance will direct you to your space. Do not board a train until you have checked your ticket with the car porter or other authorized employee. Get on the right train! Look for the number of your seat, berth, or roomette. Be sure you are in the right car. Then, if someone else has your space, notify the porter at once. He will check the tickets and either correct the error or call the conductor. Never trade places with a passenger without authorization by the conductor since he keeps a chart of passengers, their destination, and tickets.

On the Move

Plane or train travel is the ideal time to learn to use a timetable. Start at the front and read the directions and explanations. Note the change in time from east to west and west to east. As a businesswoman who travels, you must learn to read timetables.

Now is a good time, too, to brush up on your geography. You'll find that many time-schedule folders can be good reading.

On a plane, directions will be flashed: *Fasten Seat Belt, No Smoking.* The stewardess will look out for your comforts, serve a snack or meal, and help you if you have any discomfort. Buzz for her if you wish help. Relax and enjoy yourself.

Train travel is reading and resting time. You should plan to entertain yourself. Be courteous, poised, and considerate of the rights of other travelers, but avoid conversations which turn into life histories.

Don't expect the lounge car to be a get-acquainted club. Take your book or select one of the magazines in the lounge. This doesn't mean you have to be stuffy, but do avoid starting a get-acquainted routine.

Card games on trains can be expensive. Before you join a group be sure you know exactly what the stakes are. Some people take for granted a money settlement in a card game. You'll be wise to stay out of these *casual* games.

Train Meals

Eat lightly when traveling. A waiter announces each meal, so you can decide when you want to go to the dining car. Allow for a delay in crowded cars. Wait at the entrance of the dining car for the steward to seat you.

Read the menu and know what you will be charged for the meal. Look at the list of sandwiches, salads, and omelets. Perhaps this type of meal may suit you better. Leave a tip of at least 25c, even for a small bill. Tip 20% of bills over $1.00.

Pay your own way.

Pay your own meal check. It is natural to visit with other guests at your table, but you are on an expense account and you are a businesswoman. Pay your own way.

Until you gain experience, remember to keep your own counsel. Don't discuss your name, address, work, and other personal affairs with train acquaintances.

Business Travelers

You may travel to the same city with someone else from your company. Pay your own way in all transactions, even when the co-worker is a man. Do not expect to be entertained either en route or at your destination. Be gracious but ingenious enough to have plans for the dinner hours and for evenings. If a group dines together, pay your share. Remember that the only reason you are together is for business, and that you, too, have an expense account.

If a company official asks a group to dine, write your thank-you note to him or to his wife if she is present.

When in doubt as to accepting favors, make your decision according to common sense, fair play, and professional stature. Never allow an exception to occur in your standards of womanliness. It's good business to set your standards high.

Arrival

Plane travel means no tipping until you claim your luggage at the designated spot and get a porter to carry it to the airport limousine or a cab. Tip him 25c per bag.

Airport limousine fare to your hotel is usually less than a personal cab.

Train travel means tipping the porter in your car. For a parlor car seat, tip 25c to 50c, unless the porter has given you extra help with your luggage or has brought you a writing table or other supplies. Check your belongings before you leave.

Overnight travel means a tip for the car porter. You aren't expected to be lavish in your tips but, whether you get extra service or not, a tip to your porter is part of the expense of travel. Allow 50c a night if you have a berth and 75c to $1.00 a night for a roomette.

Arrival in the City

If you need a porter for luggage, get a claim check and tell the porter to meet you at the taxi stand. Remember that there is a *definite* charge for each bag or package which a porter carries for you from train to taxi. This charge is usually 25c per bag, plus a bit more to *sweeten* the service. Perhaps you can carry your hat box or small bag. Ask the porter to get you a cab or ask the cab starter to get a cab. Tell him your destination because he may have to put other passengers in your cab. Be sure your bags are in your cab.

Arrival at the Hotel

Pay your share of the cab fare and tip the driver 10c minimum or 25c for fare over $1.00.

Check with the driver to be sure your luggage is left with the doorman to be brought into the hotel.

Go to the registration desk. Show your confirmation for a room, and register your full name, company name, and address. Ask about the room rate so that you know what you will pay. Ask the bellman to inquire at the mail desk for your mail.

If you are not able to get into your room, ask a porter to check your bags. Give him 25c when he returns your claim check. This type of delay means you will have to use the ladies' lounge to freshen up and the pay phones to make your contacts. Everyone has to put up with delay in getting into a hotel room now and then. Find out when you can get into your room and plan to be at the hotel at that time.

A bellman will take your key and luggage to your room. There may be a woman floor clerk who will take your name and will handle your mail and telephone messages without your having to go to the main desk.

The bellman will show you how to regulate the heat and will explain other services. Tip him 25c for each bag he has carried.

Your Hotel Room

Unpack and hang up your clothes. If you need hangers or other room supplies, telephone the housekeeper, and give a 25c tip to the maid who brings them. If you must report any complaint about the room, telephone the housekeeper.

Some clothes lose wrinkles if hung in the bathroom. Often, hot water in the tub or shower will create the needed steam. A light-weight steam travel iron is handy if you do much traveling. Check for a sign in the bathroom or call the desk to be sure there is alternating current. The direct current found in some hotels will destroy the thermostat on an iron.

You'll find a hotel directory on your dresser which will give you information about meals, pressing, and other services. Usually, a house physician is listed and suggestions are given for emergencies of fire and accidents. You'll feel more at home if you learn about your hotel.

If permitted on the expense account, phone the valet or pressing service to come for your clothes, and say when these will be needed.

Now look over your scheduled activities and telephone to confirm appointments, if time permits. It is always a courtesy to make this telephone contact to be sure you are welcome.

Try to set up contacts at reasonable hours. Be sure there has been sufficient time to sort the mail and start the wheels rolling before you arrive. Do get to your appointments on time. Get down to business, and leave. Everyone is busy. Don't expect to be entertained. Do invite the person to be your guest if your appointment extends to luncheon time. Try not to ask for favors.

Brief yourself by looking at the map of the city which you'll find in almost every hotel room or in the telephone book. You can learn a lot by studying the map.

Evenings

Keep up your report and expense account each evening. Then plan to make the most of your free time to see the city. A sight-seeing bus is a wonderful way to see the famous features of a city.

Look through the little magazines in your hotel room to see what events are featured. But remember that theatre tickets cost more when purchased through the theatre desk in the hotel than at the box office at the theatre.

Keep your door locked when you are *in* or *out*. Leave your key at the desk when you are away from the room, unless you plan to be in and out a great deal. If there is a clerk on your floor, always leave your key with her.

Guests

On business trips you may ask a woman but never a man to come to your room for a conference. Don't go to a man's room unless there is a group in conference. Some people may insist that a hotel room can be used for business guests, but don't do it until you are experienced enough to make wise decisions. Some hotels are strict about entertaining in your room.

If you want a member of your family or a friend to share your room overnight, she must register at the desk, or you should notify the desk clerk and pay the extra rate.

Meals

Where will you eat? You'll often find two or more dining rooms in the hotel. The prices vary in different rooms from the convenient, thrifty coffee shop (tip 10c to 25c) to the night-club room with high costs, entertainment, and sizable tip. Perhaps you'd prefer to try a restaurant that is famous for certain foods. If you go to dinner at 6 P.M. almost any restaurant is all right for a woman alone. But look out for high prices! Of course, you can always order lightly or even leave, after a look at the menu, if the prices are too high.

When you dine in the hotel, you may sign the check with

. . . but never ask a man to come to your room . . .

Perhaps you'd prefer to try a restaurant famous for certain foods.

your name and room number, to be paid later with your room bill. Of course, this charge won't cover the tip so you must add 15% of the total bill when you sign it.

If you order a meal served in your room, you can sign the check or pay for it. You must tip at least 50c plus 10% of the meal to pay for this extra service.

Other Services

Telephone calls may cost 15c to 20c. You are responsible for the calls made from your room. Separate the personal calls from those to be turned in on your expense account.

Wires, letters, packages delivered to your room call for a tip of 15c to 25c.

The beauty shop in the hotel is usually reliable, but the prices are not cheap. The hairdresser expects a tip of 50c, the manicurist, 25c.

If the maid gives you extra service, as extra cleaning up or extra linens, tip her 25c to 50c. If the doorman gives you extra service, tip him 25c.

If you ask to have someone paged in the lobby or if you are paged, tip the bellman 25c.

You'll see that you can get a great deal of service at a hotel, but you pay for it.

Incidentally, a radio or TV set ordered for your room is a personal, not a company, expense. Most hotel or motel rooms are now equipped with a radio or TV set and there is no extra charge.

Money

Be sure you have enough money to check out. If in doubt, see the credit manager before check-out time to get permission to cash a personal check. For this, you'll need identification such as a credit card, a voter's card, company card, or driver's license.

Check Out

Be sure to check your ticket for leaving time and know the check-out time at the hotel. If you must stay longer, notify the hotel clerk of the hour you will leave and be prepared to pay for the overtime. Perhaps you could check out of your room and check your bags in the hotel checkroom to save this extra charge. The transportation desk at the hotel can give you information on plane, train, or bus schedules and assist you in making reservations. They can also give you information on the airport limousine time schedule. In some cities the airport buses stop at the hotels and in others you must go to a central terminal.

Telephone the bell captain to ask for a bellman to come for your bags. Allow 15 minutes. Look through the closet and drawers for forgotten items. Wait for the bellman. Then go to the

Tip the porter . . . tip the driver . . . tip the waiter . . . tip the . . .

cashier's window and ask for your bill. Check it over and question any item you don't understand. Pay the bill and take the receipt. Never forget this valuable piece of information. If you expect mail, leave a forwarding address.

Tell the bellman whether you will need a cab or the airport limousine. If a private car is calling for you tell him the hotel entrance from which you will leave. He will take your luggage to the transportation indicated. Tip the bellman for his services and you are ready to leave.

Back Home

If you have kept a running report and expense account, you may be able to complete these on the trip home. It is so much easier to get these records straight as soon as possible, before you forget or lose your enthusiasm for the trip. Be sure your report is complete, accurate, and sent to the right people.

If you have left something in your room at the hotel, write or wire the hotel manager describing the article, and telling the number of your room and where to send the article.

Write thank-you notes to those who were helpful to you or entertained you. *Business requires the same etiquette as personal affairs. It's good businesss to express appreciation for courtesies.*

Reminders

Traveling on business can be stimulating and interesting if you plan what you *must* do and what extras you *can* do. Traveling can be expensive if you entertain or shop. It may be worth it, but remember that personal extras are not included in the expense account.

Never forget you are a company representative and can contribute to good or bad publicity. When on company business you are *at all times* a company representative.

Never forget you are a company representative.

CHAPTER 14

Public Speaking Is Part of the Job

H OW do you rate as a public speaker? Can you stand on your feet and talk to a group of people easily and convincingly? Or are you scared to death at the thought of giving a talk before even a small group? It may comfort you to know that many experienced speakers get "butterflies" before beginning to talk. Almost every speaker has dreaded public speaking at first and has had to work at doing a good job.

You'll find that the ability to talk easily to a group of people plays an important part in the recognition and success of a person in business. In fact, being able to speak in public is so important that many companies urge promising employees to take courses in public speaking. But, to become proficient, you must take every opportunity to practice. You'll find it pays to accept opportunities to talk to small club and church groups so that when an important occasion arises you are ready to do a professional job. There is nothing so helpful as practice to overcome fear of talking to a group. Each time you give a talk, you will gain confidence.

Many experienced speakers get "butterflies" . . .

The businesswoman who can express her ideas clearly in terms others can understand will gain recognition as a leader. The ability to write well is important, but, often in the business world, speeches, articles, and books are written by ghost writers who take the ideas of the specialist and turn them out in readable form. In public speaking, you, the person, impress the audience not only by what you say, but how you say it.

In public speaking, success depends on your ability to:

Get the attention of the audience by your appearance, voice, and opening remarks.
Gain the confidence of the group because you know what you want to say and say it.
Create interest by keying your talk to the understanding and interest of the audience.
Show your enthusiasm in actions and words.
Hold attention by developing a main idea with illustrations and supplementary ideas.
Build acceptance by your friendly attitude and your way of seeming to talk with each person.
Crystallize your ideas into a clear unit which can be used in some way by each person in the group.
Establish good public relations for your company.

Get Attention

Your appearance, your voice, and your opening remarks should get the attention of your audience.

Pay special heed to your appearance when you are to talk to any group of people. Dress becomingly and suitably for the occasion. When people have to sit and look at you, be sure that you present an interesting picture. Beware of distracting features such as a wobbling feather on a hat, large, dangling earrings, a low-cut neckline, or startling colors. Both men and women are affected by your appearance and judge your common sense by the way you dress for the platform. Most of us form snap judgment of a speaker during the first few minutes. If our opinion is negative, the speaker must be very good indeed to change that opinion.

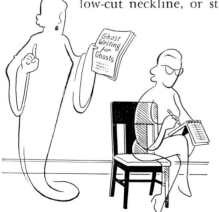

Ghost writers turn out the information in readable form.

The length of your skirt, the hang of the hemline, the appropriateness of your shoes, the becomingness of your hat are judged. Yes, from tip to toe you are on review. *Look your best.* Then you can be at ease, forget yourself, and concentrate on your talk .

Your voice may invite confidence or antagonize an audience. First of all, *be sure* you can be heard. Nothing is more irritating than the small voice that reaches the first row only and leaves those farther back thoroughly bored because they can't hear. The high-pitched voice is disturbing and gives an impression of weakness. With a little effort and perhaps a few voice lessons the pitch can be lowered to a more comfortable level for the listener. Equally bad is the booming voice that pierces the ear drums and vibrates through the room. This is apt to be the case when a microphone is used. Watch your audience and you can tell by their reactions whether you are pitching your voice right. Your voice and manner of presentation will create a definite feeling of friendly acceptance, indifference, or actual antagonism.

Your first sentence should give the audience a capsule presentation of what you intend to say, and your opening remarks should set the stage for your talk.

Your opening remarks are important. Here you should analyze the purpose of your talk and project the purpose in a condensed clear-cut statement. Learn these introductory remarks and do not deviate or ramble by injecting some spur-of-the-moment ideas. How many times have you been bored by a speaker who tried to tell a joke, or commented on the audience or on personal experiences, and so rambled on and on? Didn't you wonder if that speaker really had anything important to say?

What a feeling of confidence and expectation is engendered when a speaker states easily and effectively the purpose or main theme of the discussion and then proceeds to develop that theme.

Gain Confidence

You can gain the confidence of the audience if you know what you want to say and say it. Whether your talk is for five minutes or an hour, organize your presentation so that the audience recognizes you as an authority. Don't apologize, hesitate, or show diffidence in expressing your opinion. If you aren't qualified to speak, by all means don't accept the appointment.

Create Interest

Create interest in your subject by keying your remarks to the understanding and interests of your audience. This necessitates a pre-understanding of the type of group you are to address, their interests, and the purpose of the meeting. Think of the many times you have lost interest in a speaker who used illustrations that did not apply to the audience. You felt as if you were hearing a "canned" talk, and you were irritated, embarrassed, or bored by the whole thing.

Know your audience and talk *with* them not *at* them. Bring them into your talk so that each one feels your remarks are addressed to her. Remember the importance of *you* and minimize the use of *I*. Avoid technical words that have no meaning to a group, but do not resort to simplification that belittles the intelligence of the audience.

Show Enthusiasm

Show enthusiasm for your subject. Emerson expressed the importance of enthusiasm when he wrote, "Nothing great was ever achieved without enthusiasm." Let your facial expression, your voice, and your words show that you are enthusiastic. This enthusiasm is easier to express when you talk, instead of read, your remarks. For this very reason, you are more sure of holding the attention of the group and of spreading your enthusiasm, if you speak freely on your subject. You may use notes to outline your talk. In fact, your audience will feel more at ease if you refer to notes than if you hesitate and fumble. Scientific papers are usually read, but even these should be presented with natural enthusiasm.

Needless to say, supersalesmanship and high-pressure enthusiasm may amuse rather than impress an audience. Don't try to overact or oversell. The audience should feel that you are sincere in your enthusiasm.

Hold Attention

Hold the attention of your audience by a well-planned development of your idea. The title of your talk should be expanded into a theme in your opening remarks. The main part of your talk should further expand this theme and give proof or reasons for your opinions. Do not try to develop too many unrelated ideas. Plan your talk as a unit, with every point related to the general theme so that you strengthen and enlarge the central idea. A variety of illustrations may appeal to different members of the group and, thus, make the connection between your idea and their own experiences or interests. In this way, the body of your talk clarifies your theme and passes on some thought that will be helpful to each one who hears you.

Build Acceptance

Build acceptance and understanding by your friendly attitude. Be sure you do not talk over the heads of the audience or talk down to them. Take your audience into your circle of friends and make them feel that you have their interest at heart.

Summarize

Summarize your presentation by drawing together the points of your talk. Then you will leave your audience with a clear-cut picture of your idea-theme which can be applied in some way to the interest and actions of each one in the group.

Public Relations

Throughout your entire talk remember that, as an employee, your number one job is to cause your audience to have an enhanced opinion of you and your company.

Whatever the occasion or the type of talk, you will need to consider how you can get the attention of your audience, gain their confidence, create interest, show your enthusiasm, hold their attention, build acceptance, crystallize your ideas, and establish good public relations.

Television

A television appearance is similar to a talk before a group of people, in that you get and hold the attention of your audience by your appearance, your voice, and your message. You can use notes but these must be disguised so that your reference to them is not obvious. You should give the impression of chatting with each viewer in an informal, friendly fashion. It is true that some

Distinct plaids, checks, or floral patterns should be avoided.

formal speeches are telecast, but it takes an important person with an impressive message to hold the attention of an audience.

Some directors insist on rehearsals to time the interview, to get the position for all action and the sequence of this action. Some directors insist on make-up and give definite directions for the type of costume you should wear. Clothes of medium colors are usually best. Pastels are preferred to white, and dark or medium colors are better than black. Distinct plaids, checks, or floral patterns should be avoided. Since the audience sees you, you must be relaxed, natural, and friendly. Charts must be large and easy to read. Booklets and other illustrative material must be placed so that the viewers can see them easily. Tilt the top of a glossy photograph or a booklet with a shiny cover slightly toward the camera to avoid glare. If there is a close-up shot of something you are holding be sure to keep it steady, down on the table and tipped toward the camera.

Timing is more important than in radio work because the cameraman must be able to follow your actions and emphasize certain points with close-ups. Move at a pace he can follow easily.

Be gracious and enthusiastic and give the impression that you are a friendly person who has a message to tell and tells it.

Your voice must be controlled as in radio broadcasting. Your message should be clear, concise, and keyed to the audience that usually follows the program .

Radio and TV Talks

When you are invited to speak on a radio or television program, you assume the responsibility to put on a good performance — one that will be of interest to the type of audience that usually watches or listens to that program.

Many business positions will give you an opportunity to participate as a guest speaker on such programs. A radio or TV talk reaches a large audience and influences a great many people, either favorably or unfavorably, toward your company. Isn't it worth your time to prepare for such an important occasion?

Your voice is your most important asset in putting across your message. An attractive voice will hold your listeners. Even an interesting message given in an unattractive voice is apt to lose the audience. These unseen people can turn the dial to another station without warning the speaker. Your audience doesn't have to listen. Your voice and your message must hold them.

Since your on-the-air voice expresses your personality, the quality and use of the voice become important in all appearances. Wouldn't it be wise to do everything you can to develop a good speaking voice and to use all the techniques at your command?

Breathing Techniques

Breathing technique can make or break a voice on the air. By learning correct breathing you can sustain your voice, use it emphatically, project it, control it, and give it flexibility and interesting variety.

Correct breathing is full-chested breathing from the diaphragm so that all available air space is uti-

Your audience doesn't have to listen.

lized. This prevents "gaspy" breathing and irregular pauses to take a breath.

Do you breathe correctly? Place your hand just above your abdomen, crosswise of your body, immediately below your ribs. Now breathe in and out. Your hand should move out and in with each inhalation and exhalation. If not, you have work to do to improve your breathing habits and to make your voice effective.

Try this exercise. Lie down on your back on the floor. Breathe deeply. Now place a heavy book just below your ribs in the center of your body. Make the book move up and down with each breath. Add another book and another to strengthen your diaphragm. Keep at the exercise every day until you have full use of all the air space in your chest. Every great singer and actor has mastered this deep breathing, along with the ability to control a maximum of air capacity and thus give the voice full range and volume.

When you have controlled breathing, you will be able to master these important phases of broadcasting: (1) controlled level of voice; (2) natural phrasing or the division of sentences into easily read and understood phrases; and (3) strong sentence ending.

Controlled Level of Voice

Before air time, the engineer will ask you to talk into the microphone so he can adjust his control to the level (strength and pitch) of your voice. Just before the broadcast relax your

Add another book and another . . .

shoulders, chest, jaw, neck muscles, and abdomen. Then, take less than a full breath, smile, and you are on the air. With this technique, you will not explode your first word or crack or stutter into a beginning.

During the program, breathe naturally. Keep your voice smiling! Talk to a person, not to a vast audience. Remember to keep the position in which your voice was tested. Don't lean closer or draw back, and don't weave from side to side. The engineer will do his best for you, but you must cooperate and keep your test position.

Natural Phrasing

Proper phrasing is dependent on breath control. Take a tip from the top flight announcers and go over your script several times in advance of the program. Read aloud and notice where the natural pause comes. Punctuation should indicate a pause, but it is wise to mark the script to show pauses and to underscore the words that need emphasis. Reread the script to see if these marks make your talk sound conversational rather than preachy. Be sure you have a complete thought in each phrase so that your sentences are not chopped into meaningless segments.

Sentence Ending

The sentence ending is important. If you have good breath control, you will not *run down* at the end of a sentence. Have you ever heard a speaker who dropped her voice so that you were never sure of her last words?

Remember that the *punch* of most sentences is contained in the last few words. Be sure to have enough breath to give the punch!

Tone Control

Tone control is important also in a pleasant radio and TV voice. Be careful that nervous tension before the mike does not cause you to pitch your voice so high that it sounds weak and immature. If you relax, you are more apt to keep your voice in a low, pleasing register. If possible, have a recording made of your voice so you can hear it and criticize it honestly. Would you like to listen to such a voice?

Enunciation and Pronunciation

Careful enunciation and a normal rate of speech also are important in radio and TV. Slurred words and dropped endings such as "g" and "ing" are slovenly habits. An average rate of speaking is 150 words per minute but 175 may be natural for you.

Correct pronunciation of words is essential. Some listeners are sure to have a dictionary and consult it if you mispronounce a word. A radio or TV performer is supposed to speak correctly.

The Smiling Voice

The conversational tone sounds friendly and is one of the most essential and effective of all speech techniques. Can you read, and sound as if you are not reading? Can you make each listener think you are chatting with her? Practice the *smiling voice*. This means you should smile when you talk. Even when there is a studio audience, even when your knees are shaking, smile so that your voice reflects a warmer, friendlier you.

Don't be afraid to pause as you do in talking to a friend. When a question is asked you in an interview, don't jump in before the question is completed. Take your time.

Voice flexibility makes a more interesting voice. Monotones are dull. A good announcer covers a range of tones within a few words. Ask a friend to comment on your voice over the air, or when you listen to a recording of your voice, check your range of tone.

All of these qualities of voice and habits of speech are important in getting and holding the attention of your radio or television audience. You, your personality, your rating as an authority are judged by how you sound when you are on the air.

Plan for the Script

Most television shows use an outline script for interviews or other kinds of informal programming. This preparation is usually directed by the television producer in collaboration with the participants. He may ask for one or more pre-program conferences before the presentation is aired.

If, however, you write your own radio script, write it as though you were talking, that is, *conversationally*. Read it aloud to see if there are awkward sentences or words that make you stumble. Change these so you can read smoothly. Watch for sounds that you find difficult to say. Does "s" whistle? Do you stumble over "statistics," "specifically," or other words?

Avoid long, rambling sentences. Make your sentences short and clear and use connective words to avoid choppy sentences. Use strong verbs that denote action and omit superfluous adjectives.

Read your script aloud to see if it sounds the way you talk. Is it conversational?

Time your script so that you can give the complete idea in the allotted time. You can play safe by having additional copy to use if time permits.

Keep your method of presentation light rather than heavy. Be careful of jokes unless you can make them sound natural and really funny.

As to a plan for the script, follow the established rules for all talks:

Know what you want to say and to whom you are talking.

Give a brief statement of the purpose of your talk. Then enlarge on and illustrate your points.

Build up one idea rather than attempt to introduce several unrelated ideas.

Finally, summarize so that the audience grasps the main features of your idea.

The Format for the Script

Use 8½ x 11-inch plain paper, typewrite the script, and doublespace. Soft paper is less crackly than stiff paper. Leave a wide left-hand margin for the name of the person giving each separate speech. Staple the corners together, but tear them off just before the broadcast. Then you can drop a

Enthusiasm is easier to express when you talk, instead of read, your remarks.

page on the floor as you read it on radio. Number the pages and check the sequence before you begin.

The Prepared Script

If someone writes a script for you, provide an outline of what you want to say. Be sure to read the script. Change the phrases to sound like you and delete words that are hard for you to say. Then check the content because you must assume the responsibility for the talk you give over the air.

Ad Lib

Most interviews are ad lib. This style requires experience, skill, and a plan to be effective and interesting. The logical approach is to prepare an outline or notes on the information or message that will interest the audience. Jot down suggested questions. Go over the outline or questions with the interviewer so that you both understand the plan of the program. If there is a subject which you do not wish to discuss, such as price and regulatory laws, tell the interviewer. Then you won't have to avoid a question when you are on the air.

When the interview begins, answer personal questions briefly so that there will be time to give your particular message. Watch the clock and plan the length of your answers to cover your subject. Avoid any statement that will embarrass the interviewer or antagonize the listening audience.

Broadcasting and Telecasting Etiquette

When you are invited to be on a radio or TV program, be sure you know the name of the station, the address, the name of the interviewer or person who conducts this program, the time, and the type of program.

Acknowledge the appointment by letter, telephone, or wire. If you are traveling, telephone the station to let the program director know you are in the city, and to verify the time and the address.

Arrive about 30 minutes before the program or at the time designated by the station.

Take two copies of your script if you are to read it, or have two copies of your interview outline and a set of leading questions or well-planned notes.

Discuss with the interviewer your part of the program, policies concerning the use of trade names, the time of your part on the program, and other details. Know what you can and cannot do. Can you offer booklets? Should requests be sent to you or the station? Know the rules and abide by them.

The announcer or director will tell you whether you are to stand or sit for the interview. Most likely, he will check your voice to know what volume is necessary for the particular microphones. Then you will wait quietly until your turn to come to the microphone.

Watch for the sign, "On the Air." The red lights on the TV camera tell you that "you're on!"

Do not rustle papers or make unnecessary noise. If, during your talk, you must cough, turn your head and cover your mouth. Say "Pardon me," and go on.

If you choke up, turn your head, take a deep breath, and be careful to prevent an exploding word.

If you fluff a word, don't be alarmed. Even the best speakers fluff at times. Either ignore it or say, "that is to say . . .." or "I meant to say. . . ." Be at ease and don't let a fumbled word upset you.

Watch for the signals of the announcer or program director.

Watch for the signals of the announcer or program director. A circular motion of the hand means *speed up*. A stretching motion with both hands means *slow down*. A cutting motion across the throat with one hand means *cut* or *stop*. A circle formed by the thumb and first finger means *okay*.

Watch for the signal that you are off the air before you speak or comment on the show. Don't take a chance on having your unplanned remarks go out over the air.

Thank the announcer and program director and leave the room so that another show may go on. Studios are busy places. If you wish to have a tape or a recording made of your broadcast, ask the station about this service and the charge. The cost is not large but you should pay for this service.

Consumer Meetings

Whenever you accept an invitation to give a talk to a group of people, you assume the responsibility to give a message that will, in some way, help each person in the audience. Competition is very great. In radio, television, the theatre, lectures, books, and magazines so many experts speak or write on so many subjects.

Have you something to offer that is new, interesting, useful? In many positions, you have an opportunity to learn about some activity or work that needs telling. If you have a message, you may wish to tell it because this will help to sell a product or because you can give help as a civic service.

Let's see some of the background work that must go into each talk and some of the platform work that is essential for an effective talk.

Basic Background Information

Who is in the group? Is it worthwhile to give the talk to this group? Are their interests such that your message will have meaning? Sometimes a program chairman asks a speaker, in desperation, without thought of profit to the group or to the speaker.

When is the meeting? Will this talk interfere with more important work? Will it take one of your few leisure evenings?

Where is the meeting? Are the facilities adequate to give your program? Will transportation time and cost make this meeting too expensive?

How long are you to talk? Is this to be a 15-minute talk as one of several speakers or as a fill-in between luncheon and a social hour? Sometimes groups do not consider the value of a speaker's time. They do not mean to be careless, yet they do not always accord to a free speaker the courteous treatment given to a paid speaker. This is ironical, but too often true.

What have you to say? Is your message important? Can you adapt a former talk to this group or must you work up new material?

The *who, when, where, what, why,* and *how* must be weighed in the light of your work and your company's policies before you decide whether or not an invitation should be accepted.

Thorough Preparation

If you are to give a talk, start early to prepare for it and make a serious effort to give a star performance.

The theme or purpose of the talk is the first consideration. Then, thinking of the type of audience, decide what approach will be best.

After the theme and the approach, next consider the method of dramatization. Will you use illustrative materials, charts, or exhibits? Without some dramatization it is difficult to make a lecture or talk interesting enough to hold the attention of a group.

. . . or as a fill-in between luncheon and a social hour?

If you use illustrative materials, are these large enough to be seen, easily handled without awkward motions on your part, and interest-provoking? We live in a dramatic era. People want entertainment along with their education. You will be expected to give your message with a flare and a bit of sugar coating or you may lose your audience.

The plan for the talk should include a strong descriptive introduction, the main presentation with illustrations, then a summary or conclusion.

Learn the introduction, so you don't ramble. Outline the main portion, so you develop the theme logically. Then memorize the conclusion, so that your talk finishes on a strong note and the audience feels the impact of a completed message.

Is your voice good for public speaking? All the suggestions given for radio talks apply to all public speaking. Your voice should have volume to carry, tone qualities to please, and character or range to hold the attention of the audience. If a microphone is to be used, be sure you know how to make the most of this amplifying system. A roar or blur will spoil the best of talks.

If you need notes, ask for a podium. Make arrangements for a good display of your props and personally check your display material.

Give the chairman a written statement to use in introducing you. Include your name, business affiliation, experience, and, of course, the title of your talk.

Platform Technique

If you must sit on the platform, consider how you appear to the group. Don't cross your legs. Do keep your skirt properly arranged. Try to relax, but don't forget you are on review.

When you begin to talk, *smile.* Put the audience at ease by your attitude of confidence and assurance. Acknowledge the introduction briefly, "Thank you, Mrs. _____." Begin your memorized introduction, and give your whole attention to what you have to say and to the reaction of the group to your message. If you see the proverbial doubter, direct some of your most effective efforts toward her. If you get a smile or nod, you can relax. You have succeeded.

Don't be upset by an interruption or hitch in the use of your props. Laugh at yourself, and your audience will accept you as one of them. People are sometimes critical of the too-efficient expert, but are friendly toward the person who doesn't pretend to know all the answers. A bit of humility, a sense of humor, a spirit of camaraderie, these win your audience when aloofness, superiority, and hauteur might build a wall between you and them.

For the climax, give your strong conclusion just as you learned it. Don't add extra ideas or let your talk trail off into anticlimactic or weak words.

Be prepared to talk to some of the audience after the program. Be patient, courteous, and gracious. These aftermath chats can be trying, but it's part of the show.

Do write a note to the program chairman. Write your report to your supervisor. Then take time to analyze your presentation. Jot down your opinion of the meeting and what you would do differently next time. Next time? Yes, when you are in business, public speaking may become an important part of your work, particularly if you are a good speaker.

Professional and Scientific Meetings

Talks at professional and scientific meetings may be more formal than those given to the general public. Frequently, scientific papers are read. If slides or charts are used, these should be large enough to be seen and the data should be selected to give one idea or point. If you ever address a scientific or professional meeting, make your paper or talk interesting and direct. See that your presentation is well organized and well illustrated.

For added consideration, avoid a large stack of notes which discourages the audience; try to memorize the opening and close, even if you read the main section; show your enthusiasm for the subject by facial expression and voice; and limit your talk to the time allotted to you.

Sales Meeting

Sales meetings, small and large, play an important part in many business organizations. Selling ideas, products, or promotions may require the combined skills of many people and the ingenuity and showmanship of a theatrical production.

If you can, attend several sales meetings in your company and in other organizations to see the devices used to dramatize, impress, and sell.

Women have great creative ability. If you are asked to participate in a sales meeting, use your woman's initiative and originality to prepare and present your part of the program. Your effectiveness will depend on your knowledge of your subject, your enthusiasm for your work, and your ability to create a feeling of confidence and enthusiasm in your audience. Never try to fool a salesman! Know what you have to say. Speak from experience and make your message helpful.

The Purpose

Understand the purpose or objective of the sales meeting and your part in it. Is the purpose to introduce a new product, to explain a promotion plan, to inspire confidence, or to stimulate greater sales effort? There may be a major objective with several minor objectives.

Preparation

Get complete information about the audience, who they are, how many there will be, and their positions in the company.

Get a clear picture of the entire program and the names of the other speakers.

Understand your allotment of time and your position on the program.

What is the physical setup of the meeting place? Is there a stage? Is there work space?

What is your specific assignment and what points are you to develop?

Plan of Action

Decide on the specific point you wish to emphasize. Outline your message.

Decide on the technique to dramatize your presentation. Find out how the other speakers will dramatize their points so you will

Rehearse, practice, and rehearse some more.

not duplicate these methods. A good sales meeting should contain a variety of kinds of showmanship, such as charts, playlets, slides, puppet shows, contests, professional actors, famous people, and demonstrations. It should include original stunts that attract attention, make a lasting impression, and stimulate action.

Adapt your presentation to the spirit and tempo of the meeting. Overdone dramatics at the wrong time are as bad as lifeless, weak presentations.

Make a time schedule and a definite plan.

Rehearse, practice, and rehearse some more so that you use no notes. You must be a real authority. Sometimes the whole program must be rehearsed so that the show is coordinated and timed to the minute.

Check your props and be sure everything works as it should and that nothing can go wrong at the last minute.

Your appearance, your voice, and your attitude can win or lose your audience of salesmen. Adopt a friendly, cooperative, but professional, approach. Do not brag or take undue credit. Your success depends on your womanliness and your ability to gain the respect of the audience. Never resort to off-color stories, crude statements, or any lessening of your standards. Modern salesmanship is based on highly-developed techniques, not on burlesque or slapstick. Your ability to speak well and to put across your point will be a major test.

Your reward will be the satisfaction of a job well done. In fact, the successful participation in a sales meeting may be one of the most stimulating and satisfactory experiences of your work in business.

Check your props . . .

CHAPTER 15

Select a Good Team

YOU as a beginner have thought in terms of your own work, your ability to please your superiors, your skill in following instructions, and your judgment in getting help from the right people. Did you ever think that in your first years in business you may have the responsibility of hiring and training an assistant who will look to you as a superior?

Many young girls do have to select or have a part in selecting newer employees and in training and guiding these new workers. As a comparative shopper, you might be placed in charge of one or more girls in the same work. In secretarial work, you might be asked to help select and train a file girl, stenographer, errand girl, or stock girl to implement your effectiveness. In a research position, you might be required to train someone to run routine analyses or tests so as to relieve you of some of the mechanics of your work. In many other positions, girls with only one or two years' experience might be called on to reorient their viewpoint from that of one being led to that of one who must lead.

Whether or not you are required to assume this position of a supervisor, it may help you to understand the full scope of your present and future work if you give thought to what you would and should do if you become an employer.

Let us suppose that after two, three, or four years, your work has shown such effective results that you become an employer as well as an employee.

How good are you at judging people? One of the attributes of a woman executive is the ability to pick capable assistants who will work together as a team. When you are applying for a position, you are testing your ability to sell your qualifications as an efficient worker. When you are the employer hiring a worker, your ability to choose the right person is a greater test because your choice affects the profits of the company, the cooperative spirit of the co-workers, and your success as an executive. If you fail to choose wisely, you must assume the responsibility for your lack of judgment. A poor choice is an injustice to the applicant, an expense to the company, and trouble for yourself.

Do you need more help? Each employee must pay for herself and make a profit for the company. Her expenses include not only her salary and the use of equipment and supplies but also the cost of time spent for supervision. Therefore, you as an employer must be sure that a new worker will increase the efficiency of your department. This calls for an analysis of the job to be done and a decision as to what kind of help will be most effective in producing the desired results.

Someone must do the pesky jobs.

What kind of help do you need? Should you hire unskilled or skilled help? Would the best unskilled help take over troublesome details and be more useful than poor skilled help that you could hire at the same price? You may find that a skilled person dislikes to do routine work, and that details of filing, typing reports, clean-up, are neglected or cause irritation. But an unskilled person might take pride in organizing and executing these tasks. Don't fill your team with experts of the same caliber. Someone must do the pesky jobs.

How efficient are the present members of your team? Before you hire a new person, analyze your staff to be sure each one is doing the kind of work for which she is best fitted. Often you will find that someone has shown marked ability to do a kind of work outside of the assignment given her. You can take advantage of the new interests of your group by rearranging work schedules and assignments. Is there an opportunity to begin a new activity or to enlarge an activity? Perhaps this is the time to discontinue some activity once needed but no longer effective.

One of the tests of an executive is the ability to analyze the work and workers in her department and the willingness to shift work and workers in order to make a more effective team.

Should you promote some member of your staff and fill her position or should you fill the top position? If there is an opportunity for promotion within the ranks, you will create a better spirit of cooperation by filling top positions from your present staff. Often someone who has been loyal and efficient within your department will be challenged to do a better job in that higher position than a newcomer with more experience. The loyalty of the present worker and her familiarity with company policies are telling assets. Promotions within the ranks build loyalty.

The reputation and efficiency of your department depend on your evaluation of the present operation and employees and your ability to adjust the work before deciding what new help is needed.

The following story illustrates the importance of getting the right person to assure the right results. A father, busy with his newspaper, was besieged by his small son to tell him a story. The father, wishing to finish his paper, tore a map from it and cut it into pieces. "There, son," he said, "see if you can put this map of the world together." To his surprise, the son soon showed him the map in perfect shape. When the father asked how he had learned the map of the world, the little boy said, "Oh, I don't know the world, but I found a picture of a man on the other side. I knew if I got the man right, I'd have the world right."

Before you start to hire a new employee, write down the qualifications needed for the position.

1. Work to be done:
     List major and minor work.
2. Location of position:
     Travel or not.
3. Is the position permanent or temporary?
4. Is there training on the job?
5. Are there opportunities for advancement?
6. What inducements for security can you offer?
7. What prestige or professional advantage does the position offer?
8. Education: Diploma. Type of degree. General. Vocational.
9. Experience: Number of years. Kind.
10. Personality:
     A productive *self-starter,* with initiative.
     A leader with ambition to make a career.
     Socially adjusted.
     Capable of meeting people.
11. Skills:
     Writing, selling, etc.
12. Salary scale:
     Other monetary considerations (hours, vacations, etc.) .
13. When position is open:
     Other specifications.

When you have analyzed the position, you are ready to look for the right person.

How Do You Contact Applicants?

College and university placement services are most effective in contacting new graduates. Unfortunately, these services do not always have records of former graduates with experience who might be qualified for your position. It is well to have a personal contact with the college placement personnel so that they are acquainted with you and your requirements. Be sure to send to them your specific requirement for the position. Perhaps, in a telephone call to the college, you can give added emphasis to your needs.

When the college sends the qualifications of an applicant to you, be sure to evaluate the facts in terms of your needs. A persistent mention, in the records, of a weakness or a strength in an applicant is indicative of a fact. If only one faculty member mentions a characteristic of the applicant, this may be due to the type of the course or to the degree of compatability of the faculty member and the student.

If you are not interested in the applications sent to you, return them to the college at once. Give your specific reasons for not wishing to consider these applicants.

When the position is filled, be sure to notify the colleges you contacted. As an added measure to establish good understanding between the colleges and your work, you should take time to write the colleges about their graduates who have succeeded in your department.

Commercial personnel and employment services often specialize in applicants for certain types of work. *High school principals and commercial teachers* also may be able to suggest applicants. Be sure to give a complete description of the position and the requirements. You will find it pays to take time to know counselors in one or two employment agencies so that they do not bother you with applicants not qualified for the position. Emphasize essential requirements as compared to variables which you would consider. An overzealous employment agency can cause you wasted time and embarrassment in refusing applicants. A good employment agency often can get you in touch with a very desirable applicant who might not be willing to confide to anyone else the desire for a new position. Establish with the employment service the question of who pays the fees. Usually the applicant pays the fees. Sometimes, the company pays or divides the fees when the applicant is hired.

Professional associations may operate a placement service or may list notices of positions in publications. For positions requiring specific professional skills, contacts with the special professional association may be very satisfactory.

Your staff members, others who work with you, and friends may be effective in contacting applicants. There is always danger, however, either of causing resentment if you fail to hire the person recommended or of building a nucleus of trouble by having two close friends in one department.

The company personnel service may hire all employees, may screen them for your final decision, or may delegate to you the hiring of persons for your department. A good way for you to learn the techniques of interviewing is to work with those who are trained in the personnel management. Whether this department selects your employees or not, you can get help from them if they understand your work and your requirements.

A newspaper advertisement may be effective in reaching a person for a specialized position. Take time to write a specific description of the work and the qualifications. It usually is best to have applicants send their letters to a post office box number or to a code number at the newspaper. This allows you to screen the applications. Then you can send impersonal notices of disinterest or make inquiries before you ask an applicant to come for an interview.

Policies and Practices

Never underestimate the importance of good public relations when you interview an applicant for a position. Whether you hire her or not, you can make a friend for the company.

If you wish to hire someone who is employed, how can you proceed ethically? Should you contact her employer or ask the applicant to notify her employer of the proposed change? This depends on company policy and how well you know the applicant's employer. Some companies have mutual arrangements not to pirate or raid the other companies without discussing the offer with the department head under whom the person works. No one likes to lose a good employee, but a good executive will not stand in the way of a real opportunity for one of her helpers. Perhaps you will have such an experience yourself. Then you will know that if you cannot offer one of your girls a chance to advance, you will win a friend by giving your blessing and good wishes for success, even though it is with another company.

If you find the applicant's employer is not willing to release her, you will have to decide which is more important, the good will of the other company or the desired employee.

It is good public relations to be ethical in hiring personnel away from another company, just as it is good public relations to be ethical in all transactions with all applicants.

The Golden Rule of Interviewing

If you conduct every interview as if you were the applicant, whether you have asked the applicant to come for an interview or she comes without an appointment, you are being tested even more than the applicant. You represent your company as well as yourself.

Put the applicant at ease. Be sympathetic and try to help her get into the right job. Be friendly. Give your entire attention to the interview. Start the conversation with a general subject such as her home town, her school, or mutual acquaintances.

Avoid trick questions or statements that will antagonize or discomfort the applicant. Don't try to test her skill.

If the applicant's data sheet or application letter shows she is not qualified for the position, explain why you cannot hire her. If possible, suggest how she should contact employers who might be interested in her qualifications. Be sympathetic and helpful. Make a friend.

If the applicant's data sheet indicates good qualifications, you should proceed to find out as much as possible about her personality and ability. This is a test of your judgment.

The cooperative spirit of your staff may be upset by adding the wrong person. Personalities play such an important role in teamwork that no skill or ability is so important as to be worth jeopardizing the *working rapport* of your team.

An application letter or data sheet will show the applicant's education, training, and experience. The real test of your ability to interview wisely comes in evaluating her personality in relation to the personalities in your group.

Take time to visit with the applicant. Gain her respect and confidence. Do not take notes during the interview. Later, you may wish to rate her or write comments on her data sheet.

Whether you hire her or not, you can make a friend for the company.

The Importance of Personality

In the informal interview you should be able to judge whether or not the applicant has good *horse sense* and can meet easily people of her own age and older. Is she emotionally stable or does she show nervous strain?

Her personal appearance should tell you a great deal about how she will fit into your team. However, be careful to consider the financial status of the girl and to recognize that her present surroundings may not require the type of clothes she will need in the new work.

Note the tone of voice, diction, choice of words, and general use of English. What of her eyesight, hearing, her posture, skin, weight, and other signs of good or ill health?

Judge her loyalty to her school and to her former employers. *Loyalty* and *enthusiasm* are good traits for any employee. Bitterness, disillusionment, discontent, and suspicion expressed in the interview should be weighed to determine how much this reflects a defect of character.

"What do you like to do?" This question should lead to a discussion which will indicate whether the girl likes to be with people or prefers to work alone. Take time to ask about her experiences with organizations, her hobbies, and her outside interests. Has she traveled? Can she type? Has she had experience in sales work? Does she enjoy writing? Can she drive a car? Select your questions so that the answers will indicate the abilities for your special need.

By gentle questioning, you can get the applicant to talk about herself and to express phases of her personality that are not shown on her application sheet.

"What are your ambitions for a career?" "What are your plans for the future?" These or similar questions must be asked in order to lead into the next discussion.

Judge her loyalty to her school and to her former employers.

In hiring women, one of your responsibilities is to determine the marital status of the applicant. If a girl is engaged or married, you have a right to discuss how this will affect her work. Does she have dependents who will restrict her work or prevent freedom to travel or do night work? Has she religious scruples against a type of work? These questions require tact and a frank attitude so that the applicant understands the reasons for your questions.

If possible, have members of your staff or someone who works with you meet the applicant and have an informal chat when you are not present. Perhaps they can show the girl something of their work and give her a chance to ask questions about the work and the company. This often gives you an opportunity to observe how the new girl would fit into your team. It also gives your co-workers a sense of responsibility in selecting some new person with whom they will work.

If the applicant must work with both men and women, plan to have her meet and chat with a man in the organization. Notice how she meets and talks with this man. Is she shy? coy? bold? or natural and at ease? Later ask the man his impression of the applicant. Very often you will find that this masculine viewpoint is a valuable check on your own estimate.

If the applicant looks promising, you may wish to ask her to have luncheon with you and one of your co-workers. This is an excellent occasion to judge social adjustment and general culture.

Supplementary Information

Usually you will be required to have one of your superiors interview the applicant before a final decision is made. Do put the applicant at ease by praising this company officer and his or her interest in the welfare of your department.

References from applicants may be investigated before or after the interview. Sometimes, there are company policies about contacting references before hiring an employee. Generally, a letter is written similar to this form.

Miss ———— has applied for a position in the ———— department of this company and has given your name as a reference.

The position includes (state type of work).

We should appreciate any information you can give us relative to your opinion of the ability of the applicant to fill this position.

We assure you that any information you can give us will be strictly confidential.

The Offer of the Position

If you wish to offer the applicant the position, explain to her the general policies of the company and determine whether she seems willing to accept these policies. In other words, will she be a loyal employee and will she be proud to work for the company?

Explain the hours of work, vacations, increases in pay, opportunities for advancement, and other factors not related to the work itself. It is wise to see if the applicant will need help in finding a place to live. And surely she will wish you to explain the expenses incurred in the work and the allowances made for these expenses.

Some employers ask the applicant what salary she expects. Other employers state the range of salary allowed for the position. It is seldom wise to have an applicant accept a salary very much lower than she expects or is receiving because this may prove a point of dissatisfaction later. If you have set a fair salary for the position, it is poor policy to take advantage of an applicant by making a low offer. A scale of salaries based on skills, experience, responsibilities, and performance, without special exceptions, is of paramount importance for a good team. Therefore, the new employee must be offered a salary suitable for the position and in balance with salaries paid for a similar kind of work in the company.

The position may be offered at the time of the interview or an indication given that the position will be offered within a certain time, as a week or two weeks.

Many employers confirm the offer in writing and ask to have a written acceptance. Very few business positions require a formal contract.

Is she shy? coy? bold?

Of course, if there is a delay in making a definite offer, notify the applicant at the specified time and give the reason for the delay. It is not fair to keep an applicant in suspense and possibly cause her to miss a chance to secure another position.

Be sure to set a definite date for beginning work and state what expenses will be paid. Usually, expenses incurred in moving to a city are not paid by the company. For some positions an allowance is made for basic expenses, if an employee must live in a hotel while looking for permanent quarters.

Set the stage for a successful start in your department by making the new employee feel she is welcome. Let her know that you and all the other members of the group are looking forward to having her on your winning team.

You, the beginner of today, may be the employer of a not-too-distant tomorrow. As an employer or as a trainer and leader of other people you will find that all the advice and guidance which you have received will take on new meaning. You will be on your way up the ladder to a position as the young woman executive in business.

CHAPTER 16

Advancement Is a Challenge

WHERE are you going? Do you want to succeed in your chosen work and climb to an important position as a specialist in your field or to an executive position?

Some people claim that women in business lack ambition to succeed because their goal is marriage rather than professional achievement. A look at the records shows, however, that we are living in an era of expanding opportunity for women in many fields of business where marriage does not interfere with their business careers. Records of businesswomen show that success in business often makes a more successful marriage, whether the woman continues her work or not.

So, where are you going in your business career? Have you set a goal? Are you ambitious to prove your ability to succeed? Do you take pride in your accomplishments and welcome each opportunity to test your prowess? Are you willing to give more in time, thought, and effort than you are paid for? Unless you honestly can answer these questions with "yes," you are probably one of the many young women who wishfully hopes for success but does nothing to gain it.

Should you stay with your company or seek a new position? First, analyze your attitude, your ability, and your accomplishments. Then, weigh your opportunity for advancement with your company. If you are drifting along in a routine position with no opportunity to step into a more responsible one, perhaps you should look elsewhere. Analyze yourself critically. What is your objective? How far are you from your goal? How can you reach that prized position?

To stay in one position too long may deaden your initiative. A person who takes a new position that is more challenging and requires more skill and more initiative is respected for her ambition to mount the ladder of success. But be sure you have made the most of your present opportunity before you consider a change. One who flits from job to job may receive rightly the reputation of a restless visionary who isn't willing to master difficulties or overcome hardships. When you find your work has become routine, with no opportunity to advance, perhaps that is the time for you to make a decision to change positions, even though you have no new position in sight.

Do you need more schooling in your specialization or in some related field that seems more interesting to you? It takes courage to stop, look, and listen to your good judgment. Few people reach success without will power to make sacrifices and to concentrate on the necessary preparation for a top position.

If you aim for an executive position, are you willing to assume the responsibility and to stand the pressure that comes with such a position? More money looks enticing, but you will be expected to earn it. Do you want the prestige of being head or supervisor of a department? When you assume leadership of one or more people, you must have the qualifications of a leader. Do you hope for security? The more responsibility you have, the greater is the test of your ability to hold the position. There is no security unless you earn it. Do you want happiness and the satisfaction of a job well done? This is probably the most powerful reason for wishing to succeed in your work. With such a reason, the trials, problems, and pressures become a challenge, not a hardship.

More money, more prestige, more security, more happiness and satisfaction, these are reasons for seeking a new position. Unless the change results in more happiness and satisfaction, you will not have gained the position that gives you real opportunity to develop your best abilities for a business career.

Are there barriers that prevent you, a woman, from advancing to an executive position? Women are in executive positions in almost every field. These positions may include direction of the work of a few people or of many people. Your ability to succeed, your determination, and your breadth of vision will override barriers. There are not enough qualified women for top positions. That is a challenge to you.

The Woman Executive

As an executive you must be able to select, train, and lead those who come under your direction. You must inspire loyalty in those in subordinate positions and earn the respect of top management. This requires many qualities that must be fostered and developed. These qualities include the ability to look ahead, to make a plan, to weigh values, and to set up the necessary machinery to carry out the plan.

You will need to further the habit of clear thinking, concentration, and persistence. This is essential in one who directs a department or a program of work. Women tend to be emotional and unpredictable in time of emergency and stress. Remember that emotional conflicts sap the energy that should be directed to productive work. As a business executive, you can't afford to give way to tears, nerves, or other signs of feminine weakness. You must be dependable. You must be able to differentiate between

As a business executive, you can't afford to give way to signs of feminine weakness.

essentials and nonessentials. With good judgment and calm analysis of situations you can build confidence in your staff. Most executives have their moments of indecision. But when you must lead, you must get the best advice possible, then have the courage to decide on the course to take, and inspire your staff to accept that decision and to work for a successful accomplishment of the objective.

The Importance of Time

Time is the essence of business. Time schedules, timecards, timed plans, and timed work are part of most business positions. The higher the position, the more important is the ability to analyze a situation quickly and to make a sound decision in time to put the plan into profitable action.

Some women resent this pressure of working against time. They spend their energies fighting the idea, rather than organizing their work to comply with the demands. Don't get into the habit of telling everyone how busy, how overworked, and how tired you are. Too many women develop this boring habit. They try to impress everyone with their own importance by a recital of pressing work. The woman who is too busy to relax and do some constructive thinking is either a poor organizer or she is too egotistical to delegate authority.

As a new executive, you can learn from those who have already succeeded. They have discovered that it pays to take time to think, to plan, and to organize. Time is important. Pressure is great. But never become too busy to think.

. . . it pays to take time to think . . .

Ideas Pay Dividends

To be a leader in business you must be creative, original, and productive of ideas. You must have vision to foresee future needs and to project a plan to meet the situation.

Are you willing to work on the suggestions of others or do you like to take a problem and work out the solution?

When you are an executive you must not only originate ideas but you must be open-minded to the ideas of others. Accept each suggestion with the hope it will work. Avoid preconceived decisions. Try the *it-can-be-done* approach. Weigh all sides of the question before you reject the idea. Many famously successful ideas were laughed at by the public until some wise person gave the originator an opportunity to prove the idea was sound.

As an executive, you are expected to toss out ideas to your staff, to suggest, to encourage, and to guide. If the plan does not succeed, accept the responsibility for either an unsound idea or poor judgment in directing the action. If the idea does develop into a worthwhile action, promotion, or plan, give the credit to those who made the idea succeed. Your stature as an executive depends on the success of your staff. You actually gain in prestige as you build up the efficiency of your staff and publicize their successes.

Another feature of ideas is that they must be put to work to be successful. It is not enough to have ideas. You must have the *know how* to put these ideas to work for the good of the company.

Enthusiasm and Loyalty

If you are happy in your work, you are more apt to succeed. Enthusiasm for your work and loyalty to your company smooth the way for your advancement.

A maturity of judgment to understand company policies will help you interpret these policies to your staff so that each will accept the edict with enthusiasm and loyalty. If you set an example of loyalty, you can demand loyalty of those who work under your direction.

Your enthusiasm and interest in your work will give you an inner drive that will carry you over the rough spots. Self-pity, emotional reactions, hurt feelings, sensitivity to slights, and petty actions have no place in the busy life of a woman executive. Good health and enthusiastic participation in the work to be done minimize the troublesome annoyances that can grow to overshadow the really worth-while objectives of your work. Enthusiasm and loyalty will keynote happiness for you.

Knowledge

If you would advance to a responsible position in business, you must have not only technical or specialized knowledge but also diversified knowledge. Then you will understand the many phases of work which must be coordinated to make a company successful. This means that you must continue to study and advance in your specialization. Take advantage of every opportunity to become informed in related fields. That will give you the ability to coordinate your work with the objectives of your company.

Develop your skill to read fast and pick the *meat* from the many publications, reports, and other printed matter that relate to your business or business in general. Train yourself to retain facts and to sort and sift the mass of information into significant knowledge as against insignificant chatter.

Organizational Ability

When you first entered business, no doubt you often questioned a rule or policy and thought you could make a better decision. As you advance to an executive position, you begin to realize how carefree were your first days and how your problems have increased with your responsibilities.

Can you set up a project or plan, analyze the needs, and organize the steps necessary for completion of the plan? Many people who are successful in a field of work cannot direct the work of others. There's a difference between a skilled technician and a skilled leader, and between a leader and a driver. The

And there is a difference between a leader and a driver.

leader inspires the workers and gains their respect so that they work willingly and are happy in their work. The *driver* overlooks the importance of good human relations and considers that the result justifies the method of getting the job done.

Organizational ability requires an understanding of human nature as well as an analytical mind to sift important objectives from unimportant details. Do you like to work with people, to teach, to guide, to lead? Can you recognize latent ability and plan work to bring out and develop the talents of your staff? These traits are essential in any executive position.

Human Relations

Human relations become a Number One problem to anyone who directs the work of others. You must decide what qualities will make you respected as a good leader as against the easy-going *good fellow* or the *fair weather friend.*

A study of case histories reveals that the cause of failure in an executive position is more often due to the inability to handle people than the inability to handle the technical and special skills of the job.

The leader must set an example for her staff. She must inspire confidence and earn respect and loyalty.

Square-dealing is essential in a leader. If your staff knows you are honest, you are interested in their welfare, you give credit for good work, you try to correct errors by private rather than public criticism, and you judge each person on merit rather than favoritism, then you will gain the willing cooperation of each person. You will be able to depend on each one whether you are there to supervise or not.

If you are a good leader, you will delegate authority and responsibility for certain work to each member of your staff. Talk over problems with them and listen to their suggestions. Perhaps the desire to show appreciation for your confidence and trust in them will be an incentive to greater effort and greater success in their work.

Your good judgment will be required to decide when to say *no* to a plan or idea. Can you explain why this is necessary? Can you give a counter-suggestion that is more promising?

If you are an executive, you must *assume the responsibility* for the work of your staff. You must take the blame and accept the criticism of management. If you have misjudged a person's ability or failed to train her sufficiently for her work, you must be willing to accept the blame. Admit your error. Analyze the cause of the failure and take the necessary precautions to avoid a repetition.

If you are responsible for the work of others, you can lessen the chance of misunderstandings and confusion by making clear-cut requests and assignments. Discuss the plan with the workers. Be sure the problem is understood.

If you must correct or discipline someone on your staff, take time to have a conference in private so that you and the employee are able to discuss both sides of the problem. Never attempt to discipline anyone when you are angry. Start the interview with a statement of the good features of the work so that the employee is prepared to accept your criticism of the faults or weaknesses. Be firm but fair in your discussion so that the employee understands what is expected in the future. Every disciplinary measure should help, not break, either the individual's spirit or respect for you.

Self-control in time of stress, humility for honors received, and appreciation of the ability of others will make your work with men and women more effective and will win for you the respect of management, your co-workers, and those on your staff.

Keep Growing

Competition in business is so great that no one dares to rest on present accomplishments. If you would advance in your chosen work, you should widen your interests and your appreciation of skill in many fields. Women tend to limit their circle of friends,

Every disciplinary measure should help, not break, her spirit or respect for you.

their scope of reading, and their attendance at lectures and meetings outside their field.

Too often, women do not consult specialists who can be of great help. These specialists may demand a high fee for a special short-term job, and women are apt to consider the size of the fee rather than the worth of the service. The experienced executive is able to evaluate the worth of specialized service and to put the service to work to accomplish the objective. It pays to be open-minded to the advice, service, and help of the experts. Your growth in your work depends on your ability to make the most of every opportunity to improve the effectiveness of your work and the work of your staff.

If you would advance in your work, take an *inventory* of yourself! Are you using all of your ability or are you giving just a half-hearted performance? Do you need more training under an expert? Do you have maturity of judgment or do you rely on your femininity to carry you ahead?

You may overrate yourself or you may be a severe critic, but if you would advance to a more responsible position, be honest in your self-analysis. You are the only person who can decide what you are and what you must do to improve your rating.

Where are you going? The answer is yours. Neither chance nor luck will decide. You can advance if you accept the challenge.

CHAPTER 17

Financial Security Is Good Business

THE first pay check is one of the thrilling experiences of your life. *Your* money! The freedom to choose how you will spend that money gives you confidence that you are launched on a career. You are a businesswoman.

Your money! Yours to spend! You can buy the hat or purse or shoes you have dreamed about. But will you? You may find that the money you worked for takes on a new value. You may be content with the knowledge that you can buy frills and extras *if* you so desire. You have the freedom of choice. You can make the decision as to how you will spend and how you will save.

During the first year of earning your own living, the idea of independence looms large in your thinking. There also begins to grow a desire for security and, with it, the thought of savings. Most women have an inherent desire for security.

Security depends on many factors — spiritual and physical health, good friends, and, of course, adequate finances for today's and tomorrow's needs.

It has been said that "security is a state of mind." We might add that in this, *the state of the pocketbook* plays a telling role.

Perhaps you have had little experience in money management and therefore, the thought of building financial security for to-morrow is a bit appalling. Many women claim little knowledge of money affairs, real estate, stocks, bonds, and other types of investments and savings. But there are many others who have built up their financial safety by wisely budgeting their spending to cover both today's needs and tomorrow's security.

The Budget

What do you get for your money? What do you want to get? Do you ever have the alarming thought that you must have lost ten dollars because you can't imagine where it went?

Let's think of a budget as your method of spending your own money in the way that gives you the greatest satisfaction. Your budget can be very simple or very detailed, according to your wishes. You'll need records in order to make out your income tax, so why not look over the many budget books at the bookstore and select one that appeals to you? Each day put down what you spend. Keep this record for a month or so. At the end of that time, examine your record to see if you are happy with the value you received for the money you spent. Then is the time to try planned spending by setting up the ideal sum you want to or must spend for each basic item. These include rent, food, clothing, doctor and dentist, gifts, transportation, recreation, income tax, social security, and savings.

A budget is simply a chart of what money you are sure you will receive (salary plus other resources) and what money you are sure you must spend for your living needs. The difference, large or small, is what you can plan to save or to spend for the extra things most important to you.

For the sake of your peace of mind, you'll want to set up a fund for savings against emergencies, illness, vacations, and future security.

Don't be discouraged if that first allocation of your salary doesn't work out. You may want to make several changes in your plan of spending during the year, but you have made a start in

A budget is a chart of what you will receive and what you must spend.

a businesslike manner. Your records of spending will show what you got for your money and suggest what you can do to get *more* for your money.

Sample Form for Budget

Month:
Income:
- (1) Salary: (what is left to spend)
  Other:
  Total: (amount you have to spend)
  (Consider *take-home pay* only. This is your salary *after* deductions for income tax and social security.)

Expenditures: (essential expenses and planned spending)
- (2) Rent:
  Food:
  Transportation:
  Clothing:
  Church and Charity:
  (The costs of these items are fairly well established and can be watched closely.)
- (3) Health:
  Entertainment:
  (Doctor, dentist, drug and beauty supplies — expenditures for these items can seldom be determined in advance. Provision should be made for them by setting aside a reserve fund.)
- (4) Miscellaneous:
  (Watch this column. If you spend too much on miscellaneous perhaps you should divide this heading so you can see what is *essential* and what is *nonessential*.)
- (5) Savings:
  (As your income increases, your savings should increase. At first, food and rent take the lion's share of your pay check. It will be a temptation to spend more on rent and clothing as your salary increases and to drift along with little or no addition to that *security fund*. But the older you grow the more you will realize the importance of having money at work for you. It is fun to receive interest on your savings rather than to pay interest to someone else for the use of borrowed money.)

You'll want to set up your budget so as to make daily entries and get totals for the month. If you take a few minutes each evening to keep that record up to date, you'll know *how well* you are living within your budget.

If you make a game out of this record-keeping and test your ability to set a goal and reach it, you'll find a budget doesn't take the fun out of spending, after all.

You'll get more for your money by thinking ahead when you are away from temptation. And you'll consider every impulse to spend when you know what it will do to your financial plan.

Would you rather have that expensive hat than more money for your vacation?

When you set up a goal or purpose for your spending, you'll learn to think through what you want. You'll live within your income and have a sense of security in that small reserve tucked away in the savings account or the insurance policy. A budget is good experience, too, for later business and family life when vital records, long-range plans, and a *cushion fund* become more important and real.

Filing System

Start some kind of a filing system for important papers. This can be a shoe box or a set of envelopes bound into a file. Or you can purchase a simple file folder which will make it easy to keep your papers shipshape. Keep receipted bills, canceled checks, the record of your social security number, insurance policies, storage ticket (for winter coat), rent contract, and birth certificate.

If you do not have your birth certificate, ask your parents to get it or write to the County Recorder at the court house in the county of your birth for information about getting your certificate. This may become a vital statistic in proving citizenship, and age. You may need it when you haven't the time to hunt for it or when your parents are no longer able to give the necessary information.

Safe-Deposit Box

If you have bonds, stock, insurance papers, and other important records, perhaps you should investigate the rental of a safe-deposit box at your bank. The cost of such protection is low for the security it gives you. And you won't have to worry about the loss of your most valuable papers through fire or theft. As a businesswoman, you should learn to use business methods for your personal affairs, just as you do for your business affairs.

Bank Account

One of the problems of the beginner is the decision as to the best way to pay bills and to keep money available without danger

of losing it or having it stolen. Your first thought will be to open a bank account. Be sure to select a bank that has government protection on deposits. Investigate the required balance and the service charge at different banks. Ask, also, about the check-writing plan by which a definite charge is made per check. Then see if you can limit your checks to the minimum so as to use the fee-per-check service which is a low-cost plan. Inquire, too, about the plan by which a checkbook of a specified number of checks may be purchased for a specified sum which pays the service charge. This is a popular plan with many young women.

Perhaps you will find that a cash basis is the best. You could use a safe-deposit box for extra cash and pay out-of-town bills by a cashier's check or draft from the bank, or by a money order obtained from the post office. If you pay in cash, be sure to keep the receipted bills.

If you decide on a checking account, a teller in the new-account department of your local bank will aid you in starting one. You'll be asked to fill out an identification card and give references. Fill out a deposit slip as directed on the forms and take your money and the slip to a teller's window where deposits are handled. The teller will record your deposit in a passbook and give you a checkbook. If ever you do not have your passbook with you when you deposit money, always make out a duplicate deposit slip to keep for your record.

You can send your money to the bank if you are paid by check. Write on the back of the check your signature and "For deposit only at (name of bank)." Fill out duplicate deposit slips and mail them with your check to the bank. The bank will return one to you for your record of the deposit. However, most banks have special forms for mail service which they supply upon request.

Use a checkbook correctly. Be sure each check is made out correctly and each stub is filled in at once. Avoid writing a check for less than $1.00. In order to be certain of your exact balance at all times, deduct each withdrawal from your deposit. Do not overdraw your account. The bank will likely refuse payment of the check and make a charge for doing so.

If you lose a check made out by someone else, notify that

person. If one of your own checks is lost, notify the bank to stop payment on that check, then issue a duplicate. The original can be endorsed and cashed by the wrong person only by forging the signature, of course, and would not be honored by your bank when presented against your account.

When you receive a check, do not endorse it until you are ready to cash it. Then write your name (in ink) on the back *just as it appears* on the face of the check.

Ask to have your canceled checks mailed to you each month. Then take time to compare each check with its stub, where you have recorded the amount and the name of the receiver.

Be sure your book balance agrees with the bank's statement of your balance. Are any checks still out? Did you deduct the bank's service charge from your balance? If, after rechecking your figures, your balance does not agree with the bank statement, go to the bank and ask for the bookkeeping department. Someone there will recheck your balance with the bank records.

Sending Money

Of course, you shouldn't risk sending currency in a letter. It is far from safe and you have no receipt or proof of your payment.

If you have a bank account, you can send a personal check out of town. But there may be a delay in the out-of-town bank's honoring your check until it is advised by your bank that you have on deposit sufficient funds to cover the specified amount. If time is important, you can have your bank *certify the check* by having stamped across it a guarantee of payment. When this is done, the bank in effect withdraws the amount of the check from your account and holds it until payment is demanded. There is a charge for their service.

If you do not have a bank account, you can give the cash to a bank and ask to have a *cashier's check* or *bank draft* drawn for the sum and made payable to the receiver. There is a small charge for this service. The canceled check is returned to the bank, not to you.

A *postal money order* is another safe way to send money. At a post office you can fill out an application blank stating the name of the receiver, the address, and the sum of money. The postal clerk will make out the money order for you; you keep the receipt and send the money order. There is a small charge, and these orders are limited to a maximum of $100.00. If the order is lost, you may have a duplicate made out by presenting your receipt at the post office. The receiver may endorse and cash the postal money order at his post office, or in most cities at his bank, if he wishes.

The fastest way to send money is by *telegraph.* You may go to a telegraph office, make out the money order form stating the sum of money, the name and address of the receiver, and your name and address. The fee for this service at the telegraph office is higher than for any other form of sending money, and you must pay also for a telegram to the receiver. The receiver must take the telegram and proper identification to the telegraph office to collect the money. This service is fast and effective in time of emergency.

Credit

Charge accounts, installment buying, and borrowing money are types of credit which you may establish if you understand that you are using someone else's money and must pay for this service.

When you pay *cash* for your purchases, you can shop around and get the best buy. You are apt to weigh the real need, too, when you take money out of your purse to buy goods. Cash transactions allow you to determine at a glance your balance or cash reserve.

If you establish a *charge account,* you must give references from stores where you have had credit formerly, your place of employment, your bank, and, perhaps, someone who has an account at the store. The advantages of a charge account include: the establishment of your credit rating in an inter-store credit system; easier return of goods; less need of carrying a large amount of cash; and better service in terms of advance notice of sales.

If a charge account leads you to unwise buying, it is a costly service. A large monthly bill may prove that cash-and-carry is a safer system.

Installment buying has become an accepted method of spreading the payment of a large purchase over several months. This may be a Deferred Payment Plan, Budget Plan, or Thrift Plan.

Whatever the plan, read the contract before you sign it. Know how much this credit is costing you. Figure out how much you must pay for each dollar of credit you receive. Take time to read the *entire* contract. You can be sure the merchant reads every contract he signs. Beware of any seller who tries to rush you into signing before you have time to study the contract. If you question the charge that is asked for the deferred payment, shop around and find out what another store charges for a similar service.

Is it worth the extra cost? Will this debt make you save money to pay up the bill? Will the article you buy be worn out before it is paid for? Remember when you sign a *promise-to-pay* contract, you are taking a bite out of your future pay checks. If you must buy something on an installment plan, make as large a down payment as possible and pay up the debt quickly to save extra interest payments.

There may come a time when you have to borrow money. Most business is run on some borrowed money. But the borrower must weigh the profit made on the money or the need for the money against the price paid for use of the money.

If you must borrow money, be sure to go to a legitimate lender such as your company's credit union, an employee's loan association, a bank, a legalized loan company, or your insurance company.

There are state laws which limit the rate of interest charged on personal loans. But there may be considerable difference in interest rates among different lending organizations.

Usually, the company credit union gives the employees the benefit of cooperative financing. Thus the rate in some cases may

If a charge account leads
you to unwise buying . . .

be lower by comparison than the rates on outside borrowing. Additionally, of course, you may be able to set up some special repayment arrangements if necessary. A bank may charge 5 to 6% interest and require some security. Commercial loan companies charge up to 3% or more each month on the unpaid balance. At 3% the rate amounts to a theoretical 36% a year! If you have a life insurance policy, you may be able to borrow a specified amount against your policy, and the rate of interest is worth your investigation.

If you do borrow money, be sure the need is important enough to pay a premium for the use of the borrowed money. Know exactly how much this money costs you, the penalty for failure to make regular return payments, and the state laws governing the lending company's operation.

Is it worth that much to you? Can you afford to borrow? Wouldn't it be better business to start a savings account so you'll have an emergency fund to use? Then you can borrow money from yourself and pay it back into your savings account at the same rate of interest you'd be required to pay a loan company. Try it. You'll see that it is hard to pay interest on borrowed money, but that it is better to pay yourself than someone else.

Save To Spend

If you think of savings as *saving to spend,* you'll have more fun tucking a bit away each payday. Saving for the sake of hoarding doesn't appeal to most of us. Saving for future spending may mean next month, next year, or in twenty years, but you have a purpose for putting money aside which makes it easier to save.

If you are a good saver, you may be able to put aside 10 to 15% of your pay check. If you have heavy financial responsibilities or if you have weak will power when it comes to passing up the spur-of-the-moment impulse to spend, your savings may be too small for that vacation, insurance policy, dental bill, or long-range savings plan.

Not tomorrow but *today,* start to save for a definite purpose. If you really want something, you'll find it is easier to save to satisfy that want.

Let's say, then, that 85 to 90% of your today's earnings go for today's living. That leaves 10 to 15% for savings and investment. You'll find that the safe and sure savings systems pay relatively low interest rates. These are postal savings, savings accounts in banks and in savings and loan associations, and government bonds. Good quality corporate bonds pay somewhat higher rates of interest. Then, too, the common stocks of many financially strong companies are available for investment. Although these stocks are subject to day-to-day market fluctuations, they can be purchased for their stability of dividend payments, as well as the opportunities they provide for participating in any future growth of their businesses. Dividends are geared to earnings and may vary from year to year. Well-established stocks may yield from 3½ to 5%. Any stock or bond that pays an unusually high interest rate is generally subject to greater market risks (which you must be prepared to take if you invest your savings in an attempt to follow a get-rich-quick plan).

Whether you save a small or large amount, you should determine how your money can work best for you to return the most with the security you must have.

Income Tax

"In this world, nothing is certain but death and taxes." So wrote Benjamin Franklin. It is true that everyone who earns money or spends it pays some form of tax.

Probably your very first pay check will be whittled down by a payment on your income tax as well as on your social security. The one is forced investment in this country, the other is forced investment in your future security.

In most business positions your company is authorized by the government to take a predetermined amount from each employee's pay check to pay for these two forms of security.

The rate or percentage of your salary that goes into income tax changes in accordance with the terms of the tax laws passed by Congress. You should know the current law so that you pay your share but no more. For be-

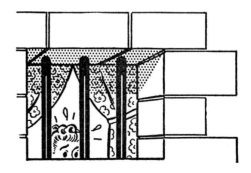

It pays to consult a tax expert if there is any doubt . . .

ginning salaries, the tax return form is very simple. If you have outside sources of income, the tax form becomes more complicated.

It pays to consult a tax expert in your company or at the tax collector's office if there is any doubt about filing your income tax return. It is foolish to overpay, but there is a penalty for underpayment.

Social Security

Federal Old-Age and Survivors Insurance benefits are known as Social Security. In most kinds of work in business, you will come under this savings plan. Deductions will be made from your salary at a prescribed rate. You can get a copy of this act and the benefits to which you will be entitled from your company's payroll department or by writing to the area office of the Social Security Administration.

When you start to work you will be required to register for Social Security and you will receive an identification card and number. Keep the card and write your number in your record book. You must use this number in reporting your income tax and for reference in making any future employment contracts.

Social Security is a government-controlled savings plan by which the employer and each employee contribute an equal share, in the employee's name. Under 1961 Congressional action, payment provisions were made for $3\frac{1}{8}\%$ on the $4800 salary ($150) for 1962, and for gradual increases up to a maximum of $4\frac{1}{2}\%$ for the year 1969 and thereafter.

These benefits are of two kinds, retirement benefits and survivor benefits. The *retirement benefits* represent a monthly payment or annuity. Your benefits will depend on several factors, such as rates of contribution and length of employment. However, this monthly insurance payment is likely to be a relatively small sum which will help, but not satisfy, your desire for security upon retirement.

Pension

If you continue to work to retirement age, you may be entitled to another form of security — the *company pension*. More and more, current thinking seems to be that some form of payment to the worker who is retired at a certain age is part of the normal cost of business. The various types of this deferred compensation, to provide protection in old age, are the pension, the sharing of profits, stock options, stock bonuses, or insurance, according to the policy of the company. These benefits which private industry grants to employees may be provided entirely by the company or cooperatively by company and employees.

Looking Ahead

It may be that even if you receive the maximum social security benefits and a liberal company pension, the combined sum will not be adequate enough to make you economically independent at the time of retirement. It therefore becomes important to consider a program which can make your retirement income adequate for your needs.

Perhaps the thought of retirement when you are in your 60's seems too remote for consideration. But the years fly by, and none of us can foresee exactly what lies ahead.

Whether you *save to spend* or save for old-age security, it is never too early to set up a plan for spending and a plan for a nest egg.

Savings Account

Your budget is your plan for spending and saving your *take home* pay. Whatever your pay check, you'll feel more secure and more like a businesswoman if you have a savings account and deposit a definite sum in the account each payday. It will be fun to see your savings grow.

If your company has an Employees Credit Union, you may find this the most convenient place to open an account, or you may want to go to the same bank where you have a checking account and safe-deposit box.

Go to the savings account window and ask to open an account. You will be given a signature card to fill out as in the case of a checking account. Be sure to use the same signature for all records. Avoid nicknames. Fill out a deposit slip for savings and hand this with your money to the person at the savings account window. Have the amount recorded in your *passbook* or bank book. Take your passbook with you every time you make a deposit or withdrawal.

Most banks do not require an advance notice for a withdrawal, as a matter of practice, although they can legally do so. Just make out a savings withdrawal slip and hand this into the savings window with your passbook.

Be sure you know what interest you will receive and when this will be recorded in your passbook. The rate of interest on a savings account is low ($2\frac{1}{2}$ to 3% is typical), but most banks insure individual deposits up to a maximum of $10,000, through an agency of the federal government. You may deposit as little as a dollar at a time or as much as you can spare from current spending. This makes a savings account a made-to-order way for you to build up a comfortable reserve.

U. S. Government Bonds

Your company may have a salary deduction plan by which you sign an agreement to have a certain amount deducted from each paycheck and applied toward the purchase of government savings bonds. You designate the amount of the deduction and the size of the bond you wish to buy. This is a rather painless way to save because you can designate the amount to be withheld and you don't have the chance to spend it.

Government savings bonds may be purchased also at any bank or post office and you can redeem them without notice. They are the safest kind of investment, but the interest rate is low. If you cash a bond before the maturity date you do not get the full rate of interest. Among savings bonds, the *E* bond is the most popular for the small investor. This pays $3\frac{3}{4}\%$ interest if the bond is held until maturity in 7 years, 9 months. You need not pay any tax on income from these bonds until you cash them or until you redeem them at maturity. However, the government allows you to keep these bonds for an extended period with the same rate of interest continuing.

Keep a record of each bond by number, maturity value, and the date at which it matures. Keep your bonds in your safe-deposit box. If you should lose a bond, ask at the bond department in your company, a bank, or a post office for instructions on filling out the required report to recover the value of the bond or to secure a substitute bond.

Insurance

Insurance is a plan by which a large number of people pool their money for mutual protection against various risks and contingencies. The loss suffered by one person will be spread over the entire group. The cost of any type of insurance is figured mathematically on the probable risk involved, and rates are fairly uniform in different companies for the same type of insurance.

As a beginner, get advice from an experienced person on the best insurance companies. You may wish to talk to representatives of two or three companies before finally deciding upon an insurance plan that suits your needs.

Don't overbuy insurance, but get the protection and planned investment that is best for you.

Property Protection Insurance

You may want protection against property loss by fire and theft. The rate on fire insurance is determined by location and the amount of protection needed. Consider the value of your clothes and other belongings to see if you can afford to risk destruction of them without protection. You may want to insure a fur coat or rings against theft and, if you travel much, you may need additional protection against loss of baggage and other property.

Accident and Health Insurance

You may decide to buy group insurance in your company or you may prefer to buy accident and health insurance from a company which specializes in this type of policy.

Read the policy before you sign the agreement and know what the penalty is for nonpayment of premiums.

Fire, theft, and accident and health insurance usually is sold at a rather low rate. This may tempt you to buy more than you can afford unless you study your budget and determine the amount of money you can spend for this kind of protection.

Protection and Investment Insurance

When your budget is in good working order and you begin to see the pattern of your financial affairs, it's time to consider what kind of personal insurance you need and what you can afford.

Now's the time to talk to a representative of a reliable insurance company to help you decide what you should buy. Don't let the insurance *lingo* confuse you. Different companies may have slightly different clauses or modifications in their policies but, actually, there are just five major types of life insurance.

Do you want protection or investment? If you have dependents, you will want the insurance that leaves money for them in case of your death. This is a *protection*. While you are working you may find you can afford to buy a policy that will pay you cash later in your life. This is an *investment*.

In the case of life policies, the younger you are when you take out the insurance, the lower the rate for the service.

Here is a condensed summary of the five kinds of life insurance showing which kind gives the most protection and which has more investment value:

Term Insurance is protection for others because a cash payment is made in case of your death within the term. The term may be one, five, ten, or even twenty years during a period of stress or special responsibility to dependents. This policy does not have savings or investment features but at the end of the term you can convert or change to another kind of insurance. The rate remains the same during the term of the policy, but if you renew it, the new rate is based on your increased age. This term insurance seldom builds up a loan or cash value. Therefore, this is a protection insurance, not an investment policy. The cost of this insurance is generally cheaper than other kinds which provide some investment benefits and cash surrender values.

Ordinary Life Insurance (straight insurance) is protection for the person you designate to receive the face value of the policy in case of your death. This is protection for a lifetime rather than for a limited period. The premiums must be paid as long as you live. The rate is low and the younger you are when you buy the policy, the lower the rate. This type of insurance builds up a cash value and you may borrow a certain amount against the policy, according to a table of values.

Limited Payment Insurance has protection and investment value. This insurance allows you to pay higher rates for your life insurance during your productive years to pay up the entire cost. Then you have this protection for your lifetime without further payments. The face value of the policy is payable only at your death. The cash value of this policy is larger because the premiums are higher.

Endowment Insurance is very popular for businesswomen because this is a form of savings and investment. The 20-year policy is favored because the rate is reasonable and a 20-year period for making payments goes quickly when you are working.

If you decide to buy an endowment policy you can select the sum you wish to have after a certain period, say 20 or 30 years. The larger the sum and the shorter the period for payments, the higher is each premium. The older you are, the higher is the rate for each premium, too. If you are just beginning to work, inquire into an endowment policy to see if this isn't a good way to help you save.

When the endowment policy is due, you can take the surrender value as cash or as a guaranteed life income, or you can leave it with the company on interest. Read the clauses in the policy that list the choice of settlements, but you don't have to decide on the plan until the policy is paid up.

A Life Annuity is another popular investment policy for a businesswoman. In this plan you pay a lump sum or regular payments to be invested by the insurance company for a certain number of years so that at a designated age you will receive an income for life. An annuity policy is popular because it provides an assured income after retirement.

You may decide you must carry protection insurance (term or life) while you have dependents, then *convert* or change the invested money to an annuity insurance to take care of yourself in later years.

There, briefly, is the insurance picture. But there are many clauses and extra provisions on each policy which are important to you.

Be sure you know what you buy.
What is the loan value?
What is the cash surrender value?

What is the penalty for lapse of payment?

What must you pay and when?

How much can you save by making annual instead of quarterly payments?

Are there dividends as in participating or mutual companies? Can you take these in cash, apply them toward more insurance, or apply the dividend toward an insurance payment?

Is there a *double indemnity* clause? (This means double payment for accidental death.)

What exceptions are there?

We live in an era of high taxes and rather low investment yields. Most women retire at sixty or sixty-five, and all desire economic security and independence after retirement. Whether you are married or single, the thought of later life and what it holds for you looms larger and larger with each succeeding year. We all want to be assured that we will have an income at the time it is needed, and we want to provide that income with a minimum of outlay and with the maximum of safety. With high income taxes, you may have difficulty building up sufficient capital to make investments in real estate, stocks, bonds, and other securities. Perhaps for you, the safest plan is to consider an investment type of insurance in the form of endowment or annuity policies.

The larger your savings, the more you can diversify your investments. You'll be wise to have a speaking acquaintance with several kinds of investments so that you can select different types.

What exceptions
are there?

Stocks and Bonds

Since most of us like to dream a bit about our future, suppose you jot down what you hope to be earning ten years from now and how much you hope to have saved. Now write down what you are earning today and how much you are saving. If you have been working for several years you might write down, also, your beginning salary and your percentage of savings. Now see how your present rate of savings compares with what you expect to have in ten years. Is it a discouraging picture? It probably is unless you have started a systematic savings program. It is so easy to put off until tomorrow what you should do today.

Your first set-aside probably will be a savings account, then some government bonds, and, of course, some protective insurance.

A look at the balance in your budget will show how thrifty you are. Perhaps you are saving all you can or perhaps you find there are loopholes in your spending so that you aren't making the best use of the money you spend. You'll have to decide how thrifty you want to be.

Surely it is not good business to owe money and pay someone a higher rate of interest than you receive on the money you have in a savings account. This means that if you have borrowed money, the soundest plan is to pay your debt as soon as possible so you don't have to pay that interest.

Now let's suppose that your budget is in good balance and your savings account shows you can withdraw $100 or so to invest in some way to earn for you a higher rate of interest. Perhaps you are ready to consider investing that $100 in bonds or stocks of some corporation or municipality.

You understand that when you buy a government bond you are lending money to the government on the promise of a definite percentage of interest on your money and the repayment of your principal at maturity. Do you understand that cities and corporations also sell bonds to raise money and that they pay interest to the persons who buy them?

Have you ever tried to read the report of the New York stock transactions in the daily paper? It's worth trying. And it becomes most interesting when you own some stock and can watch the daily sales and the rise (and fall) in the daily price of *your* stock.

Perhaps your company needs money to finance expansion of the business or a building program. The officers of the company may decide to sell bonds or stocks to the public. The company officials must file a formal registration with the required information for the Securities and Exchange Commission (SEC). If the company's registration is approved, the stocks or bonds are put up for sale. You and hundreds of others will have a chance to lend money to the company or to invest in its stock with the aim of putting your money to work for you.

First you must have confidence in the financial soundness of your company, the wisdom of the officers, and the future growth of its business. Then you will want to weigh the price you will have to pay for the stock or bonds against the income you will receive to see if it makes them reasonably good and attractive investments.

Buying an interest in your company will give you an added reason for knowing more about your company and working to contribute to its success.

What of stocks and bonds of other companies? This is where you need the advice of an expert, whether he is in your company or in a good investment company. Just as you go to a doctor when you are ill, or to a lawyer when you need legal advice, so you should consult a broker with a reputable investment company for advice on investing your money.

Your broker will want to know your financial plan and how much you want to invest. He will ask if you want safe investments, income investments, or if you are willing to take a risk on the growth of some new industry which may bring you high future returns, or nothing. He will then discuss the income you can expect from various bonds and stock.

Let's stop a bit to consider just what are bonds and how do they differ from stock.

Bonds

Bonds generally are the most stable and *safest* of all securities. If you buy a bond issued by a corporation, you lend your money and get a pledge or contract from the company to pay you a definite rate of interest until the maturity date of the bond. At maturity, the par value of the bond will be paid you. If the company fails, the bondholders must be paid the debt owed them before any money is paid to the stockholders.

Corporations, states, and cities, as well as the government, sell bonds to raise money. Securing funds through the sale of bonds is recognized as an established business procedure.

A bond usually carries a series of coupons for the promised interest at definite payment dates. If the interest is 3%, then on a $100 bond you will *clip* a coupon worth $1.50 at two specified dates each year, normally at six-month intervals. Any bank will cash the coupons for you.

Stock

If you buy a share of stock in a company you become a part owner. Some companies, such as United States Steel and American Telephone and Telegraph, have "millions of shares of stock and hundreds of thousands of stockholders or owners."

What return do you receive on *common stock*? That depends on how much the company earns. Each year the company's board of directors decides what dividends will be paid and when. If you are a stockholder, you and other stockholders elect the directors for a definite term. Thus you can play a part in deciding who shall direct the affairs of the company. If the company is on a sound financial basis, the directors (*your* directors) usually will declare a dividend on each share of stock. If business has been very good and profits have been larger than usual, an extra dividend may be declared. In this way a company divides the profits among the shareholders. The larger the dividend payment, the more attractive the stock may become to some investors. You would naturally prefer to invest in stock that pays a steady or increasing dividend year after year rather than one that pays a more spectacular dividend one year and a small one or none the next. An investment broker whose business depends in part on his knowledge of individual company positions can advise you as to which stocks are sound or steady and which stocks are variable and insecure.

Sometimes a company issues *preferred stock*. This differs from common stock in that the dividend is fixed so that you receive a steady income from preferred stock, just as you do from bonds. This means, however, that you do not get the advantage of a good business year in terms of a larger dividend. Those preferred stocks which have cumulative dividend requirements are usually *safer* than common stocks because you don't assume the risk of declining profits of the company.

Questions

What determines the price of bonds? The corporation and the market set the orginal unit price based upon the par value and the interest rate. The value or selling price at any particular time depends on the demand for the bonds and the amount the buyers are willing to pay for them in relation to the general level of interest rates.

What determines the price of stocks? The price originally may be $1, $10, $15, $100, or more, depending upon the expected rate of return based upon prospective dividend payments. The price of each share fluctuates from day to day with the *market,* that is, how much the sellers are willing to take for their shares and how much the buyers are willing to pay for them.

Who can buy stock? Anyone. You may buy one share or as many as you can afford. You may buy shares in several companies. In fact, your broker probably will advise you to diversify your investment among industries as well as companies within an industry.

What does it cost to buy stock? You pay the price at which the stock is selling, plus a small commission. This charge is standard. It is established by agreement of all member firms of the Stock Exchange so you know the charge before you buy the stock. Stocks that are not sold through the Stock Exchange are subject to state regulations, also.

Are stockbrokers licensed? Yes.

Do you want to invest in stocks and bonds? The decision is yours, but a good investment broker will advise you to get your money affairs in order. Look to a savings account for the cushion against emergencies. Think of insurance as protection and investment. Property ownership may be wise if your position is secure and stabilized. After you have taken care of these *safety* investments, you may want to consider the relative safety of bonds or the income features of stocks.

It has been said that too many women cling to security and fail to investigate the ways to make their savings earn the best returns. As a businesswoman you should welcome every opportunity to understand how business is financed and how money makes money. Many women are good managers. Are you?

What do you want out of life? Now is the time to set your standards and decide where you are going. You'll have to develop a sense of values and be a good buyer. Now is the time to set up a plan for saving:

Save regularly.
Keep careful records so you know how you spend.
Use your savings *first* for security, *next* for investment.
Get expert advice.
Investigate before you invest.
Avoid speculative investments.

CHAPTER 18

How the Married Woman Succeeds in Business

HAVE you decided on a career in business, or is marriage the career of your choice? Why not combine the two careers? Many women do, you know, and make a decided success of both. Granted — such a combination of jobs requires a stalwart heart and a heap of common sense. But success in either business or marriage is won only with conscientious effort.

Usually a girl has a plan or dream for the future which includes a home of her own, a husband, and children. But many girls want more than that and they have been trained vocationally and intellectually to do more than that. They want to test their ability in some paying position to see if they can be self-supporting before

marriage and can continue a career after marriage. There is a challenge to work in the business field where competition is keen and success must be earned.

A pay check of your own gives new meaning to the value of money. The experience of working for pay gives you a better understanding of people and of the problems of living in an adult world. Perhaps this work experience will help you think more seriously about the responsibilities of homemaking.

Today, most businesses not only retain girls after they are married but also hire married women. Management recognizes that, usually, eligibility for a job is not based on whether a girl is or is not married. The real test is her attitude toward her work and how well she can manage her work hours and her out-of-work hours. There are some positions where the experience of living in a happy family unit makes a young woman more successful in her business work.

If you decide on a career as well as marriage, you should realize that there are real advantages, but there are real problems, too, which must be faced.

Advantages of a Career and Marriage

Money is the usual reason for a girl continuing a work job after marriage. The need for two pay checks instead of one may be due to obligations to one or both parent families; past debts; a determination to improve the living conditions, as with a better home; better food and better clothes; or more travel and better education for children. It is true that the cost of supporting a wife and establishing a home is too great for most young men making a start in their career. You'll find there is little truth in the old saying that "two can live as cheaply as one." In fact, living for one isn't cheap!

If you are a businesswoman you should be able to manage his and your pooled resources so that you can set up a workable budget. This includes a cushion against emergencies as well as funds for essentials and planned savings.

Needless to say, the money advantages of continuing to work after marriage must be weighed against the cost for extra clothes and other work expenses, the need for paid help in the home or for special services, and other expenses incurred by your out-of-the-home work. Extra money is a powerful reason for continuing to work but there may be other reasons, too.

The *stimulation* and *challenge* of a business job may be so important to you that you will decide to continue to work after your marriage. A girl who has organized her life around a challenging position may find that trying to keep interested and busy in housework in a small home is too great a contrast to her former life. The change from the drive of business to a slower pace — from the stimulation of working with many people to a lack of contacts — may make the ambitious girl restless and introspective. This is especially true if you live in a large city. Long hours spent alone in a small space may be depressing even when that space is your new home.

Ambition for a career makes some girls elect to go ahead with their career even after marriage. If you feel a strong urge to have a real career rather than just an interim position, you must weigh carefully the cost to yourself and to your marriage. You'll have to establish values and decide whether your career or your home will come first if there is ever a reason for a choice. Perhaps your career will fit in with your marriage plans. If not, you may be able to change your type of work so that you can have a successful career because you are happily married not in spite of what happens to your marriage.

Assistance to your husband in a business partnership may be possible by adapting your skill and ability to direct help in his business. A girl with a flare for advertising can often turn out the best copy of her life when she is working with her husband. If you have ability at designing, buying, stenography, business management, personnel direction, or other special skill, this talent may be an excellent reason for combining your career with your husband's career.

Other advantages claimed for dual careers in business and homemaking are given by successful career women. Some say they can be better companions to their husbands if they are out in the business world. There they learn to speak the same language and to take an interest in the same subjects as their menfolk.

Again, a woman who works may gain an appreciation of her

husband's problems so that she can be more sympathetic and helpful. She should be able to understand, for example, that business demands must be met even if these require overtime hours; salary raises are seldom given as often as seem merited; a promotion to head of a department does not come until after a rather long period of experience; conversations about work may be more interesting than fashions in hats or the latest gossip; the hours of work are not to be interrupted except in case of emergency. In other words, the working wife may be able to profit by her experience and be more understanding and companionable than the stay-at-home wife.

Problems of a Career and Homemaking

The advantages of combining a business career with marriage seem attractive, and success in both jobs has been scored by many women. However, you should never underestimate the very real problems that arise when you add the responsibilities of your business position to the responsibilities of managing a home. A husband usually wants a well-run home and a cheerful wife who is ready to meet his friends and enjoy his leisure hours with him.

The physical and nervous strain of two jobs is great. When you are in business you know that working hours are crowded with many demands. Some days you become tired physically and mentally as well as emotionally. In some kinds of work, one or all of those types of tiredness may increase as your responsibilities on the job increase. In fact, the higher you go in your career the greater is the demand on your energies. If you add this strain to the duties of a wife, can you do justice to both jobs? Is your health good enough to handle both? Have you developed a philosophy of work so that you can leave the stress and strain of business behind when you change your role to homemaker?

If you continue your career after marriage, you will have to adjust your home life so that your work will not suffer. This may mean that you will have to consider your health more seriously, live more simply, entertain less elaborately, and reorganize and streamline your housework more efficiently.

Hours of work may prove a problem after marriage. Will your hours at home fit in with those of your husband so that you will have the maximum amount of time together? Does your work require you to be present at meetings and social affairs that will keep you away from home at mealtime or evenings? Perhaps you should sacrifice some of the advantages of salary or prestige in your present position and try to secure a position where working hours are more compatible with your married status.

The place of work is as important as the hours of work. Can you live in a location that will be convenient to your husband's work as well as yours? Overlong time and too much money spent in getting to and from work can prove a real disadvantage.

Extreme circumstances may require a married couple to work in different cities. Before you consider such a plan, you should determine whether the need is great enough to warrant this drastic separation. Some employers object to such a living arrangement because it is apt to foster emotional instability and absences from work.

A traveling position may prove to be unsatisfactory for the married woman. If a husband must travel and be away from home a great deal, this may be a good reason for his wife to continue to work. But if you are the one who must travel and be away from home a great deal, you should consider seriously whether this is a good type of position to combine with marriage.

Many business concerns object to hiring married women for traveling positions because this type of work often demands sudden changes in plans and long periods of time away from home. And it may have other features that are not acceptable to most married couples. In your first years of married life you would be wise to consider whether a traveling position is worth enough to you to make up for the sacrifices of home life which travel demands.

The financial success of the wife may pose a problem. The "head of the family" is the traditional title given to the man.

Will your hours at home fit in with those of your husband?

Before you decide to continue your career you should be sure that your work will not make your husband feel inadequate. Will he be jealous of your success? If you earn more than he does, will he be resentful and become indifferent to his home? Will he be oversensitive to imagined neglect? Will he lose his initiative and his drive to succeed? Will he turn to some person or pleasure that makes him feel more like the dominant male?

A financially successful woman has a definite problem when her husband is less successful in his work. Case histories are legion to prove that men find it difficult to accept a minor role. Perhaps at first it will be all right if your salary is larger and your position better, but will he become discouraged if you continue to be the major success?

It is possible for both members of the marriage team to establish sound habits of thinking so that each complements and supplements the other in their separate careers as well as in the home. A selfish or thoughtless attitude on either side may prove a definite disadvantage to a business career after you are married.

Children and a work schedule may be hard to reconcile. Much attention has been given recently to the importance of family relationships. When a mother works out of the home, very serious consideration must be given to the welfare of the children. If your salary is sufficient to pay for a good full-time helper who will give a sense of security and stability to the children, you may be able to adjust your dual job satisfactorily. And there are day nurseries and day schools for older children that may

Will he lose his initiative and his drive to succeed?

be substituted for reliable help at home. But illness and other emergencies often complicate the problems of the working mother.

Some business concerns grant a leave of absence to a woman for a period before and after a child is born. Management recognizes that men as well as women have family responsibilities that may interfere at times with work. But in all fairness to other employees, a company cannot entrust a responsible position to a woman who must be absent or who asks for special privileges too often. Therefore, the care of children is a constant problem to the working mother.

Whether or not you can have a successful career and also raise healthy, happy children depends on many factors: your salary; the type of care arranged for the children; the type of work and its demands on your time and health; and the cooperation and help given by your husband or some other member of your family. Perhaps most of all, the real test lies in your own efficiency and your ability to manage your time and energy so that both your job and your family profit by this dual role.

Home or Part-time Work and Marriage

One way to continue in your career after marriage may be to bring your work into your home, or to select part-time work until you can carry on two full-time jobs at once. Some stenographers have established a profitable business by specializing in expert typing for individuals or businesses. Manuscripts, reports, briefs, and other sizable typing jobs may bring in considerable revenue.

Consultants in various lines of work have made a success of production of booklets, plans, and projects in a home office.

The care of children is a constant problem to the working mother.

Writers of feature articles and stories, as well as radio and television scripts, often work at home for a fee or a salary.

The home office or workshop can be used to develop a career if you are persistent and sincere in your desire to succeed. This requires scheduling of time and a regular routine for work and initiative. The girl who decides to follow her work career at home must be able to withstand the temptation to let interruptions interfere with her work.

Part-time work may prove a better plan if you can agree on an acceptable work period and on the amount of work required for that period, so that both you and your employer are satisfied with the arrangement.

Preparation for the Dual Career

You will see from this brief discussion that success in business and homemaking requires an understanding and agreement between your husband and yourself and also between your employer and yourself.

The wife-husband understanding. This dual role of career woman and homemaker must be acceptable to the husband. Will he recognize that your job requires the same loyalty to the employer that his job requires? Will he be willing to share the household tasks so that only half of the homework becomes your share? Can you hire help to relieve you of some of the housework? Two full-time jobs may be too much to attempt to do well.

Discuss with your husband-to-be the question of the name you will use in business. A woman sometimes continues to use her unmarried name because it is easier in the business situation. Will this be agreeable to him?

Decide on the method of banking and sharing expenses. Some couples solve this problem by a joint bank account for deposits and withdrawals.

Will he be willing to
share the household tasks?

Sometimes the woman's salary goes into a separate fund for savings, vacations, and special purchases. A settlement of the financial problem of two pay checks may seem unnecessary before marriage, but it can become an issue later on.

Your employer and you. Your employer should be told about your plans to marry so that there can be an agreement about your work before you make plans to continue in your position after marriage.

There may be very good reasons why your employer will *not* agree to your continuing in your present position if you marry. It may be that your employer could offer you another position in the company which would be acceptable. Or, after hearing of your plans and your future husband's acceptance of your dual role, your employer may decide that you can continue in your present position.

Whatever the outcome, you must play fair and tell your employer about your decision to marry. Secret marriages and marriages without notice to the employer have done much to foster the opinion that women are unpredictable and are not dependable enough to promote to topflight positions.

Marriages without notice . . .
. . . have fostered
the opinion that women
are unpredictable.

When you are in business you owe a responsibility to your employer to explain your plans for marriage even though you may feel that this is a strictly personal arrangement in your life.

Your professional standards should caution you to avoid any act that would harm your reputation or might in any way hinder the chances of success of other women in business. Your business associates have a right to expect of you ethical standards of conduct which extend even to plans for your marriage.

The following letter was written by a woman executive to her staff of young women in several cities when one of their co-workers was married secretly. The letter gives several reasons why the girl who marries without telling her superior hurts herself, her co-workers, and other girls who hope to be accepted in the business world as conscientious applicants for executive positions.

The fourth member of our group has just been married without warning, so I am going to try to do the impossible and explain to you why I think a secret marriage is wrong for a businesswoman.

I write as one who honestly feels that homemaking is the finest profession for women. A happy marriage is the ultimate goal of every normal girl. I write also as one who has been instrumental in helping to build our staff from one unit with one woman to eight units with 18 trained women.

Whether or not a girl wishes to announce her engagement publicly is her own business. Personally, I think a girl misses a lot of fun if she omits this experience. To get married without telling anyone always (yes, always) results in the question, "Why did she do it?" People are human and curiosity is a normal trait. Everyone begins to speculate "Why the suddenness" with the result that the young woman in question is hurt. She is put on the defensive. She is asked to explain and justify the supreme moment of her life.

You can argue that it is no one's business but your own, but I have never known a single case of an unannounced marriage when there did not arise at least one unpleasant controversy. In every case, in later years the girl wished she had waited a day, a week, or a year so that her family and friends were prepared to join together in wishing the young couple happiness and success.

Now professionally, our staff is like a chain, as strong as the weakest link. The officers of our company have talked to me of the unusually fine young women on our staff. We have built up a reputation for clear thinking, fair play, and womanliness. We have the respect of the men of our company. This may be whimsically expressed, but I like to think that men treat me like a man, yet never forget I am a woman. This is the standard I have for you, too.

We are in a new profession and men are still somewhat skeptical of women in business. Management hesitates to pay women on the same scale as men because women don't have a long-range view for their work. The manager of your plant has backed you and has publicized your work more than that of some of the older basic departments. You surely do not want to break his faith in you and our staff by an unprofessional act.

If you have done a good job for your company, you can imagine that it should be a bit difficult to fill your place if you decide to leave. If you have pride in your work, you surely want to see it go on without faltering. If you expect to continue your position after marriage, you should realize that management has the final decision.

I think you'll all agree that our company has a remarkable *human* spirit and much family (company) pride and loyalty. I feel that the manager of your plant will consider always your welfare of vital importance and he will make adjustments to assure your happiness. But girls, give him a chance to continue his confidence in you as a business-woman so that he can make those adjustments that will mean success for you and continued respect for you and all of your co-workers on our staff.

As for myself, I hope you can trust me to want your happiness, even when I can see the problems of training a new person to fill your capable shoes. So, if you are planning to be married, please let your manager and me know a month, a week, or a day before you take the step. Don't make it difficult for us to make it easier for you to find real happiness.

This is my thinking on the *unannounced marriage* problem, as one businesswoman to another.

Questions for Decisions

Do you want to continue your work after marriage?

> First consider whether you want to work just to get more money for a short time or whether you have ambition and determination to make a successful career of your work. Your answer will determine the type of position you should accept.

Does your husband-to-be agree to your combining a career with homemaking?

> If he accepts this arrangement of two career people in the family and takes pride in your achievements, you are very likely to succeed in your dual role.
>
> If a husband resents his wife's success and refuses to accept the necessary adjustment in their plan of living, an undue burden is placed on the woman and she must combat mental as well as physical fatigue.

Does your employer agree that you may continue in your position after you marry?

Your employer has the right to decide whether your marriage will interfere with your present work.

Marriage should bring to a woman greater understanding of the needs and wants of the people who represent the customers of most business organizations. Social adjustment, financial security, and real womanliness can be expected of the career woman who uses her experience and abilities to combine business life and home life. It is not an easy task, but it is challenging and productive of great accomplishments.

Index